ENERGY'S DIGITAL FUTURE

T0324454

CENTER ON GLOBAL ENERGY POLICY SERIES

CENTER ON GLOBAL ENERGY POLICY SERIES

Jason Bordoff, series editor

Making smart energy policy choices requires approaching energy as a complex and multifaceted system in which decision makers must balance economic, security, and environmental priorities. Too often, the public debate is dominated by platitudes and polarization. Columbia University's Center on Global Energy Policy at SIPA seeks to enrich the quality of energy dialogue and policy by providing an independent and nonpartisan platform for timely analysis and recommendations to address today's most pressing energy challenges. The Center on Global Energy Policy Series extends that mission by offering readers accessible, policy-relevant books that have as their foundation the academic rigor of one of the world's great research universities.

Robert McNally, *Crude Volatility: The History and the Future of Boom-Bust Oil Prices*

Daniel Raimi, *The Fracking Debate: The Risks, Benefits, and Uncertainties of the Shale Revolution*

Richard Nephew, *The Art of Sanctions: A View from the Field*

Jim Krane, *Energy Kingdoms: Oil and Political Survival in the Persian Gulf*

ENERGY'S DIGITAL FUTURE

*Harnessing Innovation for American
Resilience and National Security*

AMY MYERS JAFFE

Columbia University Press

New York

Columbia University Press
Publishers Since 1893
New York   Chichester, West Sussex
cup.columbia.edu
Copyright © 2021 Amy Myers Jaffe
Paperback edition, 2024

Library of Congress Cataloging-in-Publication Data
Names: Jaffe, Amy Myers, author.
Title: Energy's digital future : harnessing innovation for American resilience
    and national security / Amy Myers Jaffe.
Description: New York : Columbia University Press, [2021] | Series: Center on
    Global Energy Policy series | Includes bibliographical references and index.
Identifiers: LCCN 2020041676 (print) | LCCN 2020041677 (ebook) |
    ISBN 9780231196826 (hardback) | ISBN 9780231216753 (pbk.) |
    ISBN 9780231551847 (ebook)
Subjects: LCSH: Energy policy—United States. | Energy industries—Technological
    innovations—United States. | Automation. | Big data. | Energy security—
    United States. | National security—United States.
Classification: LCC HD9502.U52 J337 2021 (print) | LCC HD9502.U52 (ebook) |
    DDC 333.790285—dc23
LC record available at https://lccn.loc.gov/2020041676
LC ebook record available at https://lccn.loc.gov/2020041677

Cover design: Noah Arlow
Printed and bound by CPI Group (UK) Ltd, Croydon, CR0 4YY

Contents

Preface and Acknowledgments

Afew years back, I was sitting in the cafeteria of the Google headquarters with longtime friend Alexander "Andy" Karsner. He
suggested I needed a change. We kicked some ideas around. I said
I would like to write a book. We both felt at the time that Silicon Valley was on a
collision course with the Texas oil industry and that neither knew enough about
the other to make sensible future investment decisions on new energy technologies. Andy and I had organized an academic retreat for leaders from both sectors at an inn in Napa Valley. Each side was shocked and amazed to hear what
the other was doing. Afterward, Royal Dutch Shell pursued a joint venture with
one of the hydrogen firms in attendance. Other companies pursued relationships
with big-data providers. It was as though two meteors had collided, and neither
could go right back onto its old trajectory.

Andy has guided my education on the intersection of tech, energy, and climate change for several years now. To get this book off the ground, we organized
a study group of business leaders, leading academics, and policy makers on the
"Tech Enabled Energy Future" as part of my work at the Council on Foreign
Relations. The study group greatly expanded my knowledge, facilitating the
contents of this book. I am grateful to the study group for its dedication to the
purpose of open-minded learning and to the companies that hosted us on our
Silicon Valley tour, including Applied Materials, Google X, and Carbon 3D. My
thank-you on the study group exercise would not be complete without mention-
ing Evan Michelson and the Alfred P. Sloan Foundation, which generously supported the study group, this research, and my other research over multiple years
and three academic institutions. Nicole Alexiev and Shelbi Sturgess provided
organizational muscle to the study group endeavor while my research associates

Dylan Yalbir and Ben Silliman provided important research contributions, as did my fantastic summer intern, Stefan Koester. I also thank Lucy Best and Michael Collins for their outstanding research contributions on China's energy strategy and Liz Economy and Steven Lewis for their expert counsel on China's unique internal politics.

I want to thank the Council on Foreign Relations for the opportunity to work on a book project. I also thank Caelyn Cobb, my editor at Columbia University Press, for her steady guidance and Patricia Dorff, who spent countless hours advising and encouraging me during the drafting process. I offer a special thanks to my research associate Gabi Hasaj, whose intervention on the challenge of completing a manuscript in the middle of a pandemic was invaluable.

I also owe special thanks to friends and mentors who have played a guiding role in the process of researching and writing. It is only fitting that Edward Morse, my longtime mentor and friend, was the first person to read the manuscript and give treasured advice. Jason Bordoff, director of the Center on Global Energy Policy at Columbia University and an enthusiastic friend and supporter, also provided much appreciated encouragement for the book project and a frequent forum at Columbia to try out my new ideas regarding tech and peak oil demand. My dear friend Alison Cowan was instrumental in guiding me into the excitement of sleuthing the mysteries of the Edison-Ford partnership on an electric vehicle and other archival treasure hunts, and we are both indebted to Paul Israel, director and general editor of the Thomas A. Edison papers project and research professor at Rutgers University.

Several of my academic research collaborators offered significant research contributions to the book, notably including Lew Fulton, Daniel Scheitrum, and Zane McDonald for their intrepid persistence to our joint modeling on peak oil demand. Other important research collaborators include Kelly Sims Gallagher, Paul Griffin, Joan Ogden, Mahmoud El-Gamal, Likeleli Seitlheko, Hany Abdel-Latif, Marianne Kah, Rosa Dominguez-Faus, and Nathan Parker. Steve Currall and Jagdeep Bachher gave me the time and platform to pursue my interest in the intersection of sustainability, climate change, and finance and helped me think outside the box on what the future might bring. Their insights were supplemented by my ongoing discussions with Joe Barnes, Rene Aninao, Andrew Lebow, Matt Rogers, Jareer Elass, and Albert Lee.

I learned most of what I know about energy markets from the trenches, starting when I was a young journalist and continuing today. Many smart and generous people from the international policy world, from the energy industry, and from Silicon Valley took the time, and still take the time, to help me understand complex issues. I definitely need to thank them for my success, but so many talked to me on the basis of anonymity that I offer this blanket acknowledgment. You know who you are; know that I greatly appreciate your time and assistance. Ditto my original team at *Petroleum Intelligence Weekly*, with a special shout-out to Ira Joseph, Isabel Gorst, and the late Alan Troner.

Often people ask me how I became an energy economist with no formal PhD educational training. In actuality, that is only technically correct in terms of conferred degrees. In terms of hours spent learning economics with a dissertation adviser, my many joint publications with Ronald Soligo could constitute a lengthy tutorial. He was a patient, able instructor. The fact that both Kenneth Medlock and I have prizes in economics is no coincidence. Besides our own incredibly fruitful collaboration with each other, we were both lucky students of Soligo.

Throughout my work in energy and geopolitics, many luminaries have helped make my journey a successful one. In the sciences, Neal Lane, the late Richard Smalley, Daniel Sperling, and Robert Powell were able mentors. Ambassador Edward Djerejian, the director of the James A. Baker III Institute for Public Policy, taught me valuable lessons on the power of storytelling in public diplomacy and the art of negotiation.

Then there is the shining beacon of my career, Secretary James A. Baker III, who showed me by example so many lessons for my life I could write a book on the subject. Most important, he showed me the value of not speaking or acting in haste. His invaluable instruction in the art of patience greatly contributed to this book and to my life.

And to the shrewdest human being I know, Dr. Falih Al-Jibury, who sat with me for countless hours in the hotel lobby during the meetings of the Organization of Petroleum Exporting Countries and imparted much wisdom on international relations, I owe you a debt of gratitude.

Finally, here is where I get to say in writing that I fully understand that if I had married someone else, my life would have been a duller and less fruitful endeavor. An inveterate self-starter, my husband Rick Jaffe has been the rock from which all my incredible forays, including this book, have sprung forth. I would also like to add that this book would not have been possible without countless hours with my beloved Rebecca listening to my complaints, correcting any faulty understanding of electricity markets and storage systems, and sharing a laugh. I thank Jordan for his quiet presence, without which writing a book might have been a harder challenge. And to Daniel, with whom I check all ideas, energy and otherwise, your wise counsel has improved my life and this book invaluably. "Nothing gold can stay," to quote Robert Frost, but love of family is eternal.

Finally, in addition to my family, I feel it is important to dedicate this book to Richard Smalley. He believed that the single greatest challenge humanity faced was meeting the world's burgeoning energy needs with clean, renewable energy. "If you believe with me that we absolutely need to provide the planet's 10 billion people with the potential to pursue a fulfilling lifestyle, where they have a roof over their heads, enough food to eat, sufficient mobility, communications, and the capability to build homes and develop cities," he proffered, "then, you will agree that we have to revolutionize the world's energy system. We need cheap, clean energy in vast amounts"—an effort he came to name the Terrawatt Challenge.[1] Smalley's vision was that electricity should become the ubiquitous fuel of the twenty-first century, based on a decentralized, local energy storage model where everyone on the grid would have a personal storage appliance that could ensure delivery of uninterrupted power. This distributed system would be supplemented by rewiring the electric grid with superconductors that could enable cross-continent and even worldwide electrical transmission, taking advantage of time zones, climate variations, and large-scale sources of power such as nuclear energy. Smalley was ahead of his time. A sample of the system he envisioned was built by Tesla in South Australia in 2017.

Richard Smalley hoped, in his final years, that he would inspire a future Einstein of energy, up for the challenges of tomorrow. This book is my own attempt to spread the word and encourage others to be part of the solution, exploring or harnessing new technologies to achieve the highest possible outcome for our planet. Richard Smalley's vision of distributed electricity and small-scale battery storage is just the tip of the iceberg of the impact digital innovation will have on how we produce and use energy.

• • •

I put the finishing touches on this book in the midst of the unprecedented lockdown of the United States and other major economies in light of the COVID-19 pandemic and then, no less important, amid historic protests related to social injustice. This is not a book about those events, the consequences of which will take years to unfold. But both those historic turning points draw attention to the pressing challenges we face both in addressing climate change and in bringing affordable, reliable energy equally to all segments of society. Without access to energy, other vital needs like clean water, food security, and health care become nearly impossible.

I am technocentric, not Malthusian. I believe there is a generation of new energy scientists, engineers, policy analysts, economists, and political activists who are well placed to push for the changes needed and to succeed, especially because of the opportunities that digital energy can create. This book is aimed to provide some context, if not inspiration, for their work.

So much is in flux that one must keep an open mind that the future can be one of positive change. History is a teacher in this regard. Progress often comes in the wake of destruction of old ideas, landscapes, and institutions. For the digital energy revolution, as the coming pages will explain, many of the long-standing principles around which the energy sector was organized will see their demise.

Abbreviations

ADNOC	Abu Dhabi National Oil Company
AI	artificial intelligence
ALAM	Association of Licensed Automobile Manufacturers
AVs	autonomous vehicles
b/d	barrels per day
BCM	billion cubic meters
BECCS	bioenergy with carbon capture and storage
CAFE	corporate average fuel economy
CCS	carbon capture and storage
CCUS	carbon capture utilization and sequestration
CNPC	China National Petroleum Corporation
CO$_2$	carbon dioxide
DARPA	Defense Advanced Research Project Agency
EBA	European Battery Alliance
EOR	enhanced oil recovery
ESPO	East Siberia–Pacific Ocean
EVs	electric vehicles
eVTOLs	electric vertical takeoff and landing aircraft
F & D	finding and development
FDI	final decision investment
4DS	four degrees scenario
5G	fifth-generation mobile wireless technologies
G20	Group of Twenty
GDP	gross domestic product
GHz	gigahertz

GPS   Global Positioning System
IAMs   integrated assessment models
ICE   internal combustion engines
IEA   International Energy Agency
IMF   International Monetary Fund
IPO   initial public offering
IRR   internal rate of return
ISO   independent system operator
ITU   International Telecommunications Union
IWG   Interagency Working Group
LTE   long-term evolution
MIT   Massachusetts Institute of Technology
MoMo   mobility model
NPC   National People's Congress
OAS   Organization of American States
OEMs   original equipment manufacturers
OPEC   Organization of the Petroleum Exporting Countries
P2P   peer-to-peer communication
PHEV   plug-in hybrid electric vehicles
PIF   public investment fund
R & D   research and development
SCC   social cost of carbon
SDS   sustainable development scenario
SRM   solar radiation management
SWIPT   Simultaneous Wireless Information and Power Transfer
3D   three-dimensional
TOE   tons of oil equivalent
UPS   United Parcel Services
V2G   vehicle to grid
V2H   vehicle to home
VMT   vehicle miles traveled
WTI   West Texas Intermediate

Introduction

I began my journey thinking about energy as a problem the way most Americans of my generation did: sitting in a gasoline line with my father. The year was 1973, and the Organization of Petroleum Exporting Countries (OPEC) had imposed an oil embargo on the United States in retaliation for its support of Israel in the 1973 Arab-Israeli war, causing pandemonium across the nation. Companies and consumers alike scrambled for oil supplies, and the panic buying sent oil prices up over 600 percent. A U.S. federally imposed gasoline allocation system led to lines at the pump across the country, and "Sorry, no gas today" signs became a common sight. The oil embargo and its negative economic aftereffects ushered in an age of oil scarcity that would color U.S. energy policy for the next thirty years.

I was a teenager at the time, so I am not sure the geopolitical implications of the situation are what struck me. But I do recall the anxiety they created in my father, who was insistent I rise at 5 a.m. so we could get to the one gasoline station in our New England town before the rationed fuel for odd-numbered license plate cars ran out. My father couched his request that I get up and sit with him at Gulf Oil as a practicality. He claimed if the process of lining up down Humphrey Street and then filling up took a long time, he would not have time to come back to the house to get me to take me to school. But I am guessing now what I intuitively knew as a child—that he simply wanted company. Starting the morning with several hours in a gas line made for a long day.

I would not realize the impression that experience had on me until many decades later when I was already a professor writing about U.S. energy and climate policy. It was 2001, and my daughter Rebecca was assigned an essay at school to consider how the terrorist attacks of September 11, 2001, might influence the course of her life. To complete the assignment, she had to interview four family members about historical events that had happened when they were her age. My father-in-law, who lived with us, told her about the world wars; my husband, how the Vietnam War influenced his decision to study religious philosophy abroad; my mother, by telephone, about working on a farm as her contribution to the American war effort during World War II. Rebecca needed one more, and at first I told her nothing much had happened in the 1970s, except that we all learned disco dancing. Then it struck me. The 1973 oil embargo and subsequent fall of the shah of Iran in 1979 had provided a formative historical backdrop to my life.

In retrospect, the ramifications of the 1973 Arab oil embargo made a bigger impression on me than I realized. You see, I have been steadfastly writing about the energy problem since 1975, when my high-school American history teacher, Alan Shapiro, entered my essay on the 1973 oil crisis in a statewide essay contest. I won third prize. Unbeknownst to me, a career was being launched. Who knew I would still be thinking about the energy problem forty-five years later?

Many younger-generation Americans today come to the subject of energy out of concern for the contribution that burning of fossil fuels has on global climate change. It is important to consider the energy problem today in terms of that environmental context. But today's geopolitics of energy goes beyond carbon emissions and the viability of global climate agreements. As I will discuss in this book, energy politics covers a wider range of topics, including economic competitiveness, trade, strategic and military preparedness, and culture. It is clearer than ever that technology is a key component in solving global energy challenges of affordability, access, and greenhouse gas emissions. Technology is, however, agnostic. It is the context within which human beings use that technology that sets its value—both positive and negative.

The advent of new, advanced digital technologies will transform the global energy system in the coming decades. These changes will be revolutionary—not just in the way that the 1973 embargo was revolutionary, but in a manner similar to what was experienced more than a century ago when mass distribution of electricity and mass-produced automobiles were first established. The United States needs to embrace this change, or it risks being unprepared for the ways the digital energy revolution will alter the geopolitical landscape. New rivalries will emerge in this new digital energy world order, creating challenges for U.S. foreign policy and national security. In its response, the United States needs to consider how to optimize its own deployment of digital technologies to enhance democratic institutions and promote solutions to climate change, enabling its continued global leadership role and preparing a positive outcome for future generations.

THE GEOPOLITICS OF DIGITAL ENERGY

The dominance of oil in the global energy system has influenced global relations for decades. Now, a new wave of digital energy innovation, driven by the convergence of automation, artificial intelligence, big data, and the Internet of Things, will usher in a new geopolitical order of winners and losers. Industrial capability, rather than the current geography of oil, will take on an outsize role in this new energy world.

Historically, U.S. primacy in energy innovation has been instrumental in catapulting U.S. military and economic power on the international stage. Innovations from American entrepreneurs such as John D. Rockefeller, Henry Ford, and Thomas Edison, combined with rising U.S. oil production, helped the Allied powers achieve victory in World War I. Later, America's Manhattan Project, which harnessed nuclear fission, played a decisive role in America's national security and power during World War II and its aftermath. Today, a new wave of digital energy innovation, driven by the convergence of automation, artificial intelligence, and big data analytics, is poised to remake energy and transportation systems, potentially conveying on the leader in digital energy both military and economic superiority, just as energy and manufacturing innovation did a century ago. Therefore, it is a vital national interest that the U.S. maintain its leading role, requiring special attention from policy makers.

Surprisingly, it has become increasingly difficult for the United States to maintain its global energy technology edge. One reason is that China is positioning itself to lead in this new digital energy world order by pursuing a massive industrial program in revolutionary digital energy technologies, especially those with dual-use military applications. The United States has yet to fully mobilize, to the potential detriment of future U.S. global competitiveness and national power. By contrast, Europe is responding with a major green industrial energy initiative of its own.

The stakes are high because China's domination of digital export markets could allow Beijing to establish its own rules for cyber intrusion that could be contrary to Western democratic values and interests. At issue is not just the economic welfare of the United States, therefore, but the survival of America's core values of individual freedom, human rights, and privacy. The regulation surrounding digital energy technology will also be critical to addressing climate change.

That China's vision of how to deploy smart technologies differs from that of Western democracies has contributed toward increasingly uneasy relations between Beijing and Washington. During the Obama years, from 2009 to 2017, China considered climate change an area of strong bilateral cooperation and aimed to preserve a good working relationship in light of other areas of conflict involving more difficult issues such as intellectual property rights, North Korea, and other territorial disputes in northeast Asia. The breakthrough in U.S.–Chinese cooperation on energy and climate change generated trust and laid the groundwork for a concept of parallel efforts in which both superpowers committed to contribute similar but independent action. The strategy was productive, underpinning wider success in establishing a global climate action agreement in Paris in 2015.

However, in the years since Chinese president Xi Jinping ascended to power, China has forged a surveillance state that has ushered in a toxic mixture of political authoritarianism with digital surveillance and tracking technology. Xi's "third" Chinese revolution has been rooted in a severe deepening of centralization of power and authority of the ruling Chinese Communist Party and a more pervasive presence of the state in the daily lives of all Chinese. Digital technology has been utilized to tightly control the flow of ideas, commerce, and finance inside and outside China. Facial recognition software actively tracks the movements and activities of China's population. A data-intensive social credit system, backed by the National Credit Information Sharing Platform, invasively monitors and influences behavior by rating individuals with a social score that is used to judge their standing in society as well as their access to financial credit. In practice, the social credit score goes well beyond employment, income, and credit history to include the quality of people's social networks and their social behaviors. The system can be utilized to punish any individual who strays from the edicts or philosophy of the Communist Party by denying credit, a job promotion, and even the right to own a house.

The danger of China's system is not just to its own population, because Beijing has demonstrated its inclination to export its authoritarian and digital surveillance practices along with its equipment to neighboring states and other trading partners. The inclusion of surveillance technology in China's export products threatens the strength of the liberal world order that is based on democratic principles and the individual right to privacy. It raises the stakes in the competition between the United States and China in the digital export market. The challenge for the United States will be how to take the lead in countering China's repressive digital vision and replace it with a democratic values–based global deployment of digital technologies that will not erode democratic governance and principles. At the same time, the United States still needs to maintain a strong working relationship with Beijing on matters of high global importance such as climate change, global health, and conflict resolution, as well as cooperate within multilateral efforts that underpin the global financial system such as the G20 and the World Trade Organization.

Given the complex nature of the U.S.-Chinese bilateral relationship, my belief is that, first and foremost, the United States must lead by example. The choices made on how best to regulate emerging digital energy technologies such as on-demand travel services, self-driving vehicles, electricity storage, and the Internet of Things will dramatically influence outcomes for human rights, individual privacy, and personal security. It cannot be an accidental process. It is increasingly clear that the use of artificial intelligence, automated vehicles and drones, e-commerce, and smart, computer-assisted household electric and appliance systems comes with strings attached, requiring an ethical and moral element that will determine our future in almost every sphere of daily and political life. It is too important to leave to chance.

China has looked to American and European models in constructing its market economy, including in recent years its approach to air pollution and greenhouse gas emissions. Chinese scientists and policy makers have collaborated with the California Air Resources Board and other American research counterparts, for example, and established a working group, the China-U.S. ZEV Policy Lab, in 2017 to partner on policy studies related to the deployment of low-emission or zero-emission vehicles. When California governor Jerry Brown hosted a global climate action summit in September 2018, China sent a high-level delegation and hosted a pavilion that highlighted China's efforts to reduce its carbon emissions. That China has sought information about California's environmental policy practices demonstrates the positive gains that can come when the United States leads by example. China, like California, is further along than the United States as a whole in establishing a market system for carbon pricing and has put in place regulations and subsidies aimed to incentivize low-carbon or zero-emissions vehicles.

Even with friendly California–China relations on climate change, California-based firms still need to worry about broader U.S.–China trade issues. Several U.S.-based American tech firms have been victims of intellectual property theft by Chinese parties and have found policy differences regarding the Communist Party's censorship and surveillance rules that have thwarted export business. The Trump administration's response to some of the competitive pressures posed by Chinese firms was to raise tariffs on Chinese solar panels and tighten restrictions on exports of sensitive technologies to Chinese firms, but America cannot outcompete China through protectionist measures alone.

The United States has shared global interests with China that must still be cultivated even as the United States mounts an economic policy to promote its own products and services. The United States needs to make sure it is building capacity from within. A key metric for the United States in achieving digital energy leadership will be how new technologies are deployed in the United States and other democratic societies. I spent considerable time researching this topic as part of my work at the University of California, Davis, where the university took an active role advising policy makers from the state of California on sustainable transportation. For five years, I met regularly with automakers, oil companies, cleantech executives, tech entrepreneurs, and state regulators. I sat on several state scientific and policy commissions. I ate sustainably, rode a bike, and drove a hybrid electric car. I took long walks in Asilomar State Park. That time convinced me of the need for a better understanding of the technologies coming in the energy sector and their pluses and minuses. This book aims to lay out the choices that need to be made regarding the deployment of those technologies and to offer some insights about how to ensure desirable outcomes as we revolutionize our transportation and electricity generation infrastructure with automation and digitization. The changes will be as astounding as those seen by our great-grandparents in the early 1900s, but we need the unintended consequences to be less damaging to the planet.

GEOPOLITICS OF CLEAN ENERGY

In the coming digital energy age, the geopolitics of energy will shift from control of access to natural resources to domination of patents, technology, and skilled workforces. Geography was destiny in the oil age. Reserves were distributed unevenly around the world, creating anxieties about access and transport routes. The United States positioned itself to address that challenge by incentivizing development of its own oil and gas resources while maintaining the naval power to ensure its unchallenged access to foreign resources. But now, in the changing energy landscape, navies will matter less. Instead, ingenuity and industrial capacity will have an outsize role. The ability to finance, deploy, and operate smart electricity infrastructure and automated vehicles will be the key to competing for new markets and consumers, especially in a world concerned about climate change. The United States must recognize this shift and embrace it. With energy such a vital input into economic activity, the world's major economies are focusing on energy innovation as a major feature of economic policy.

The U.S. Senate recognized the importance of promoting greater innovation in energy technology deployment and manufacturing by putting forward the American Energy Innovation Act in early 2020. The bill failed to progress because of a dispute over proposed amendments, but it highlighted an area of bipartisan consensus that the United States must act decisively to maintain global competitiveness.

The United States needs to take a comprehensive approach and develop a deliberate energy innovation strategy. We do not think of the United States as having industrial policy, but in fact we often spur attributes or goals for the economy through laws, regulations, tax policy, and public investment. A focused industrial policy on digital energy would bring together funding for research and development in strategically important sectors such as automation, battery storage, and advanced nuclear power with market-driving incentives that could enhance widespread adoption of new technologies through regulatory frameworks, tax policy, and government stimulus. What is needed on the regulatory end is a restructuring of the incentives for electric utilities and electricity pricing that promotes use of emerging, energy-saving, digital technologies. On the transportation side, restrictions on the operations of automated vehicles are necessary to ensure they do not contribute to a sharp rise in carbon emissions. Measures such as these are needed to guide optimal outcomes that advance the digital energy age in a manner that does not sacrifice individual rights to privacy or limit the potential for environmental gains.

U.S. policy makers face a formidable task in addressing the twin challenges of economic vitality and climate change. Consideration of how to take into account the changing world of energy must be part and parcel of any debate about restoring American manufacturing and fortifying U.S. infrastructure. Today, the United States remains unsurpassed in its development and manufacture of advanced semiconductors. That success finds its roots in a government-organized program that created the legal and budgetary architecture for public-private partnerships in the 1980s. A similar program could be instituted today in digital energy technology. It could enhance existing publicly funded technology incubators and regional research centers that are already advancing industrial and regional ecosystems in certain parts of the United States, such as northern California.

U.S. clean energy and technology companies currently have a global edge, but without a supportive policy atmosphere to foster markets at home and abroad, the United States could inadvertently cede the major global economic and strategic advantages it currently enjoys in the energy, military, and technology spheres and jeopardize its ability to sustain a premiere role in global economic activity, trade, and innovation.

U.S. ENERGY LEADERSHIP

Both the U.S. economy and U.S. national security have benefited significantly from American energy innovation over the past decade. Accelerated energy technology innovation has contributed to a renaissance in both traditional oil and gas businesses and greener technology firms. U.S.-led improvements in alternative fuels, smart devices, energy-efficient vehicles, green building design, battery storage, and small-scale smart-grid solutions, to name a few, have offered consumers around the world new options to meet surging energy needs. At the same time, the U.S. oil and gas industry has made innovations of its own. By improving hydraulic fracturing methods and combining it with horizontal drilling—both guided by supercomputing, enhanced data analytics, and automation—U.S. independent oil companies have been able to produce oil and gas from America's vast unconventional reserves. The industry's success has allowed the United States to unleash a giant wave of competitively priced oil and gas exports to the global market. By leading simultaneously in energy technology and exports, the United States was able not only to enhance its economy but also to strengthen ties to its important trading partners. At the same time, expanding exports of U.S. energy supplies and green technology constrained the petro-power of authoritarian states such as Russia and Iran, buttressing U.S. allies and enhancing U.S. global power.

Anticipation of the digital energy revolution is already reshaping the geopolitics of oil and gas and empowering major economies like the United States, Japan, and China to reduce geopolitical rivalries with each other over oil supplies. The declining allure of access to large oil fields in risky locales has made it harder for countries like Iran to solicit support against U.S. sanctions and made it easier for the world to ignore humanitarian crises in oil states like Venezuela and Libya. Similarly, as stricter carbon emission restrictions and alternative energy technologies increasingly characterize European energy markets, Russia is losing its ability to use its westward energy exports as a geopolitical tool. Sans an energy weapon, Russia has turned increasingly to military buildups and cyber confrontations in Europe and the Middle East. Iran's desperate lashing out against international shipping in the Strait of Hormuz and at Saudi oil facilities in 2019 can be viewed in the same context as Tehran's response to the waning importance of its oil and gas.

Ironically, against this backdrop of the possibly fading age of oil, the United States over the past few years has pinned its hopes for the coming years on the idea that its shale oil and gas will usher in an age of energy abundance that America would dominate. But competition to rising U.S. oil and gas exports has come from multiple directions, creating huge headwinds for U.S. shale companies during the early days of the COVID-19 crisis in 2020. Ultimately, it is in the long-term strategic interests for geopolitical oil rivals such as Russia or Saudi Arabia to continue to take actions to preserve their petro-power by ramping up pricing and export strategies to squash competition from U.S. oil and gas. The United States will have to navigate this threat to its own oil and gas sector through skilled multilateral diplomacy, while at the same time positioning its economy over the longer run for the energy transition.

By the same token, U.S. cleantech policy must take into account that China's embrace of digital energy innovation as part of its new industrial strategy, called China 2025, could turn out to be even more challenging to American preeminence. China's push in clean energy innovation will mean it can be a rival energy exporter to the United States. The Trump administration envisioned a resurgent U.S. global leadership bolstered by America's vast supplies of affordable fossil energy. In Trump's energy-dominant America, U.S. foreign policy hoped to tap America's energy wealth to help the United States maintain its global leadership and influence through U.S. energy exports unfettered by excessive government regulation. But failure to recognize the impact that a global energy transition to lower- or zero-carbon-emitting fuels could be detrimental to the long-term interests of the United States. By focusing on traditional energy and withdrawing from global engagement on climate change, the Trump administration set the United States backward as a global economic competitor, because there will be increased opportunity to sell products linked to green energy to markets already embarking on the energy transition or considering doing so soon. Moreover, as more countries impose carbon taxes or pricing, exports of fossil energy will be penalized. Finally, as new energy-efficient technologies take hold, this could potentially shrink opportunities for petroleum-based fuels from the United States, which generally cost more to produce than those in the Middle East and Russia.

China is already staking out its position to promote and thereby dominate the green energy market, creating a giant industrial complex armed with cheap solar panels and intelligent drones, smart-grid and distributed-energy technologies, and Chinese electrified and autonomous vehicles. The country's energy pivot, expected to include investments of more than six trillion dollars by 2040, is designed to take its current national energy deficit, characterized by rising oil and gas demand amid a dearth of domestic oil and gas resources, and, with the help of a vast arsenal of rare earth materials, turn it into a global clean-energy gold mine. China dominates the global solar panel market, and now Beijing is diving in deeper to expand to a wider range of oil-saving technologies, from batteries to electric vehicles, drones, and robotics. China's ambitious Belt and Road Initiative aims to build the next generation of energy infrastructure throughout Asia and the Middle East. In many cases, these exports come complete with Chinese influence on how to utilize censorship of the internet and other uses of technology for political repression. China's energy innovation means it will be able not only to buy less U.S. oil and gas but also to offer other important economies in Europe and Africa the chance to lessen their purchases as well.

U.S. MISSTEPS

The Trump administration's withdrawal from the Paris climate agreement was a decisive, potentially costly error. The United States must reestablish fully its leadership role in climate negotiations, to ensure global carbon and energy rules are not set by other nations, potentially to the disadvantage of the U.S. economy and its exports. There is a distinct possibility now that the global architecture for carbon and energy might wind up strongly in China's favor, to the detriment of U.S. interests. So far, the inherently decentralized free economy system of the United States is a plus. The pluralism of American political culture and economic activity is ensuring that the trend toward energy innovation continues. State and local governments are actively playing a key role in supporting major industries inside their jurisdictions, including cultivating international R & D interconnectedness that keeps the United States in the game even without a major commitment at the federal level.

Still, how countries limit greenhouse gas emissions (including possible border tariffs or prices on carbon) and modulate investment in energy and transportation services (including regulations on how publicly traded companies must operate to comply with globally set targets established in Paris in 2016) will be a major feature of the emerging twenty-first-century international system. The United States must be actively engaged as a leader in global climate negotiations to reestablish America's say on how and what technologies and alternative energy will be promoted in key economies. Anything less could potentially reduce American standing in international organizations. U.S. companies have a strong role to play not only in clean technologies but also in carbon capture and sequestration, should U.S. political leaders step up to the plate with a wider range of policies. In 2019, the U.S. Congress passed a limited first come, first served federal tax credit for companies willing to capture and store their carbon emissions underground or use the CO2 for enhanced oil recovery. It was a useful policy, but more like it is needed.

Still, even with an active climate change diplomatic strategy, the United States will not be able to rest on its laurels as a past leader in energy innovation. Without substantial public funding for innovation in energy and resiliency technology development, the United States will fall behind other nations and regional groups with focused efforts such as China and Europe. The United States has responded to the challenge with greater export controls on its own critical technologies but has yet to step up to the plate with the kind of massive investment in innovation that characterized its race to space against the Soviet Union after the successful launch of the Soviet *Sputnik* satellite in 1957. U.S. failure to embrace the digital energy challenge could by analogy be comparable to

America's failing to recognize that the Soviet superiority in space could threaten its own national security and preeminent geostrategic status. China's clear intention to dominate the new digital energy market with its own brand of smart drones, cyber surveillance technologies, submarines, and automated vehicles is in no small measure related to the stakes thàt new, asymmetric warfare technologies will play in future global conflicts.

ENERGY INNOVATION AND U.S. MILITARY SUPREMACY

Since the time of Edison, American business innovation and entrepreneurship have given the United States a technological edge over geopolitical rivals and ensured U.S. military supremacy. Ford's mass-produced trucks and cars proved critical in many battles of World War I in overcoming Germany's advantageous access to European railroad transport. Over the course of the war, the United States manufactured more than 70 percent of all allied war material, with Ford Motor Company alone contributing more than the entire Italian national war effort. By the 1940s, the U.S. domestic oil industry, dominated by Rockefeller's Standard Oil, constituted two-thirds of world oil production and was a crucial factor in closing Britain's fuel deficit compared to Germany and Japan. By 1941, President Franklin Delano Roosevelt had to back away from trust busting to a "Win the War" industrial strategy that included loaning American oil to the British as part of Roosevelt's "arsenal of democracy."[1] As the war effort accelerated, Roosevelt, whose New Deal was initially decried by industry, was forced to embrace the unfettered advancement of the country's wealthiest industrialists as part of the war effort.

Now, decades later, a new geopolitical rivalry is emerging among great powers seeking to dominate critical digital technologies to be applied to energy and mobility. A new race to electrified self-driving vehicles and drones, armed with artificial intelligence, machine learning, and monster data analytics, is about to revolutionize warfare and change the nature of critical military supply chains. The U.S. Pentagon recognized this future and began funding American scientists to develop the technology for automated machines and vehicles in 2004 with a grand challenge to produce a robot car that could transverse the Mojave Desert in the American Southwest.[2] Largely unnoticed, the U.S. Congress set a goal to have a third of all ground combat vehicles be autonomous by 2015, a deadline that missed the mark in the timeline of its ambition.[3]

The U.S. private sector is certainly doing its part. Five U.S. tech giants—Amazon, Facebook, Apple, Microsoft, and Google/Alphabet—are expected to have their R&D spending reach $160 billion in the year 2022.[4] Amazon spent $39.5 billion in 2019 alone. In one sample year, all of the U.S.-based companies spent $329 billion in R & D from June 2016 to June 2017, according to one Pricewaterhouse-Coopers study.[5] By way of comparison, that is larger than the entire private sector of Japan, whose total R & D spending was $151 billion in 2018. But the focus of their product development can differ from national needs and goals. Balancing the advantages of a free market system and the proven benefits of government-directed industrial efforts is one of the United States' largest challenges vis-à-vis its geopolitical rivals when it comes to energy innovation. The United States has a long, complex history of mixing laissez-faire economics with national initiatives, as in the space race or SEMATEC, the public-private initiative to restore the competitiveness of American semiconductor manufacturing which had been surpassed by Japan in the 1980s.

I bring to this book five very interesting years living near Silicon Valley and conducting research on emerging energy technologies and sustainable investing. My office at the University of California, Davis, was located in West Village, the largest planned "net zero energy" community in the United States. A net-zero-energy facility is one that produces as much energy as it needs to use. Next to my office in West Village was a three-story solar tower that, together with solar-panel-covered parking arrays and other on-site renewable energy at the university, powered electric lights, computers, household appliances, and even the occasional electric car plug. Advanced energy conservation at West Village via energy-saving design, appliances, and smart-metered apartments resulted in a reduced energy load that was about half the typical building standards of the day. The town of Davis also collected our organic garbage—that is, food waste and plantings—to process in a biodigester on the University of California, Davis, campus that converted the garbage into usable energy by hastening the process by which microbes break down organic matter into methane, which can then be used to power electricity or converted to gaseous fuel.

West Village offers just a hint of how technological energy advances could radically transform the way businesses and individuals buy and sell energy services and the kinds of fuel sources that will be favored in the coming decades.

It is possible that someday we will collect solar energy from our roofs and have a home "digester" that transforms our garbage into electricity that we can sell back to our neighbors and friends when we aren't using it. We will become a class of "prosumers" who both produce and consume energy, much as we now both watch and generate content for social media. Our excess energy production will be stored in devices like stationary batteries or car batteries and offered for sale when we don't need it and there is demand elsewhere on the grid. If we choose not to have a personal vehicle, a solar-array-covered parking lot near our home will store vehicles we can summon at will via phone or Alexa when we need to travel—but probably not to the store, because our grocer will have a robot truck to bring food to our doorstep and a mini-robot to bring it from the curb to inside our home or office. We will 3D-print goods with less waste and eliminate fuel-intensive shipping. Yet these technologies will only help us achieve net zero emissions if we demand that they be designed and regulated to do so. If we pursue their use in wasteful ways, they could increase our need for energy.

Computer-assisted, automated energy innovation will soon become a vital national interest. Leading in energy innovation is critical to a country's global competitiveness, not only in spurring new markets, industries, and companies, but also in producing more cost-effective supply chains and boosting manufacturing productivity. It is important for military readiness and access to space travel. Over the years, it has lowered our economy's energy intensity.

To understand the nature and magnitude of the coming digital revolution and its implications, I looked both backward and forward with the help of some of the best and brightest business leaders, scientists, historians, and economists of our time. I interviewed technologists from Silicon Valley and toured their factories and headquarters. I met with senior leaders from oil-producing states and strategic planners from the world's largest car manufacturers. I delved into the archival history of energy innovation in the United States and its role in America's military ascension. The chapters that follow reflect the digital energy future that might be ahead of us and offer some prescriptions for how to mold it to our benefit. In the coming chapters, I explain the nuts and bolts of key digital energy technologies and how they could potentially reduce the need for oil through radical improvements in productivity and optimization. As part of the process, I offer an early assessment of potential gains, as well as possible land mines, on the path ahead.

HISTORY AS TEACHER

Chapter 1 lays the groundwork for how best to think about the interaction between new technologies and potential unintended consequences. History shows that national institutions and regulatory structures play a critical role in promoting the kinds of innovations that lift nations to prominence. Most people believe that Ford Motor Company's gasoline car won the day simply because it was the superior, most affordable technology, relative to other options of its time, and that we locked into the oil economy because it was the best alternative. As chapter 1 will show, electric vehicles were cheaper and less dangerous than their gasoline equivalents for more than a decade, and other factors related to military priorities and a lack of proper regulation of monopoly industries played an outsize role in oil's rise to the top. Now, one hundred years later, a new set of entrepreneurs and inventors are launching a similarly bold period of energy innovation that will create new infrastructure path dependencies and crown new geopolitical winners and losers. The history of the 1900s energy technology boom illustrates how choosing the policies that will bridle energy's digital revolution is highly material to our sustainable future, just as choices made one hundred years ago are even now hard to reverse. Chapter 2 further investigates this concept of path dependency and expounds on the efficacy of industrial and trade policy to influence outcomes.

A vast array of inventions to come, such as robot cars, smart device apps, and home battery systems could transform the way we use energy in our everyday life. A new generation is eager for change, but the difficulty of replacing an entire system of more than a billion automobiles, hundreds of oil refineries, massive international pipeline systems, large-scale centralized power generation plants, and an extensive network of transmission wires seems overwhelming. Studies on innovation explain how incumbents like the fossil fuel and utility industries continue to benefit from existing political, institutional, and structural forces that protect their interests. But we cannot blame the difficulties in making a rapid energy transition solely on Big Oil, no matter how appealing that might feel. Energy infrastructure is by its nature long-lasting and creates physical and regulatory path dependencies that are hard to reverse. As we consider how the infrastructure of the digital energy revolution will be deployed, we must consider the path dependencies of choices to ensure we do not inadvertently lock in results that are out of step with societal goals and environmental aims. The history of how path dependency has led to today's fossil fuel dominance is instructive to how we utilize emerging digital technologies purposefully to solve current and future problems, not create new ones.

Chapter 3 delves into how China, the world's most populous country, is leveraging its giant population and consumer buying power to attain top status in the race to dominate digital energy and green technologies and what its efforts might mean for changing geopolitics. China's plans stem from its increasing energy insecurity at a time when the United States is moving toward energy self-sufficiency. How these two economic and military superpowers understand and influence the energy transition will have major consequences for their bilateral relationship and for global trends.

To consider the stakes for the new technologies that are coming, chapters 4, 5, and 6 lay out how an array of smart digital advances are poised to disrupt the future of urban transportation, global manufacturing, trade, and the business of electricity generation. Since the technologies themselves are not deterministic, attention is paid to the regulatory and institutional framework needed to ensure these disruptions eliminate carbon emissions and promote democratic institutions. These chapters delve into the opportunity to utilize smart transportation solutions and advanced manufacturing and power generation technologies to tackle congestion, air pollution, and greenhouse gas emissions, but note that the regulatory and business response to market restructuring will determine just how effective new technologies and investor responses can be in providing greater energy supply resilience under the stresses of climate change. Regulatory response is also needed to prevent changes to the energy landscape from accelerating volatility in financial markets as investors begin to assess more earnestly the risks to incumbent businesses that will come from a transition to a lower-carbon global economy.

The remainder of the book covers the geopolitical consequences of the new greener, digital energy world, laying out the potential winners and losers and the actions they could take to assert themselves in global discourse amid rapid change. As new global energy winners and losers emerge from the digital energy age, the relative power of nations will change. Historically, expectations were that oil-producing countries like Saudi Arabia, Russia, Iran, and Venezuela that sit on hundreds of years of oil and gas reserves would be able to leverage their coveted oil and gas assets to gain international power and influence as oil became scarcer. But now technology has begun to usher in an age of energy abundance, as new technologies eat away at demand for oil while making it easier to find and produce. As the global economy delinks economic growth from oil intensity, the world's largest oil reserve holders could be relegated to lesser geopolitical stature and find their common interests with consuming nations are less compelling. On the flip side, the widespread advent of digitally assisted green energy will usher in a new dawn of international competition that will focus more squarely on ingenuity and industrial capability than on controlling access to raw materials. Perhaps even more striking than the loss of power by petro-states, it is becoming increasingly clear that nations that excel at automation and artificial intelligence will gain both military and economic advantages. As I will argue over the course of the book, the United States will have strategic competitors in this regard, and its energy policy needs to reflect that.

A MORE COMPREHENSIVE DIGITAL ENERGY
STRATEGY FOR THE UNITED STATES

I end with some thoughts on what the United States should do to embrace the digital energy revolution and ensure that the change is a positive one aligned with U.S. national interests and core democratic values. As in the past, managing access to energy will be a critical element in the balance of power between the United States and a rising China. Both China and the United States are using energy as an entry point to strengthen alliances and bilateral trade. China's embrace of digital energy innovation as part of its new industrial strategy is challenging America's vision of itself, with highly significant consequences for the future of trade and globalization. The United States is moving to restrict trade with China and Russia in American technologies that might have a military dual use, such as artificial intelligence and remote-sensing laser technologies such as lidar, a critical automation technology that transmits a laser pulse to measure the distance of objects. The United States is encouraging its allies to do the same.

Mirroring history, in which national security took precedence over other values during the two world wars and the Cold War, the pressure to outstrip China introduces the risk that some of the downsides to widespread digital technology adoption—such as higher consumption, environmental degradation, and violation of privacy—might not be addressed if technological dominance is the sole metric of success. This is creating tension between important goals of national security and Western values that must be resolved by thoughtful public policy.

In the future, countries that emphasize easily accessed, energy-saving technologies could wind up best positioned in global trade and national security. The new technologies are likely to better prepare countries to recover from extreme weather events and other calamities, offering security, convenience, and economic benefits to their citizens. Militaries will also need to position themselves to source energy from fuels and power systems that are ample, reliable, and best suited to fuel automated vehicles and drones, raising questions about what energy technology applications the United States should be investing in for strategic reasons. The United States cannot just rest on the laurels of its ability to produce a lot more oil and gas domestically. U.S. energy policy must also encompass future energy transformations to make sure the country is positioned for the future. To maintain its global influence and economic power, the United States needs a smarter policy that will engage a new generation of citizens to mobilize for scientific and technological innovation. Policy makers must be prepared to adjust the market design and regulatory framework not only to gain the benefits of energy innovation but also to avoid potential unintended negative consequences of adopting new energy technologies.

To ensure that energy's digital future is one that protects democratic governance and institutions while also addressing climate change, the United States must be the leader in the deployment and export of the host of new energy technologies about to disrupt the existing energy landscape. Momentum is not in favor of the United States because China's unparalleled size as the world's largest consumer market confers on Beijing an economic and strategic advantage. Still, the rigidities of the Chinese authoritarian system are a hindrance to China's success and leave an opening for the United States to harness the power of a well-designed, liberal values–based, market-oriented approach to move forward with a better paradigm that will be compelling to other countries.

CHAPTER 1

Lessons from History

Nothing Is Inevitable

One of the things many of us find most difficult to understand is the process of technological change. What makes a society shift from one form of energy to another? Not only is the current energy system massive, but it has been in place for more than a hundred years. The oil industry often falls back on these facts in its efforts to convince us how impossible it would be to modify the status quo, let alone remake it. The giant infrastructure that delivers our energy—refineries, gasoline stations, pipelines, power stations, substations, and electrical grids, to name a few—requires billions of dollars to construct and then lasts for decades. As the former chair of Chevron, John Watson, said in a typical oil industry speech in 2010, "The sheer scale of our energy needs is far beyond the capacity of any one source or technology. And under any scenario, oil and natural gas will be the largest part of that portfolio for decades to come."[1] But history has shown us that there are periods of rapid transformation, such as the turn of the twentieth century, when time seems to speed up and change comes overwhelmingly fast.

Consider how New Yorkers at the previous turn of the century switched from horse-drawn carriages to motor cars in under two decades. To our generation, gas-guzzling cars, internal combustion engines, and plastic water bottles might seem as though they are here to stay. Yet when a fellow named Steve Jobs confidently told a television news reporter in 1982 that his goal was to create a computer so small you could hold it in your hand, people who saw that interview probably scoffed because it seemed so preposterous. Today, we feel lost and naked if the device he conjured for us is not firmly in our grasp.

Classical economic theory on technology winners implies that markets will dictate the rapid adoption of the best, cheapest, and most widely available product. We assume that suppliers who can reliably furnish the best product at the largest scale and least cost will be the winner. But experience shows a more complex equation. Research on technology lock-in is instructive. Sometimes, one technology solution is chosen over another because institutional factors, such as antitrust laws, convey an advantage beyond quality or price. For example, there is an entire body of scholarly literature on whether U.S. antitrust laws promote innovation.[2] The intuitive argument is that the more competition, the greater the chances of innovation. In a market with strong antitrust laws, new start-up firms are not bought up by larger competitors, avoiding the risk that the innovative spirit of newcomers is lost. But it can also be argued that market power gives large firms the security to invest in research and development of new products by ensuring the long-range profitability of doing so. Politics can also skew outcomes: owners and workers associated with prevailing technologies often fight hard against insurgents whose inventions might make their products and jobs obsolete.[3] And, in the case of energy, as I will argue here, other national priorities, especially national defense, often dictate which technologies receive government incentives and thereby rule for decades after a threat of war has passed.

The period around the turn of the last century ushered in a time of monumental energy innovation that influenced the outcomes of two world wars and positioned the United States as a global superpower. The premiere role of energy innovation, supported by U.S. government sponsorship of research and development around the time of the two world wars, gives a historical context to the idea that government involvement in shaping energy policy serves the national interest. Thomas Edison actively pitched products from his innovation lab to the U.S. military. Henry Ford's rapid assembly-line process and engineering design team contributed to the war effort when America entered World War I in 1917. But most important, the materials that went into making electric car batteries were needed for the war effort. As a result, car manufacturing was altered during World War I and never shifted back.

The journey back in time also reveals other important truths about the energy innovation process. A host of exigencies can drive outcomes, including not only social change but also the intense personal drive of an individual entrepreneur. Oil's victory as the premiere vehicle fuel was not a given in 1910. Electric cars were widely deployed in major cities, and early gasoline engines had many flaws. Public policy failed to address the pollution and other drawbacks to gasoline vehicles.

Not only did the U.S. government support the internal combustion engine technology for its own use, but roadbuilding that supported faster, gas-guzzling cars became a national project. By the 1930s, oil's ubiquitous role was locked in with a host of ramifications, both good and bad. Once this path dependency was firmly established, it became virtually unchallengeable, leaving us today with great difficulties in returning to electrification. As we consider the future of mobility, fuller debate is needed on the consequences of automated vehicles and ride hailing to ensure there are no similar regrets one hundred years hence as there are today with gasoline cars. In the United States, the U.S. National Highway Traffic Safety Administration has begun to grant temporary approval for low-speed autonomous delivery vehicles, expected to deliver groceries in Houston and other locations. That approval has focused on safety conditions. The California Public Utilities Commission has solicited feedback from stakeholders on autonomous vehicle regulations for business fleets on a wider range of issues, including emissions regulations and social equity principles—that is, ensuring equal services are provided to all riders and neighborhoods.

The fact that transportation in cities was almost fully electrified in the early 1900s is probably shocking news to many. Gasoline vehicles were initially developed to help rural folk who lacked the electricity infrastructure get around. In 1910, gasoline was not the best technology. It was highly flawed and dangerous. Rather, electric streetcars and electric taxis, hailed by telephone, were the main means of transportation. I point that out because a desirable transportation outcome being discussed today is a coordinated system of electrified public transit combined with phone-summoned, last-mile taxi services. Had we stuck with that system for the past hundred years, the current problems of air pollution, congestion, and global warming might already have been solved.

FLAWS IN EARLY GASOLINE TECHNOLOGY

Back when we made the choice, proponents of oil like to tell us, gasoline cars were the cheapest, best, and most widely available option. The arrival of gasoline saved the day, historians of the oil industry recount, by rescuing society from mounting levels of horse manure that had become a major environmental and health hazard in cities. Then there is the oil industry's other favorite mantra: Gasoline is the fuel with the highest "energy density," which means it takes less of it than other fuels to produce the same level of travel; therefore, it is so superior no other technology could compete.

It seems obvious now that gasoline cars were a big improvement over horse-drawn carriages. Dire predictions in the 1890s warned that millions of pounds of horse manure from horses drawing carriages were overwhelming city streets each day and creating a health nightmare for the growing urban masses. According to a *New York Times* article from July 1893, neighborhoods close to stables experienced a 60 percent increase in mortality rates compared with the city average. Horseflies were another scourge that city dwellers had to grapple with because of carriages and animal droppings.[4] These health consequences were a priority for many urban policy makers struggling to keep up with the issue.

But the claim that gasoline—or the oil industry that kept gasoline flowing—was what rescued the masses is a dubious one, bordering on revisionist history. In fact, urban policy makers saw electricity, not oil, as the elixir most likely to help cities transition away from animal power. Mass transit would be one beneficiary of that shift, and by 1895, there were more than 850 electric trolley systems with more than ten thousand miles of track.[5] As one *New York Times* writer opined in discussing the monumental health and environmental problem of the proliferation of horseflies in cities in 1898, electricity was viewed as the distant technological solution: "the most hopeful token of abatement to flies in cities, however is to be found in the substitution of electricity for horses, but that is still so far off that there is every possibility that the fly question will still be discussed long after the Cuban question [referring to the Spanish-American War] is settled."[6] As it turned out, he did not have to wait too long. The Spanish-American War came to a close soon after this article appeared, and over the next decade electric streetcars and electric vehicles quickly took hold in cities. By 1902, Americans had taken more than 4.8 billion trips on electric streetcars.[7]

Even when Henry Ford introduced the Model T, his famed car for the masses, in 1908, it was not clear that the gasoline-powered engine would become the king of the road. A bruising struggle for fuel dominance in the United States between electric- and gasoline-powered automobiles persisted for more than two decades. Ford hedged his bets somewhat with the Model T, giving it a flexible fuel system that could operate on gasoline or alcohol, a dual-fuel car in today's parlance. The car found particular favor in rural markets, where electricity services were still lacking. It ran best on grain alcohol, which suited farm communities like the one where Ford was raised.

Accurate historical accounts do not paint the gasoline engine as the best and cheapest technology alternative in its early years. Print ads for the first generation of gas-guzzlers touted their "modern" and "innovative" technology. But early gasoline-powered cars had serious obstacles to overcome if they were going to win over the public. Gas-powered cars were relatively expensive compared to electric vehicles, and they came with hand cranks that made them very hard to start; women in particular were often not strong enough to start the engine using the manual crank. In fact, the American slang term "cranky" finds its roots in the frustration people felt wrangling with the infernal devices to start their cars. Even worse, the kickback from the crank handle was sometimes strong enough to break an arm or jaw. It was not an invention for the faint of heart.

A further disadvantage of gasoline cars is that while steam engines and electric vehicles could accelerate and decelerate smoothly from idle to full speed without stalling, early gasoline engines had trouble idling at a low rate of revolutions per minute. To keep from stalling, they required a more demanding gearshift that was commanded with a clutch. Many drivers found this piece of equipment hard to operate. To this day, many Americans cannot operate a stick-shift car. But in the early 1900s, the act of driving was even more daunting. A case in point: in 1912, Henry Ford, a master at public relations, bestowed a Model T upon his famous friend John Burroughs, a naturalist who had previously spoken out publicly against the evils of gasoline. Given how feverishly the press covered both men, the flashy gesture should have resulted in the kind of publicity most entrepreneurs dream about. But Burroughs had so much trouble maintaining control of the vehicle, he crashed into a barn.[8]

To make matters worse, until the advent of gas stations, filling up was also a problem. Gasoline was sold in handheld containers, ladled out from the local grocery or paint store. It was smelly and highly combustible. People literally had to worry about blowing themselves up since early cars were designed to stash the fuel in a holding tank just under the driver's seat, inches from the driver's bottom. The fuel was considered so volatile that insurance companies, cities, and companies placed restrictions on the use of gasoline in certain locations out of concern for safety or cleanliness.[9]

On dirt roads, gasoline cars also performed worse than electrics, with broken axles, overheated engines, and cracked pistons among the problems that drivers encountered regularly. Engine knock, that nagging sound produced inside car engines when fuel and air are not mixing properly, went unsolved until the 1920s.

Smoky, noxious fumes from car exhaust poured into the atmosphere, fouling the air that was already sullied by pollution from the manufacturing sector and the burning of coal and wood.

The crazy thing about how cars developed in cities at the turn of the twentieth century is that the solutions we are debating today—converting city streets over to fleets of electric taxis, buses, and trucks—was *the* system that was in place in those same cities in the early 1900s. Somehow, as a society, we lost more than a hundred years of progress by shifting from electricity to gasoline-powered machines as our dominant mode of transportation, to the virtual exclusion of all else. That makes it all the more important to understand exactly how electricity eventually lost out.

ELECTRIC CARS DOMINATED IN 1910

Most people would be shocked to learn how commonplace electric cars, taxis, and trolleys once were in the United States, and that all the American can-do they represented somehow got left at the side of the road. That should give heart to the possibility that we could make a more constructive change again, back to an urban transportation system fueled by electricity, now generated by cleaner energy sources.

Just as we consider how to deploy robot taxis today, it is useful to understand that taxis were part of the first wave of cars used in cities in the early 1900s. Ford's Model T was intended as a rural product. Before cars were affordable for most people, taxi services were commonplace in many cities, and they typically consisted of fleets of electric cars. The companies quickly changed out the batteries in a vehicle when the charge was low and then redeployed the vehicle. Operators of these large fleets usually had enough cars in service to be able to charge the car's batteries as needed. They managed the logistics of the long charging period in central locations in a manner that meant customers were not affected by the downtime.

The first electric taxi service was founded in central London by the London Electric Company in 1897. It deployed cabs developed by Walter Bersey, with forty-cell lead-acid batteries, a horsepower of three, and a fifty-mile range.[10] That same year, the Electric Carriage and Wagon Company emulated London Electric and bought a fleet of electric hansom cabs in New York City. Soon, some sort of electric taxi company was established in most U.S. cities. The first U.S. speeding ticket went to an electric taxi driver who got a ticket in May 1899 in New York City (12 mph in an 8-mph zone). A police officer who pulled the driver over was on a bicycle.[11]

By the time Ford's Model T first appeared in 1908, electric cars and delivery trucks dominated city streets. Dozens of manufacturers jostled for a piece of the action, including the Baker Motor Vehicles Company of Ohio, the Pope Manufacturing Company, and the Electric Vehicle Company, to name a few.[12] These automobiles used a variety of technologies, but most relied on lead-acid materials. Early electric vehicles had a range of around forty to one hundred miles and a maximum speed of thirty miles per hour.[13] They were easier to use and maintain than gasoline-powered vehicles. At the turn of the century, several firms were also building electric delivery wagons to replace horse-drawn vehicles, in addition to trucks, theater buses, and omnibuses.

Electric vehicles were not only widely available, they were considered cleaner, safer, and easier to operate than other alternatives. At the time the gasoline engine was being pioneered, electric cars were actually the less expensive technology. Although the limit on how far an electric car could travel before needing a recharge was less than the distance a gasoline car could go before needing a refill, the differential was not that great and was not a make-or-break factor for drivers who hardly left town and had no expectations of high-speed operation. In 1908, the Baker electric Roadster could go as fast as forty miles per hour. At its conservative average city speed of fourteen miles per hour, it could travel one hundred miles before needing a charge. Ridiculously slow, you say? Try driving across Manhattan at rush hour today and you might be wishing for that speed.

By 1912, more than six thousand types of electric vehicles were on offer, ranging in price from modest $850 town cars to luxurious $5,500 limousines (roughly equivalent to spending $22,600 to $146,000 for those same luxuries today). Magazine advertisements for electric cars featured women drivers attending social affairs, chauffeuring their husbands about, and going out to play golf.[14] Henry Ford himself bought his wife higher-end models of the Detroit Electric, a rival line, because his wife refused to drive in one of his own mass-produced cars.[15]

As is true today, for electric cars to work at the turn of the century, line voltage had to be adjusted with a rheostat device to match the vehicle's configuration of battery cells, ranging from sixteen to forty-eight 2-volt cells. A home charging setup was needed to ensure the current and voltage and to prevent the battery from overcharging. Initially, electricians had to create custom systems, but eventually Westinghouse brought to market a rotary converter and control panel that ended the practice. J. B. Merriam also offered a small 500-watt power plant, fueled by a water-cooled gas engine, which was offered as an optional accessory to the Baker electric cars. General Electric developed a charging hydrant called the "electrant," but wide distribution of charging equipment remained problematic.

Society in the heyday of electric cars faced social pressures similar to today. Groups whose jobs were on the line provided a political context to the question of alternative automotive technologies. The hay industry was a dominant feature of New England economic life; U.S. hay production topped ninety-seven million tons in 1909.[16] Hay farmers were an important political constituency, and they tended to oppose any new modes of transportation that put horses out to pasture. Moreover, early cars were considered a danger to the majority of people getting about by bicycle or horse, much as many Arizonans object to sharing the road with Waymo's self-driving vehicles. Back in the day, motorists were required to pull over and stop their cars if a horse driver was approaching. Today, people have been arrested for attacking a Waymo robot car with a baseball bat or worse.[17]

Other undercurrents of a more serious nature were also brewing at the turn of the twentieth century, an earlier troubled time when incredible technological change was undermining institutions and jobs. As Walter Reade notes in his essay about that turbulent historical period:

> As Americans struggle to make sense of a series of uncomfortable economic changes and disturbing political developments, a worrying picture emerges: ineffective politicians, frequent scandals, racial backsliding, polarized and irresponsible news media, populists spouting quack economic remedies, growing suspicion of elites and experts, frightening outbreaks of violence, major job losses, high profile terrorist attacks, anti-immigrant agitation, declining social mobility, giant corporations dominating the economy, rising inequality, and the appearance of a new class of super-empowered billionaires in finance and technology-heavy industries.

Curiously, one issue that did not make Reade's long list of social maladies, but probably should have, was America's growing indifference to the environment in the wake of technological progress.

Reade goes on to note that, following the radical technological changes of the early 1900s, the United States became the "largest and most advanced economy in the world," in no small measure because of technologies and business innovations that came from industrialists like John D. Rockefeller, Henry Ford, Harvey S. Firestone, and Thomas Edison. Doug Brinkley notes that around that time, the United States was the "greatest industrialized country," producing more than a quarter of all manufactured goods in the global market.[18]

AMERICA'S ORIGINAL TECH DISRUPTERS: FORD AND EDISON

The monopolistic tendencies of the great U.S. industrialists such as Rockefeller, Edison, and Firestone were eventually challenged by other firms, by new laws, or by the courts, and sometimes reined in. But the energy system that evolved during that period from 1900 to 1925 has endured for more than a century with few changes. The aftereffects of these industrialists' efforts to dominate markets left an entrenched infrastructure that has been stubbornly resistant to change. Countless scientific studies and computer simulations later, we are still struggling with the best way to transition to a more sustainable energy system. There is a lesson in that. Decisions made today about self-driving vehicles, ride hailing, and distributed electricity require greater public debate and scrutiny if they are going to allow the kind of "modernity" that might be desirable in another hundred years.

By all accounts, Henry Ford would have fit in well with today's disruptive institution-busting tech culture of Silicon Valley. The historian Douglas Brinkley recounts how Ford's fascination with machinery went back to his childhood years on a farm,[19] much as the current media now trace some of Telsa's high-flying achievements to the formative years that its founder and chief technology officer J. B. Straubel spent hanging out in start-up garages.[20] When Ford left his engineering position at the Edison Illuminating Company to pursue his own inventions, he confounded his early backers by spending too much time perfecting prototypes and not enough time selling his own designed car.[21]

Ford's grand vision, to assemble and sell cars for the masses, eventually required him to take on the powerful Association of Licensed Automobile Manufacturers (ALAM) and the formidable patent pool it had amassed to safeguard the entrenched interests of its membership. In 1903, after failing to negotiate a deal with ALAM, Ford refused to pay the royalties the organization had assessed on his Model A cars and publicly dared the ALAM to sue him for patent infringement.[22] By 1909, the simmering lawsuit between Ford and ALAM continued to expose Model T owners, whose vehicles violated ALAM patents, to potential liability. The *Detroit Free Press* published an editorial that hailed Ford's efforts on behalf of the common man who desired an inexpensive car, in a sentiment that reflected popular thinking of the day. "As a human figure," the paper gushed, Ford "presents a spectacle to win the applause of all men with red blood; for this world dearly loves the fighting man, and needs him, too, if we are to go forward." Ford eventually won the case and built a company that outpaced his rivals on the ALAM roster. Ford Motor became one of the most important firms in America. His path made Ford a bit of a folk hero in America as a self-made millionaire of the people, "the millionaire commoner" as Brinkley so aptly suggested.[23]

Early in his career, Ford was not committed to gasoline as a fuel. He initially designed the Model T to have a flexible fuel system that could operate on either gasoline or alcohol. Like today's dual-fuel sugar ethanol/gasoline cars in Brazil, the Model T had a lever on the side of the steering wheel that allowed the driver to freely switch the engine to accommodate either gasoline or an alcohol made from biomass like ethanol.

At the same time that Ford was working on his Models A through T designs, a then very famous Thomas Edison was also experimenting with a nickel-iron battery he hoped would revolutionize the electric car. To say that Edison was the Bill Gates or Steve Jobs of his day would not do justice to him or the dizzying number of game-changing inventions that flowed out of his lab, everything from the bulbs that light up our nights to the recorded music that lights up our lives.[24] His celebrity was more iconic than today's tech giants who are famous for one thing. He was considered a national icon and was a household name at a time when media coverage of business was less widespread than it is now.

In May 1901, Edison formed the Edison Storage Battery Company. Edison had big plans for his new battery, which he thought could be used by trolley companies and others. To extend the viability of his invention into the countryside, Edison even proposed that small windmills be attached to electrical generators. Together, they would be used to recharge batteries in cars while homeowners were asleep in a manner that would be cheaper than gasoline.[25] This model of decentralized household distributed energy plus electric car is being revisited today in the Honda House of the Future on the University of California, Davis, campus, again raising the prospect that we lost what could have been an opportunity to do things differently one hundred years ago.

As Ford and Edison became better acquainted (they had met only briefly when Ford was in Edison's employ), the possibility of an alliance on batteries became logical. Edison sent a letter to Ford asking if he would consider "gambling with me on the future of the storage battery."[26] In 1912, Ford's competitors at Cadillac made a big stride forward by developing an electric starter that could be put on a gasoline-powered engine and end the need for those pesky crank handles that customers detested. The nudge from Cadillac gave Ford and Edison extra incentive to push forward on storage batteries, not only for an electric starter to counter the competition from Cadillac but also for the development of a superior all-electric car.

Letters between Edison and Ford executives show that the Edison-Ford enterprise began in earnest and involved at least one successful test run of a prototype of Edison's storage battery. That occurred in March 1913, when the device powered a railroad car between New York and Boston.[27] In 1914, the Edison-Ford electric car venture made headlines when Henry Ford himself directly confirmed to the *New York Times* and other outlets that the two moguls were collaborating to produce a superior electric car that would cost no more than $600. In January 1914, Ford advised reporters: "Within a year, I hope, we shall begin the manufacture of an electric automobile. . . . The fact is that Mr. Edison and I have been working for some years on an electric vehicle which would be cheap and practical. Cars have been built for experimental purposes, and we are satisfied that the way is clear for success." Ford added that the new cars would be able to run one hundred miles and that his son Edsel would be in charge of the new plant where the electric cars would be built. The ballyhooed project never came to full fruition, however. Historians have differed on why Edison and Ford never completed their joint electric vehicle, but it is clear that the exigencies of war diverted the attention of both men.

GASOLINE, NOT ELECTRIC, FOR THE WAR EFFORT

Though the fighting was initially confined to Europe, the outbreak of World War I in 1914 was a significant distraction for American business. The war effort, and the engineering and administrative attention it required, reoriented priorities and pressed firms to develop factories for new machines. The war diverted many of the commodities needed for batteries and car manufacturing away from civilian use to the military. Factories were retrofitted to support the war effort. It is hard to calculate just how much damage the war economy inflicted upon the electric car business, but it is clear that even just the lead needed for bullets and other weaponry sharply reduced supplies of the metal available for civilian batteries. Similarly, copper for wiring and machinery that might have been used for batteries were also called upon for the war effort. These national priorities severely curtailed production of civilian goods and could have contributed to the decline in electric cars at a critical turning point in their evolution.[28] Carmakers had experimented with alcohol-based fuels, but that route became less promising as well, as the war disrupted alcohol fuel use by taking its toll on Europe's grain production.[29] One bright spot for U.S. domestic carmakers, though, was that gas-powered trucks were suddenly in high demand by Allied Europe's military. In Ford's case, his gasoline trucks and cars were favored to support the European war effort because the Allies desperately needed a solution to Germany's domination of rail lines to move supplies and materials. Gasoline trucks, with their ability to pull large loads long distances, were a ready solution, and Ford Motor did its patriotic duty to oblige once America entered the war in 1917.[30]

Henry Ford's brand of pacifism was unpopular at the start of the war in Europe, and he did not initially sign agreements to supply the French or British forces. By April 1917, however, when the United States entered the war, Ford pivoted, signing a deal to provide the U.S. military with Model T chassis. In 1917, the United States supplied France with fifty thousand gasoline-powered vehicles that proved critical in battle preparation for the movement of troops and supplies.[31] Ford's efforts to produce a winning farm tractor also put him in the service of Britain, which was struggling against a German submarine blockade that hindered food imports. In July 1917, Henry Ford & Son was incorporated, with an ownership stake included for Edsel; it focused entirely on manufacturing tractors to meet a commitment to provide Britain with six thousand of its Fordson farm tractors.[32] The tractors contributed to an increase in Britain's foodstuff production and launched Ford decisively into the war effort.

In comparison to Ford Motor Company's annual output of more than half a million cars, the number of vehicles sent to the war effort was small, but Ford factories were also busy producing aircraft engines,[33] gun caissons, tanks,[34] helmets, and body armor.[35] Ford sold ambulances to the Red Cross as well, after donating $500,000 to the organization to facilitate a bulk purchase of more than a hundred specifically designed ambulances, along with a thousand other vehicles designed for use in the war. More than 5,700 ambulances were made for the Allied armies. But perhaps Ford's largest contribution the war effort was when he lent an engineering team to help improve the efficiency of the Liberty engine, a standardized design for airplane engines that was badly needed to navigate the war effort. Ford's team did not disappoint, and by August 1917 Ford was producing the cylinders for all of the Liberty engines, as many as 415,377 by the war's end. By November 1917, Ford, along with other U.S. car manufacturers, undertook a massive effort to mass-produce Liberty engines for Allied aircraft.[36] Ford also volunteered to build a prototype to meet the military's specifications for a new ship for the U.S. Navy. With the war effort taking up significant time and capacity in his factories, it is understandable that Ford may not have had time for side projects like the Edison-Ford electric car. Ford would never turn back to the full electric venture.

The impact of the war on Edison's business operations was even greater. Edison's personal stature and prominent position as a proponent of arming the U.S. military gave his flagship Edison Electric a clear business advantage and a way of benefiting from its founder's leadership in technology. Edison's chief engineer, Miller Reese Hutchison, devised a marketing strategy aimed at positioning the Edison battery as the best way to power submarines for the war. In January 1911, bearing the lofty title of "Representative of Thomas A. Edison in Naval Affairs," Hutchinson began his campaign to show that Edison's nickel-alkaline storage battery would be superior to the lead-acid batteries that dominated the market.[37] If the sulfuric acid in the electrolyte of the battery came into contact with salt water, the lead batteries could produce a dangerous chlorine gas that would imperil a submarine's crew. After much lobbying over a period of years, Hutchinson obtained authorization from Josephus Daniels, the U.S. Secretary of the Navy, for the installation of Edison batteries in the L-8 submarine under construction at the Portsmouth Naval Yard in Maine. A few weeks later, Edison's storage battery company won a contract for the battery to be installed in E-2 submarines.[38]

Then tragedy struck. On Saturday, January 15, 1916, an E-2 submarine recently equipped with an Edison nickel-alkaline storage battery exploded in the Brooklyn Naval Yard, killing five men and injuring nine others. Edison's battery was blamed for the accident in the "full glare of the public spotlight." The news was politicized by detractors of President Woodrow Wilson, who had been endorsed by Edison, who served on the president's newly created Naval Consulting Board. The culprit was thought to be hydrogen gas emitted by the battery cells during discharge and recharging.[39] The catastrophe led to the cancellation not just of the U.S. government's order for batteries, but also of hundreds of orders from trucking firms and others who now questioned the safety of Edison's batteries.[40] Edison ordered all the tools and dies for the submarine batteries to be destroyed.[41] In later years, the commercial reputation of Edison's commercial storage battery was restored for other applications. But the incident and the other exigencies of war go a long way toward explaining how the Edison-Ford electric car venture lost momentum.

FORD'S ANXIETY ABOUT OIL SHORTAGES

Henry Ford did not fully abandon the idea that his cars should run on a fuel other than gasoline. Ford fretted not only that oil supplies would run dry in the future but that gasoline fumes were damaging the atmosphere. He told the *Detroit News* late in 1916:

> All the world is waiting for a substitute for gasoline. When that [oil] is gone, there will be no more gasoline, and long before that time, the prices of gasoline will have risen to the point where it will be too expensive to burn as a motor fuel. The day is not far distant when, for every one of those barrels of gasoline, a barrel of alcohol must be substituted.[42]

Ford worked with a Dow Chemical chemist, Jay Hale, on "power alcohol" to try to reduce the dependence of his products on the oil industry and to give a boost to American farmers. The effort led to the first ethanol gasoline blends[43].

As Michael S. Carolan writes in his study of alcohol-based fuels versus gasoline, "the bulk of evidence points to alcohol as having [the] greatest support among scientists and automobile engineers."[44] Fuel tests between alcohol and gasoline showed that alcohol was the superior product, improving engine efficiency, preventing engine knocking, and delivering comparable performance. It was not until 1921 that Thomas Midgley discovered the antiknock properties of tetraethyl-leaded gasoline that allowed gasoline to surpass alcohol fuel in performance.

Ford's Model T carburetors were designed to run on either gasoline, alcohol, or a blended fuel, with gasoline considered the least favorable fuel because of its low compression ratios. But Standard Oil and its lobbyists at the American Petroleum Institute instituted a malicious public information crusade to ensure that alcohol had no chance of taking off as a fuel. Between 1920 and 1933, a concerted effort was made to link alcohol fuels with the prevailing moral attitudes against alcohol of the Prohibition Era. John D. Rockefeller Sr., the churchgoing founder of Standard Oil, and his son John Jr. were both staunch supporters of Prohibition, and although they likely supported the restrictive code on moral and religious grounds, there is no doubt that the thirteen-year-long ban on producing or selling alcohol fuels helped Standard Oil protect gasoline and assert its dominance. Gasoline interests peddled the idea that every alcohol fuel station was a potential speakeasy, with Standard Oil referring to alcohol fuels as "drinkable moonshine" even though the fuel was not consumable.[45] The anti-alcohol campaign continued well into the next decade and beyond.[46]

Sadly, the electric car and alcohol fuels were not the only casualties as more Americans became able to afford a personal gasoline-powered automobile. Increasingly, as middle-class families moved to the suburbs and acquired cars, urban trolley companies began to face serious economic challenges. Pressed by the politics of the day to keep fares low, trolley companies were forced to cut corners on system maintenance, leading to increasing mechanical difficulties, which in turn drove more riders to seek alternatives. As ridership decreased, streetcar companies had trouble paying the bills. But as Jonathan Kwinty detailed in a 1981 *Harper* article, there was a concerted effort on the part of the automotive, oil, and tire industry to put the final death nail in the American streetcar system. As he memorably put it, "mass transit didn't just die—it was murdered."[47] General Motors, Standard Oil of California (later Chevron), Firestone Tire, Phillips Petroleum, and Mack Trucks, among others, were accused of forming "dummy companies" in the late 1930s and through the 1940s to buy up transit and city streetcar companies and close them down.[48] The streetcar routes they tampered with were eventually replaced with bus services, and the buses, lo and behold, required oil-based fuel and rubber tires, both core products of the accused companies.[49] The court case, *United States v. National City Lines Inc.*, alleged that the five corporate defendants had conspired to obtain control of local transportation companies in forty-four cities in sixteen states to "restrain and monopolize interstate commerce in buses, petroleum and other supplies incident thereto," in violation of the Sherman Antitrust Act of 1890. The corporations were found guilty of conspiracy to monopolize interstate commerce, but the die was already cast. By the 1950s, highways and automobile ownership became the cornerstone of American life, leaving us in the current state of congestion and pollution in need of a remedy.

THINKING FORWARD

Without any trace of irony, the tech titans are currently offering solutions, much as hopeful inventors like Edison and Ford once sought to use their ingenuity to end a crisis with horse manure and horseflies. Ensuring these new solutions do not usher in deeper problems will require some foresight. Many commentators in the early 1900s warned that gasoline automobile exhaust would pose a problem for society, but their warnings were ignored in light of the many advantages that cars seemed to offer. In the following pages, I will discuss the potential for new technologies to solve the problems facing the world today. But instead of just assuming a passive, may-the-best-man-win approach to technology, we need to be cognizant of the past. The United States' national security needs, institutional frameworks, and policy incentives will shape how these new technologies do or do not solve ongoing societal dilemmas, and incumbents will utilize the political capital they still wield to prevent outcomes that disadvantage their profits and or drain their supportive labor ranks. The campaign against public transit that conservative billionaires Charles G. and David H. Koch have underwritten is a modern-day case in point.[50] Koch Industries owns oil refineries, pipelines, and petrochemical plants. As we consider the future of autonomous cars and drones and new delivery and manufacturing systems, we need to remember Henry Ford's eventual regrets that it proved too difficult to walk back oil once every brick of infrastructure had been laid in place, from wells in the ground in the Texas Panhandle to convenience stations pumping gas on every street corner of America. We can put our cars in reverse gear, but we cannot go back in time to encourage Ford to make different choices.

CHAPTER 2

Revolutionizing the Link

Energy and Advanced Economic Development

For most people in industrial societies, energy is both ubiquitous and mysterious. How many of us really know what energy source is responsible for the illumination that brings us light when we flick on a light switch or the heat that comes on when we fiddle with the thermostat? The fuel that powers our transportation needs is less enigmatic, given how much time we spend driving up to filling stations to pump oil-based liquids into our cars. Gasoline prices are probably the most visible consumer prices in our lives because they are posted on ten-foot-tall signs on highways around the globe. Years ago, Brookings researchers did a study on social well-being that confirmed, using standard polling methodology, what one might have guessed intuitively: Americans begin to feel more anxious and unhappy when gasoline prices rise above $3.50 a gallon.[1] It turns out that this anxiety is not just a pocketbook issue. Americans intuitively suspect that rising gasoline prices could be a bad omen for the economy—and they are correct.

The fact is that energy and economic development are inextricably linked. The geographer and scientist Vaclav Smil describes the relationship between energy and civilization this way: "the course of history can be seen as the quest for controlling greater stores and flows of more concentrated and more versatile forms of energy and converting them, in more affordable ways at lower costs and with higher efficiencies, into heat, light, and motion."[2] Economists have shown that demand for energy rises as population and incomes rise. It is easy to imagine how a society would use more energy as it shifts from subsistence agriculture, which is based mainly on human energy (labor), to mechanized agriculture, which relies on a combination of human and machine labor, to industrialization, which increases the need for energy in manifold ways. Industries like steel and cement

use large amounts of energy in the manufacturing process, for example. Industrialized societies also use more energy in transportation, and a rising standard
of living among manufacturing workers allows for widespread distribution of
consumer products that use energy. This relationship between economic development and a changing structure of productive activity has been well documented
in the economics literature, most famously by Nobel Prize winning economist
Simon Kuznets.[3] Within that economic framework, the increased use of modern
energy by households is a cornerstone of the broader process of human development. The World Bank sociologist Douglas Barnes and his bank colleague and
coauthor Willem Floor found that per capita income of less than $300 per day
restricts the widespread use of modern energy services and encumbers development. Only when a population's income rises above $1,000 per capita does the
switch to modern fuels become more prevalent.[4]

The link between energy use and economic growth underpins many aspects of
the current geopolitics of oil, as well as the politics of climate change. Because oil
has been so central to the human welfare that economic growth conveys, secure
access to oil has been a national foreign policy priority for most major economies, including the United States, Japan, China, and Europe. For the developing
world, access to energy is a critical input to rising per capita income. In his 2014
book, *The Moral Case for Fossil Fuels*, Alex Epstein lays out the case that fossil fuel
use has been, and will continue to be, key to improving the quality of life for
billions of people in the developing world.[5] The fall in costs for new technologies
for the deployment of small-scale renewable energy is starting to change that,
potentially altering the pathway forward.

Until recently, the economic benefits of oil have created difficult trade-offs
where climate change is concerned. Leaders from developing world countries
have argued in the past that they cannot afford to abandon the use of oil in an
effort to lower greenhouse gas emissions and still be able to lift their citizens
out of poverty. This is where digital energy holds the most promise. Advances in
energy efficiency technology, combined with smart regulations and tax policy,
have already helped decouple energy use from economic growth in major economies over the past two decades. The transformative power of digital energy technology could accelerate and enhance this trend, making it easier for all nations
to lower oil use and thereby improve energy security and reduce their greenhouse
gas emissions. China is betting that more countries in the developing world will
want to move in this direction and is proactively positioning its state-run and

private companies to be able to export products and services, tapping its major Belt and Road Initiative (BRI), which assists nearby countries and trading partners with infrastructure development via loans and technical assistance. The United States in 2018 responded by announcing an Indo-Pacific economic vision to be managed by the U.S. International Development Finance Corporation (USIDFC). The initial sums of $25 million for U.S. technology exports and $50 million to help countries with energy production and storage are small compared to China's BRI, which has totaled over $200 billion since its inception.

The potential of digital energy to advance cleaner energy raises the stakes for how countries like the United States and China choose to implement and regulate the deployment of autonomous vehicles, smart grids, and advanced manufacturing as models for the rest of the world. As we learned in chapter 1, energy infrastructure can be long-lasting, so decisions made now about how to deploy and regulate these new, advanced digital technologies and related infrastructure will have a material influence on both the geopolitical and the environmental benefits of their use in individual countries.

Advances in on-demand services, robotics, the automation of vehicles, data-assisted logistics, smart connected devices, and advanced manufacturing are all expected to radically transform the way businesses and individuals buy and sell energy services and the kinds of fuel sources that will be favored in the coming decades. They could potentially reduce the need for oil through radical improvements in productivity and optimization. But if countries lock in digital infrastructure and applications in a way that increases oil use, then it could be harder still to undo, as happened with energy innovations from the 1900s. Thus, as the United States considers its global competitiveness in digital energy, it must also consider how best to reap the maximum potential for positive change that can come from broad deployment of the new digital services and devices.

In this chapter, I discuss the massive scale of our current energy system, which is built around a large-scale centralized system designed around economies of scale for energy technologies developed over a century ago. The idea that this vast network of oil refineries, oil and gas pipelines, power plants, transmission lines, and gasoline stations is too enormous to transition to a low- and zero-carbon world is often put forward as an argument against attempts to mitigate climate change. But as we learned in chapter 1, major transitions to new technologies such as gasoline cars can take place over a relatively short period of time. That raises the question regarding digital energy: How fast might disruptive business models and advances in digital energy technologies prompt a transition away from our current centralized infrastructure? The rapid retirement of coal plants in the United States in recent years offers a clue that change could be faster than politicians care to admit.

For decades, experts have asserted that it was downright foolhardy to build energy installations on a small scale because each one was too expensive an undertaking. A generation of energy scientists had been raised to think that nothing short of a massive nuclear plant would be capable of supplying energy efficiently to an entire city. Large was best, they reasoned, because it allowed operators to keep costs low through economies of scale for capital invested. In other words, the more energy the facility could generate, the more its costs per unit of energy would go down, benefiting consumers.

But digital energy is changing that. As my late dear friend, the Nobel prize-winning chemist Richard Smalley, used to say, we need a 'new basis for energy prosperity.' He suggested that it would be much more efficient to transport energy as energy rather than as matter and predicted that electricity would become the new oil for the twenty-first century. To facilitate this, Smalley theorized that there would need to be a decentralized, local energy storage model such that everyone on the grid had a personal storage appliance that could ensure the delivery of uninterrupted power. Such technologies now exist and are becoming cost competitive with traditional centralized power plants. For example, places like South Australia and New York City are finding that renewables combined with smart, advanced electricity storage can both save money and lower the chances of unintended sudden shifts in voltage that can lead to brownouts. As will be discussed at greater length in chapter 5, these smart, small-scale electricity systems can optimize grid performance if strategically deployed in the right locations with enabling regulatory and pricing incentives.

In this chapter, I discuss how our next set of energy infrastructure choices could create hard-to-reverse path dependencies that could lock in both technology choices and consumer behavior patterns. In launching an industrial policy intended to stimulate energy innovation, policy makers should keep such considerations front of mind. Digital innovation will be highly influenced by societal context and supporting institutions, with a diverse mix of political stakeholders trying to influence outcomes in their favor. Politicians representing districts with high employment in incumbent industries, such as the oil and gas industry, are warning that rapid changes should not be directed by government intervention because of the negative consequences for existing jobs, tax revenues, and regressive costs. Proponents of change are lobbying that disruptive technologies should be nurtured by subsidies and other incentives and steered by environmental regulations and carbon pricing to foster economic competitiveness and new jobs and to address climate change. With high stakes for the environment, social justice, and individual privacy, the rules of the road for the widespread deployment of digital energy technologies in the United States will be critical to the kind of energy infrastructure that is installed for the twenty-first century.

LINKAGES: PER CAPITA INCOME AND ENERGY USE

At the economywide level, the relationship between income and energy use has been studied extensively and underpins the mechanics of economic modeling used to project future energy demand. In an award-winning paper, the Rice University economists Kenneth Medlock and Ronald Soligo found that increases in per capita income during economic development have a direct effect on the composition and growth of energy demand.[6] Industrialization is initially accompanied by large spurts in national energy consumption. Then, as incomes rise, a decreasing share of the consumer spending shifts from food to manufactured goods, and eventually spending on fuels for transportation takes flight. As more people reach the middle class in developing countries, consumers begin to attain income levels sufficient to purchase an automobile, historically linking a wealth effect to rising fuel use.

This energy consumption effect of economic development has been seen in recent decades in China, India, and Southeast Asia, where energy demand has skyrocketed amid a booming manufacturing sector and rising personal car ownership. As Daniel Sperling and Deborah Gordon note in their book *Two Billion Cars*, the trajectory of a rising global middle class is producing an enormous global fleet of passenger vehicles that can barely be accommodated on the roads of major cities:

Today's one billion vehicles are already pumping extraordinary quantities of greenhouse gases into the atmosphere . . . and overwhelming the roads of today's cities. Billions of hours are wasted stuck in traffic, and billions of people are sickened by pollution from cars. From Paris to Fresno and Delhi to Shanghai, conventional motorization, conventional vehicles, and conventional fuels are choking cities, literally and figuratively. Cars are arguably one of the greatest man-made threats to human society.[7]

As societies become wealthier, a shift to a more service-oriented economy, combined with increased concern for the environment and technological improvements that enhance energy efficiency, brings about a flattening in energy use even as gross domestic product (GDP) continues to grow. Economic growth becomes linked in greater measure to financial services and other sectors that are less energy intensive than heavy industry. Even with the explosion we now see in personal car ownership around the globe, most industrial economies today and many developing nations have reduced their energy intensity—that is, the amount of energy it takes to generate a unit of GDP—through automobile efficiency standards, building codes, equipment and appliance energy efficiency standards, and industrial productivity gains.

In the case of the United States, the oil intensity of the U.S. economy—the measure of how much oil is needed to generate a unit of GDP—has fallen as more of the economy has switched to service industries. Bouts of high oil prices have also prompted businesses and individuals to reduce their oil use in various ways. The rise of nuclear power in the 1970s and then more efficient natural gas plants of the 1980s and 1990s pushed oil out of the power sector market in the United States. At this point, oil is hardly used for power generation in the United States, and natural gas is rapidly displacing oil in residential heating and manufacturing as well. As a result, the oil intensity of the United States is minuscule compared with what it was in 1972. It now takes 92 percent less oil to fuel one unit of GDP than it did forty-eight years ago (figure 2.1).

On the flip side, China's staggering economic growth over the past several decades has substantially increased its need for oil. Mass migrations of its populace to urban centers were accompanied by massive, energy-intensive construction of buildings and other infrastructure as well as rapid industrialization. Today almost 60 percent of China's population lives in cities, roughly triple the fraction that did in 1978. But even fast-growing countries like China are experiencing a significant decline in oil intensity. The one-time shift from rural agriculture to urban living is slowing now, and China's government is more focused on energy efficiency in vehicles, industry, and buildings. As China was increasing its GDP fortyfold between 1980 and 2010, it did so by making historically unprecedented

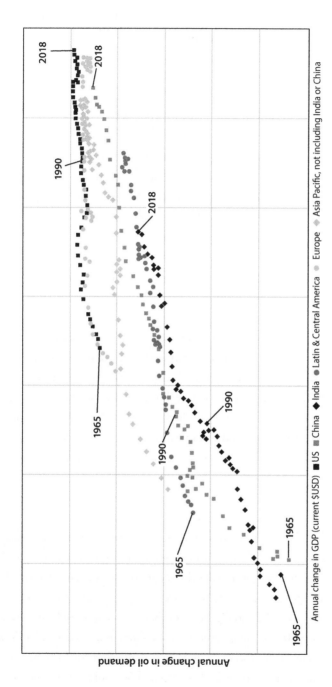

2.1 Global oil demand versus global GDP growth

Annual change in GDP (current $USD) ■ US ■ China ◆ India ● Latin & Central America ● Europe ◆ Asia Pacific, not including India or China

Annual change in oil demand

improvements in limiting the amount of energy used. The energy intensity of China's economy was reduced by two-thirds between 1980 and 2009.[8] Today, the oil intensity of China's economy is only 26 percent of what it was in the year 2000.

DIGITAL INNOVATION AND LOWER OIL USE

Digital innovation has the potential to drive the oil intensity of the U.S. and global economy lower still. The incentive to do so exists not only for environmental reasons but also to protect economic growth. The volatility of oil prices continues to influence economic activity. Many economists have studied the impact of oil price shocks on macroeconomic performance. Their studies have generally found that rising oil prices can dampen investment, productivity, and economic growth over longer time horizons. The economist Lutz Killian concluded in 2008 that price hikes that resulted from sustained demand growth for oil were even harsher than geopolitical supply disruptions.[9]

The current rapid pace of digital innovation in the energy sector holds great promise for reducing oil use and accelerating the transition to cleaner energy. That should further weaken the traditional correlation between rising oil usage and rising GDP. The convergence of artificial intelligence, big-data analytics, and automation is creating a host of opportunities to remake the way energy is used in the transportation, electricity, and manufacturing sectors. A wide range of transformational technologies, such as on-demand travel services, automated vehicles, data- and GPS-assisted logistics, decentralized electricity microgrids, and three-dimensional (3D) printing, will boost productivity in energy production and distribution while optimizing energy usage so we can all do more with less.

It has become obvious how profoundly technological changes are reshaping many aspects of everyday life, from mass communications to shopping to hailing a ride in a big city. Staggering developments that some have described as a "second machine age" are occurring that mix together a confluence of technologies ranging from artificial intelligence to robotics to connected smart devices and the Internet of Things, all to produce life-changing innovations.[10] Life with a smartphone is enriched in so many ways it is hard to list them. Soon autonomous vehicles and 3D printing will also become household words, and perhaps necessities. Few of us have given much thought to how quantum computing and big-data analytics will change our lives. But all of these technologies are hitting an inflection point where the transformational changes that are brewing could mirror gains seen during the Industrial Revolution and at the turn of the twentieth century, when mass-production techniques and the advent of electricity ushered in modern society. We are facing such an unprecedented level of change that major companies of all types need to become tech companies just to survive, let alone thrive. This will be especially true for energy. We will have an historic opportunity to accelerate the decoupling of economic growth from higher fossil fuel use and thereby forge a path of economic progress that is not linked to rising carbon emissions. The question is how to tap the digital revolution to promote this process rather than set it back.

The industrial players that currently dominate energy—electric utilities, oil companies, and automotive companies—are among the largest installed industries in the world. To date, they have generally deployed their formidable market power, political power, and in some cases state power to thwart disruptive changes rather than embrace them. Society, however, cannot afford to let the private sector keep creating infrastructure that undermines long-term societal goals. Because energy infrastructure is expected to be long-lasting, decisions made today can seriously limit the changes that can be made tomorrow—a problem known as path dependency, meaning that decisions made in the future are constrained by decisions made in the past.

Large-scale facilities such as power plants, pipelines, and export terminals cost hundreds of millions, if not billions, of dollars to build and are expected to last for decades. Because it can take many years for their owners and investors to reap the desired return on investment, there is often considerable resistance to the idea of closing such facilities before the end of their useful lives, even when newer, competing technologies beckon. Not only are we still using outdated energy technologies that were instituted in the early 1900s, but most of our regulations and energy pricing systems are also designed to sustain those technologies and the businesses that invest in them. Coaxing new technologies to market will require wholesale changes in regulations, energy policy, and pricing that are capable of breaking that self-reinforcing loop. We must be mindful, too, that decisions made today on how to regulate self-driving vehicles and how to reform electricity markets to incorporate new technologies are just as likely to lock in new path dependencies that our descendants might be chafing at years from now.

The same can be said of decisions made at the individual level. Take the number and type of cars on the road today. Because cars are a durable good that most individual owners keep for a decade or so before replacing, buying a traditional car that runs on gasoline creates yet another kind of path dependency that has far-reaching ripple effects. Prospective car buyers need to know that there will be places to refuel along the road for whatever trips they may take, no matter how long, in their new car. Without that implied assurance from multiple stakeholders, individuals will not risk the new outlay. Gas stations are plentiful, electric charging stations less so. Thus, each additional purchase of a traditional car not only bolsters the already well-entrenched oil-refining industry, it also helps perpetuate it. That purchase makes it more likely that the next buyer will also lean strongly toward the purchase of a gas-powered car. Reducing the country's addiction to gasoline by asking drivers to shift to electric cars or any other substitute is difficult until there is also an adequate support system in place to allow all those venturous early adopters to drive in confidence. Barring some change in political will, this could end up being a decades-long process, all because of these sticky path dependencies.

Imagine, for instance, that you as a consumer are open to putting a solar panel on your roof and an electric car in your garage. Is your utility willing to credit your electricity bill for the excess solar power you could be pumping back into the grid? State regulations have not been updated yet in many locations to give you the full economic benefit of upgrading to rooftop solar energy. Depending on where you live, the purchase of an electric car might qualify you for a tax break, but do you see as many fast charging stations as gas stations along your regular driving routes? Even the slightest anxiety about your ability to refuel, because the infrastructure is still fledgling, is a barrier to conversion. Even if electric cars manage to deliver a better ride and carry a lower price tag than traditional cars, individual consumers might pause before buying one if they worry that they might not be able to find a charging station during a trip. That too is a symptom of path dependence.

Our decisions on how to regulate new technologies and what kind of infrastructure we build will create the same kind of no-going-back path dependencies that could shape how digital technologies are used, once they become widely available. As we fashion strategies to unleash the power of sensors, big data, the Internet of Things, and smart connected devices, we must consider the opportunities to do our energy transition by design—that is, by creating public guidance that steers how innovations will be applied in the marketplace. What suite of policies needs to be adopted to steer problem solvers to tackle the world's greatest problems, recognizing that there will always be unintended consequences of new technologies that cannot be anticipated? How do we design cities for people rather than for cars? How do we repair our social contract so that digital technologies are providing solutions to high-value problems, like global warming or global health, and not just throwing time and money at the next Angry Bird app or, worse, mass surveillance? By studying history, can we avoid creating path-dependent applications of automation and electrical systems that worsen congestion, pollution, and greenhouse gas emissions instead of ameliorating them? In other words, how do we prevent history from repeating itself? And, how do we ensure that any innovations we are about to embark on do not turn out like those from the early twentieth century, solving some problems but replacing them with others?

VISIONARY ENTREPRENEURSHIP OR GOVERNMENT POLICY?

We know from history that technological innovation is critical to national security. But we also know that national security applications at times take precedence over social and environmental goals when it comes to the development of energy infrastructure. As we consider how energy-related digital technologies will be guided by regulation, we need to learn from the past and integrate national security with other goals for how governments should shape the adoption of these technologies into our daily life.

The overarching lesson from Edison and Ford's day is that infrastructure decisions made in the moment about a hot new technology could be here for keeps. It has been more than a hundred years since we in the United States turned our backs on electric cars, taxis, and trolleys in favor of gasoline—one reason that their widespread use is so utterly forgotten. It is stunning to think that if city dwellers had simply stuck with and improved the electric taxicabs and electric streetcars at their disposal in the early 1900s, the shift to low-carbon fuels today would be considerably easier. Had the transition to private gasoline cars not taken place, we would not be fretting about how to retire hundreds of millions of gasoline vehicles and their associated filling stations and oil refineries. It would not be an exaggeration to say that our failure to ask some tough questions then has cost us a full century in our race to build a more sustainable world.

If we had stuck with electric cars in urban settings, when the 1973 oil crisis hit we would have been less hostage to the vagaries of foreign oil. Four decades of wondering how to stop needing oil for the daily mobility of millions of Americans would never have happened. What if, in the decades since 1915, bright minds had turned to perfecting the electric car instead of perfecting the ignition systems and engine performance of the world's gas-guzzlers? Once we realized the dangers of global warming, we could have quickly switched our sources of electricity to renewables and other low-carbon solutions.

While we are at it, ask yourself, what if taxi-loving New Yorkers were still using their phones to hail rides in electric vehicles, as they did back in 1910? Nudging them to make the switch now from manned rides to self-driving, electric-fueled robo-taxis might be easier.

Instead, because none of these things happened, we face the heavy lift of having to convince multiple generations of drivers not only to abandon the gasoline cars they dote on but also to switch to a new mode of transportation that requires them to relinquish personal ownership of a car altogether. That is what energy-infrastructure path dependency means. Today's city planners and futurists, with no sense of déjà vu, are talking about moving people around with the help of a coordinated system of all-electric, on-demand vehicles that could be a modern-day version of trolley cars following set routes, supplemented with electric vehicle (EV) robotic taxis that can be more nimble about the routes they take. In effect, we would be turning the clock back a full century to re-create the system our ancestors once had, all at a rather exorbitant cost.

The choice that Ford made to market gasoline cars for excursions into the countryside lasted not just for his generation, but also for ours. Edison's vision of electricity as a basic human right has also created a massive, decades-old infrastructure that is hard to retire, even though new innovative ways to store and generate electricity are emerging. Built today, a traditional thermal power plant, using natural gas or coal as its fuel, could potentially still be in operation forty years from now. Whiz-bang energy inventions sold to our great-grandparents were amazing at the time, but they created material path dependencies that became almost impossible to budge as the years rolled on. Total domination of the world in which his business empire operated seems to be precisely what made John D. Rockefeller Sr., the mastermind behind the Standard Oil empire, tick. Ultimately, it is not much of a stretch to say similar things about the business empires of Ford and Edison. They worked hard to have their technologies "win" and to shunt alternatives aside. Their runaway success is now our failure.

Of equal concern, we seem hell-bent on letting a new generation of industrialist innovators (we don't call them inventors nowadays), running the likes of Amazon, Apple, Google, and Uber, make choices for us about what the next one hundred years of energy and telecommunications infrastructure will look like. We need to stop and consider the path dependencies that could be created if e-commerce companies create cruising warehouses on wheels to bring groceries and other goodies to our doorsteps at short notice using fossil-fuel-powered trucks. I worry that a hundred years from now, my great-grandchildren might have to write a book about how the tech boom of the 2020s unleashed a dystopic set of unintended consequences that their generation is struggling to undo. We can already see how social media are harming democracy, rather than promoting it, contrary to what their early disciples had promised. We can understand how the surveillance state being assembled in China, using facial recognition software, is worse than science fiction. Hence, we need to think harder about the structure of the energy system that we *want* to transition to, not just accept the one that is being sold to us by technology innovators or pushed by their partners. Public policy is the toolbox we must use to guide all stakeholders onto the pathway that is best for society in the long run.

How we power up 5G networks and self-driving vehicles will matter not only to the pathway of greenhouse gas emissions but also to the kinds of privacy and cyber checks that will need to be added to the monstrously large amounts of personal data probably already lacking protection. What systems we use to fuel the ever-increasing number of data centers that are being built will influence global carbon emissions. It will take an active reshaping of electricity market regulation and utility business models to get the resiliency benefits of breakthroughs in electricity software management and battery storage. This is not about having the government "pick winners," an idea often met with derision by libertarians and others who have more faith in free markets than in politicians to allocate resources. The goal of regulation is not to hurt profits. Regulation is about guiding market design so that businesses choose the solutions that deliver what we, as a society, want and do not leave us, the taxpayers and other members of the public, with the cost of cleaning up any and all messes—even unintended ones—that businesses and their new technologies unleash.

Think of it the following way: that Uber ride you just took might have been cheaper than taking your own car because hired cars are spared some fuel taxes, but you will pay for the decision in other ways—maybe higher taxes so the Navy can patrol oil regions in the Middle East or local governments can address the health costs of urban respiratory illnesses or emergency response teams can come to the aid of communities affected by climate disasters. We are paying the bill for the "externality" of that cheap Uber ride because its provider does not cover the all-in costs to society related to the service. The externality cost of a commercial activity (say, underpricing the use of automobiles) is the side effect, or unaccounted-for consequence, of an industrial activity that affects parties other than the business itself. There is no escaping the cost. We are paying for these externalities one way or another, in the form of higher health costs or the damage or impairments we experience in our natural surroundings. We would all be better off if we created systems in which the products we use generated as few externalities as possible. That is how we need to think about the digital energy revolution before it gets firmly established. Ordering Facebook now, ex post facto, not to accept certain kinds of damaging advertisements will have less chance of producing the desired changes than would clearer ground rules before the platform launched.

THE POLITICS OF CARBON LOCK-IN

The process of updating our energy system has become highly politicized. We see the disruption coming, and we cannot agree how new technologies should be deployed or old ones adapted or retrofitted. That is our challenge. We need more debate and more awareness of our options, and that includes motivating established businesses to be part of the solution instead of barriers to change.

In his book *Sustainable Innovation*, the finance professor and former entrepreneur Andrew Hargadon noted the difficulties of modernizing existing factories as opposed to simply building new ones: "The business proposition for new technologies is often hindered by direct and indirect subsidies for incumbent competitors."[11] In energy, such indirect subsidies include a labor force trained in fossil fuel businesses, local community support, and a massive web of existing infrastructure that is already amortized and thereby gives incumbents a highly favorable economic advantage. The capital assets needed to produce energy and bring it to market—power stations, transmission lines, oil and gas fields, refineries, and pipelines—have a life span of forty years or more. Roadways, freight systems, buildings, and other downstream industries are all integrated with these entrenched energy networks, forcing many innovators to integrate their products and services with the existing energy supply system.[12] In this way, energy is unlike information technology, which rapidly created wholly new markets for services that did not previously exist. If there are billions of dollars of physical energy production assets in need of replacement, it will be difficult for challengers and upstarts who work in novel ways to force that infrastructure into retirement. The paydays also tend to be smaller and slower for energy innovation than for internet-related inventions, and the capital needed to surmount incumbents is staggeringly large. As Gregory Unruh explains in his article on "carbon lock-in," the scale of the existing fossil fuel system creates "path-dependent" returns that are creating "persistent market and policy failures" that throw up barriers to innovation. For example, when politicians allocate more funding for roads and parking for existing cars but not for public transit or pedestrian centers, that blocks innovation. Regulations that give fixed profits to electric utilities for building additional power generation rather than for saving energy reduce the incentives for innovation.[13] Thus, sometimes, policy can fail to unlock the environment needed to promote new energy solutions. Incumbents often advocate for policies that best suit their market position.

Yet, regardless of how much these incumbents struggle to slow disruption, new technologies are likely to revolutionize the built environment in the industrial sector as well as the energy system for manufacturing and data centers. The question is how to manage this process to arrive at the best possible outcome.

Alexander Karsner, a successful investor in clean energy and cochair of a group I assembled at the Council on Foreign Relations to discuss technology's impact on the global energy transition, used the example of a "Kodak moment" to illustrate an important principle. "The meaning of a 'Kodak moment,'" he said, had changed over time. For baby boomers, a "Kodak moment" was a scenic moment worthy of being memorialized on film as a permanent snapshot—anything from a gathering of old friends to a breathtaking sunset. Now, a "Kodak moment" is more likely to invoke a colossal business failure, stemming from the moment in the Kodak boardroom when some of the most intelligent, highly compensated executives in the world failed to predict or understand a technological revolution their own company's best-in-class products had induced. The company went out of business because they were unable to understand the technology shift to digital photos. Executives in the traditional energy business need to be mindful that their own Kodak moment may be looming. The energy world is experiencing breakneck technological change, and the businesses they run will not be immune.

Alec Ross, the author of the *New York Times* best seller *The Industries of the Future*, identifies several digital industries as key to the global economic future: robotics, genomics, coded money and the sharing economy, cybersecurity, and big-data analytics (including precision farming and fintech).[14] All of these industries already intersect in some ways with energy production and consumption. Blockchain is already being used to help manage electricity grids. Genomics of the DNA found in core rock samples are helping oil companies in the United States improve recovery rates for oil and gas production and develop better ways to convert food waste into usable energy. Robotics is already a mainstay of deepwater drilling. Big data combined with 5G connections are core technologies for logistics and self-driving vehicles, which will likely bring energy efficiencies that human-controlled vehicles cannot offer. Protective cyber software and drones will be needed to protect critical energy infrastructure from, ironically, attacks by cyber malware and drones. One question we should be asking is, which of these technologies will change energy for the better?

I have toured around the United States and abroad to see new technologies at play and to talk to technology leaders about the world they envision in the future. At the World Economic Forum in Davos, over the past few years, corporate CEOs, global thinkers, and strategic planners have been divided on the question of whether new technologies would bring about lower demand for oil. It is hard to know whether some of the uncertainty expressed by top brass was defensive (rooted in fear of taking the air out of their stocks on the London or New York stock exchanges) or whether corporate leaders were simply in denial about all the products and presentations on display at the World Economic Forum's deep dive into the "Fourth Industrial Revolution," as WEF founder Klaus Schwab described it.[15] But it defies credulity that anyone visiting Toyota's headquarters in Japan could watch in their lobby a trumpet concert by a band of five-foot-tall, exotic Toyota robots, complete with artificial lungs that fill with air to allow them to play brass musical instruments, and still think that a quarter-century from now we will have to use exactly the same highly polluting technologies we do now to generate energy.

The dazzling technologies on display at Davos, and also in Dalian, China, home of Davos's summer confab, have made me optimistic that our energy future can yet be bright. The first time I walked by a lifelike Japanese humanoid robot receptionist in its $800 business suit at the Dalian conclave, it took me a moment to realize I was being welcomed by a mannequin that could only greet me from a preprogrammed list of pleasantries. Earlier that day, I had attended an exhibit explaining how cybercriminals might someday be able to steal my face, in yet another dark side to facial recognition software. After that, I donned a pair of virtual-reality glasses to watch a three-dimensional reenactment of a nuclear weapons test in the South Pacific, making it clear how state-of-the-art surround-sound systems will look in twenty years.

A new rage soon might be queuing for a transport drone that will shuttle from the top of one skyscraper to another to avoid the bridge traffic in San Francisco, an innovation that prompted one Silicon Valley executive to explain to me recently that drones could make "self-driving cars so yesterday." I recognize that not everyone feels that way. Even with all the thrilling changes afoot, there are still plenty of people in the energy industry who think these miraculous technologies will somehow skip right over them.

SOCIAL AND INSTITUTIONAL BACKDROP
TO SCIENCE INNOVATION

I recognize that energy innovation will not take place in a vacuum. Innovation is highly influenced by a tightly woven web of institutional actors and systems that support the development of new technologies.[16] In the world of innovation, this is referred to as the innovation ecosystem. As Richard Nelson and Nathan Rosenberg point out in *National Innovation Systems: A Comparative Analysis*, we often think of innovation systems as linear—that is, deriving directly from scientific discoveries that enable new inventions.[17] Such was the case with modern electricity, itself the fruit of years of progression in theoretical and experimental physics in the nineteenth century. Incandescent light and the invention of the telephone found their roots in Faraday's demonstration of electromagnetic induction, for example. But Nelson and Rosenberg argue that the paradigm that innovation comes directly from scientific inquiry is too restrictive. They submit that as new technologies emerge, they often stimulate scientific work that spurs improvements. As they note, the Wright brothers, who had initially worked in bicycle manufacturing, were inventors, not scientists, but their success at Kittyhawk eventually spawned the scientific fields of aerodynamics and aeronautical engineering. Edison was also self-taught. In his book *Energy: A Human History*, Richard Rhodes elaborates on how evolutionary the development of energy technology has been. In one example, he chronicles how Thomas Beddoe's experimental collaboration with James Watt, Sr., on devices for medical gasses laid the groundwork for William Murdock's large gas-lighting project years later.[18] Fast-forward to J. B. Straubel, one of the founders of Tesla and its longtime chief technology officer. He had worked on Stanford University's solar car team but honed his single-minded idea that a lithium battery could be used in a car by tinkering in his garage, hanging out with start-up engineers, and briefly working for Rosen Motors.[19]

PRIVATE VERSUS PUBLIC INVESTMENT

Today, private companies often dictate what science is needed to support their businesses and the changing needs and desires of society. Technological advance is bubbling up inside companies, not just national laboratories or universities. Some tech firms are going so far as to lean on young people to bypass years they might otherwise spend inside the ivory tower of university life and report to work immediately. As a professor, I resist that urge. Broader learning fosters creativity and invention.

I can see the merit of private-sector efforts. Industry has certain advantages where energy innovation is concerned. Company researchers doing applied research in that field may not only have a stronger grasp than academics of which improvements could yield the biggest payoffs for their employers and customers, but they also have market-tested experience in production and in marketing to scale up a product once it is developed. They may be better placed to generate improvements that involve systems design in which component parts must be calibrated to operate seamlessly with automation in an integrated manner.

It is also common to hear assertions from tech executives today that the United States does not need a national initiative on energy innovation, or cybersecurity, or anything else, because the private sector is so technically adept and has so much capital that it can beat a command-economy nation like China hands down, simply relying on the strength of the capitalist system, if only regulators would move out of the way.

That view is a little backward. Government intervention in the innovation process has proven instrumental over the years, even in the United States. As Servan-Schreiber pointed out, the U.S. government spent more on R & D than competing European governments in the 1960s, especially through defense contracts and the space program, with positive results. The U.S. university research system was stronger than other countries', with faculty who were American, producing graduates who went to American firms. Firms located in the United States were also American-owned and made goods for a growing American market.[20]

The mass movement of people and the lowering of trade barriers that have characterized globalization have reduced the impetus to chase a national industrial policy. The internationalization of business and the lively migration flows of students and job seekers have eroded the relevance of national borders for innovation, making global energy initiatives like Mission Innovation sensible and timely. Under Mission Innovation, an initiative launched in 2015 as part of the Paris climate accords, the EU and twenty-four major countries, including the United States and China, agreed to increase substantially their R & D funding for early-stage clean energy innovation. The program was intended to link business and technology leaders with governments, nongovernmental organizations, universities, and national labs to promote performance breakthroughs and cost reductions for clean energy solutions to climate change.

By rejecting the Paris accord and cutting spending on science, the Trump administration tried to put the kibosh on U.S. promotion of the multilateral effort. That decision was a mistake. The Trump administration was quicker than prior administrations to defend U.S. digital technologies against Chinese industrial espionage, a stance that could be helpful in the long run. But it did not marry that protectionist stance together with a nurturing environment for research and development and other supportive regulations that might nudge U.S. firms to position themselves for the future economy. Some of the administration's policies have been outright counterproductive to global competitive trends emerging in response to climate change and digital advances. One instance was proposing to cancel Obama-era regulations that would have forced U.S. carmakers to speed up the development of cleaner, advanced automobiles, trucks, and buses. Remarkably enough, that about-face was thought to be so shortsighted that industry giants resisted taking the feds' outstretched hand and instead negotiated a deal directly with the state of California on how to meet that state's rigorous climate goals. A second example is the Trump administration's failed effort to press utilities to stay on course for traditional, centralized, coal-burning plants when innovative, smaller-scale, distributed electricity systems across the globe are offering better resilience in extreme weather, often at a lower cost.

Energy innovation is a vital U.S. national interest. Rethinking the ecosystem of government bodies, universities, corporations, and private entrepreneurs, with each playing a role in sharpening and sustaining the U.S. technological edge over rivals, remains a pressing need for the country. Energy is part and parcel of that process, given how critical energy access and supply chains are to the military at home and around the globe. Energy powers weapons systems, communications systems, infrastructure, and vehicles in domestic control centers, on military bases abroad and at sea, and in combat theaters.[21] Defense-related R & D has also been proven historically to drive new technological advances into the broader U.S. economy.[22] Today, one has only to imagine all the commercial products that have become integral to everyday life, like GPS navigation, to fathom the contribution defense-related satellite technologies have made toward U.S. global economic success.

And here's the rub. Just as the United States moved away from major government investment in energy innovation under Trump, China is betting big that the global economy will want the products that address environmental concerns, such as solar panels and battery storage, electric and autonomous vehicles, and high-speed rail. Doing so could give it an advantage in both the economic and military spheres.

Robert Atkinson, president of the nonpartisan think tank Information Technology and Innovation Foundation, a leading U.S. tech policy entity, notes:

> To the extent the United States continues to lose technological capabilities to China, U.S. technological advantage in defense over China will diminish, if not evaporate, as U.S. capabilities wither and Chinese strengthen. It is certainly a risky proposition to assume the United States can continue its weapons systems superiority over the Chinese if 1) the Chinese continue to advance, largely through unfair, predatory practices, at their current pace or 2) the United States loses a moderate to significant share of its advanced technology innovation and production capabilities.[23]

In 2006, China announced a National Medium- and Long-Term Program for Science and Technology Development (2006–2020) that established indigenous innovation as a national priority. The program identified 402 core technologies deserving of its attention, including automated vehicles, high-performance computing, and robotics. Since then, China has launched the world's fastest supercomputer, in Wuxi, China, in 2016, and Da-Jian Innovations (DJI) has become the world's top drone maker.[24] To accelerate its development of a technical workforce and its production of bankable, cutting-edge products, China's government has made foreign access to its sizable market subject to forced joint ventures and technology transfers, while also grooming homegrown Chinese business champions to scale up inside China and beyond. As a result, competition in the global energy and tech sector has become fierce, exposing U.S. innovators to the real risk that, as they lose market share, they will have less revenue to invest in the next generation of products and services than their government-funded Chinese counterparts.

U.S. government R & D expenditures still exceed Chinese government R & D spending overall, but China is quickly closing the gap. In the ten years from 2007 to 2017, Chinese government institutions' spending on R & D as a percentage of GDP climbed from 84 percent of what the U.S. government was spending to 119 percent.[25] U.S. businesses still outpace Chinese private industry in R & D spending by a fair margin, but key Chinese companies are closing in on America's business leaders in terms of total R & D investment, with Chinese telecommunications giant Huawei now in the world's top five.

Admittedly, China still lags in the number of patents it has been awarded for clean energy technologies. It has, however, made a strong showing in key fields such as energy storage and raw materials recycling. Europe has taken notice and initiated a government-backed program of its own. The European Commission, stating the need for Europe to build a competitive indigenous battery supply chain, launched the European Battery Alliance (EBA), which has set a target of two hundred gigawatts a year of manufacturing capability in the European Union by 2025. France and Germany announced a $5 billion to $6.7 billion consortium of mainly auto and energy firms to enhance Europe's electric car battery-making capacity. The EU will contribute more than $1 billion in public subsidies. This venture supplements other initiatives on raw materials, recycling, and battery packs.

A RISING CHINA

As a rising China closes the technological gap with the United States, U.S. policy leaders are increasingly questioning whether the United States needs to update and improve its industrial and trade policies. One main concern is making the U.S. supply chain less vulnerable to shortages of rare metals and other processed components that go into smart and automated devices. Moreover, many advanced energy and transportation technologies developed by American firms for use in everyday products have dual-use direct applicability to defense and national security. For example, while drones are being auditioned in the commercial delivery sphere because of their advantages over human drivers and are also being plumbed as a way to ferry American commuters for short distances, the defense industry has harnessed the help of drones on the battlefield.

The U.S. military also avails itself of a wide variety of digital products, from robotics to cyber hacking to geospatial satellite imagery and location services, to carry out its missions. Commercial availability of these dual-use items to players in the energy and transport sector of adversary nations could prove problematic over time. As the United States faces increased cyber threats and other digital intrusions from adversaries, it must have the mechanisms in place to protect the military and civilian use of computer networks used in everyday activities. This means injecting some product export controls on key critical technologies and ensuring that the United States can continue to develop second- and third-generation technologies that will supersede those of other market entrants. This will be important both for the United States' continued economic success and for its national security.

A U.S. INDUSTRIAL STRATEGY?

It is becoming increasingly clear that America cannot just rest on its laurels when it comes to digital technologies and energy. The United States needs to take additional steps to address long-term capabilities, perhaps emulating some of what the U.S. Defense Department did to rev up the development of self-driving cars by U.S. firms. As China combines government-led investment and workforce development, the U.S. government will have to shape its own strategies to align publicly funded research with the ongoing product development strung across its private sector. That effort must focus attention on workforce development as well as basic R & D if the country is to have any shot at maintaining a critical edge.

China spent $205 billion on new infrastructure projects in 2020 as part of its stimulus to jump-start its economy in the aftermath of the government's lockdown of the economy to stop the spread of COVID-19.[26] The government is prioritizing technology such as 5G telecommunications, mass transit, and power generation infrastructure, including high-voltage long-distance transmission lines.

The United States is also making hard choices about its COVID-19-related stimulus and focusing at least in part on reducing the risk to supply chains for critical goods, including rare earth metals and uranium refining, electronics hardware, and medical equipment and pharmaceuticals. But the country needs a broader, more strategic focus on domestic infrastructure, including installations that will be needed for the new, digital energy economy. As Andrew S. Erickson, professor of strategy with the U.S. Naval War College, and Gabriel Collins of the James A. Baker III Institute for Public Policy suggest, other priorities are also needed to reclaim U.S. strategic security and economic resilience, including key technologies such as quantum computing, artificial intelligence applications, autonomous vehicles, and robotics. They argue that U.S. companies or allied country suppliers of these strategic digital technologies should be prohibited from accepting Chinese investment funding if it could "provide sensitive knowledge exfiltration opportunities or operational control."[27]

For the United States, a looming question should be how to build back the economy on a better, forward-looking footing. Doing so must include a redoubling of effort on digital energy technology. Washington-based policy analyst Sarah Ladislaw notes, in her essay "The United States Needs an Energy Industrial Strategy, and Everybody Knows It," that many well-known national politicians, including current and former U.S. presidential candidates, are voicing concerns about U.S. competitiveness. Some, like Republican senator Marco Rubio, are actively calling for a deliberate industrial strategy. Ladislaw argues that U.S. government intervention in the economy should prioritize clean energy technologies that not only position the United States to compete effectively with China in the future but also serve "shared global interests" in the low-carbon technology future.[28]

Given the long-lasting nature of energy infrastructure, U.S. industrial and infrastructure policy should be forward-looking and resist the temptation to focus on restoring the existing economy. While preserving existing infrastructure and manufacturing capacity to protect jobs is pressing, consideration must also be given to America's future global competitiveness and economic vitality. To achieve both, a careful consideration of the digital energy future is a necessity.

The U.S. economy has benefited greatly in recent years from advances in energy technologies, with large geopolitical benefits for the United States. Now, digital energy technologies are reaching an inflection point where the path forward could be different than it is today. We cannot afford to let businesses create path-dependent infrastructure that does not meet long-term, societal goals. The United States must take actions that defend its lead in energy innovation and smart and automated devices, both protecting Western democratic values and ensuring the technological edge of the U.S. military. That will require policies that guide investment and best practices for the American private sector.

U.S. industrial policy and future infrastructure investment must include a vision that acknowledges the need for fuel for current infrastructure but positions the United States for the future energy economy being pursued by its trading partners. China is actively trying to dominate the coming digital energy marketplace with its own brand of products, including smart drones, automated vehicles, and batteries. Understanding how China's policies could influence future economic trade in clean energy products and boost their relative capabilities in asymmetric warfare is an important priority for U.S. political leaders.

CHAPTER 3

China's Energy Strategy

C hina is the world's most populous country at 1.4 billion people. Over the centuries, China's large size has been a challenge to its leaders, who have struggled to maintain stable political organization, secure borders, rural economic development, and food security. In recent times, the enormity of China's population has made headlines because of the health-care challenges of a pandemic. But mostly, the country's size and massive workforce have created tremendous advantages for China's rise on the world stage as modernization and economic mobilization have taken place in the last three decades. China has successfully leveraged its size and resources to become a global force in recent years, both economically and militarily. The Pew Research Center found, at the height of the U.S.-China trade war of 2019, that 81 percent of Americans thought China's growing military power was a bad thing for the United States.[1]

China is now unparalleled as the world's largest consumer marketplace, and China's leaders are focused intently on ensuring that this stature is exploited both economically and strategically. More than eight hundred million Chinese actively use the internet. The size of China's online shopping industry has been growing rapidly and now totals over $1 trillion. China's annual production of automobiles exceeds that of the United States and Japan combined and represents more than 25 percent of global production. In 2019, new vehicle registrations reach 21 million in China, compared to 17 million for the United States and 4.3 million for Japan. China's government supports its national companies, some of which have been selected to serve as key national "champions" in targeted national security sectors. There are private-sector champions as well, many of whom have been forced to include Communist Party leaders on their board of directors or in their upper management ranks. The fate of China's giant automobile market has become inextricably intertwined with the fate of Western carmakers, including U.S. firms. U.S. electric-car maker Tesla saw its stock price surge in early 2020 as it become clear that its cars would qualify for Chinese government subsidies, just at the same time as it was losing its tax credits to support U.S. sales. General Motors, by contrast, posted its largest ever sales drop in China, now its largest market, in 2019 and must worry that Beijing is promising to curb sales of gasoline vehicles over time.

In the early years of China's economic modernization, the country was self-sufficient for oil—that is, it was able to produce the oil it needed to run its economy. But as its economic success gathered pace in the 1990s, China rapidly became a major oil importer. Beijing responded at first by sending its national oil companies in search of billions of dollars of oil and gas investments in Eurasia, Africa, Latin America, and the Middle East. But China's oil adventurism turned out badly. After spending roughly $160 billion in oil loans, oil-field development deals, and foreign oil company acquisitions, China faced defaults, corruption, and mounting geopolitical risk. The oil-guzzling nation was able to repatriate home barely two million barrels a day from all of its many foreign endeavors in Iran, Iraq, Sudan, Venezuela, and a multitude of other places or roughly15 percent of its imported oil needs.[2]

When Chinese president Xi Jinping came to power, he addressed this oil failure by purging the upper ranks of China's oil industry, as part of his national anticorruption campaign. He then turned to a new energy strategy: a massive campaign to move China's economy in a new direction by innovating in science and technology, including in clean energy technologies. In the 2000s, prior to Xi's rise, China was already dominating the solar panel manufacturing industry and had noted the importance of energy science and technology in industrial policy. But now Beijing has mobilized a larger national offensive to lead globally in everything from oil-saving technologies to batteries to electric cars. The goals of the program go beyond earlier targets to reduce China's dependence on foreign oil. Now digital energy innovation has a meaningfully strategic aspect. China is committing to utilizing these technologies for its industrial and military rise, and it is doing so in a manner that has created headwinds for U.S. jobs and threatened the intellectual property rights of U.S. patent holders. That is creating tensions in the U.S.-China relationship, prompting a rethink on U.S. trade and industrial policy.

There is no question that China's early pivot to clean energy created opportunities for the United States. Both countries were able to highlight their parallel efforts in clean energy to unpin a bottom-up approach to a global climate agreement. Xi's China offered its ambitious targets for renewable energy and energy efficiency, and the Barack Obama administration put forward its regulatory plan to clean up the U.S. power sector. With the two global powerhouses offering the same level of effort to combat climate change, they could jointly announce their bilateral commitment to a global climate pact based on their individual national pledges. This bilateral success paved the way for a global success as diplomats from the United Nations and France worked with other countries to pull together a system of similar pledges for national contributions. In December 2015, the Paris climate agreement was born, with 195 countries pledging to take part.

But the excitement of the U.S.-China bilateral success gave way to a harsher reality as President Xi took an increasingly nationalistic tone on territorial issues, human rights, and access to Chinese markets. U.S. companies started to blanch at requirements for operating in China that ranged from demands for technology transfer to participation in censorship. The U.S. public also became more acutely aware that China's economic rise was coming at the expense of U.S. manufacturing jobs. The solar industry was instructive. Four of the top five solar-manufacturing firms globally now are Chinese firms, replacing U.S. firms First Solar and Sunpower. The latter has gone through bankruptcy proceedings along with many other American solar panel manufacturers such as GlobalWatt, Evergreen Solar, and SpectraWatt.

The reality that China planned to make itself the center of the digital energy universe has increasingly come to be seen as a new challenge for U.S. national security and economic well-being. China is building an industrial complex that could give it asymmetric military advantages while simultaneously bolstering Chinese companies as tough global competitors. This chapter lays out the extent of China's commitment, potentially ranging in the trillions of dollars, and its implications for the United States. China is building an energy system that will propel its economic growth, enhance its export trade, and equip its military to better withstand and deliver cyberattacks and recover from natural disasters. The United States needs to do more than wring its hands over this new reality. It needs to make the same commitments to digital energy, but in a manner that safeguards democratic institutions and values.

CHINA'S MARKET SIZE ADVANTAGE

The growing size of China's economy, especially in the digital domain, is an asset to its national aspirations to be a global economic and military leader. China plans to leverage its giant population and consumer buying power not only to reduce its reliance on foreign industry by fostering domestic innovation, but also to attain top status in critical strategic industries surrounding digital products, including major energy and green technologies, many of which have dual-use military applications.

The size and commercial attractiveness of China's giant consumer market creates the platform for China to execute its long-range plan to gain the technology it needs not only to increase the size and prominence of its economy, but also to achieve asymmetric military advantages vis-à-vis the United States. To meet these national defense goals, China's leadership has launched industrial plans targeting critical materials and technologies that will allow Beijing to dominate globally in asymmetric warfare capabilities in artificial intelligence, robotics, autonomous vehicles, and biotech. Moreover, the Chinese leadership is able to use the market power of its giant consumer sector to do so. The country is not only attracting companies from around the world to form joint ventures with Chinese companies, but it also sets as a condition of access to its plentiful consumers that foreign companies must transfer technology know-how to China. Beijing has also tied business access to other political strings, including those that promote Chinese foreign policy and some that infringe on freedom of speech and privacy. In cases where doing business together has not succeeded in rapidly transferring technological capability to Chinese partners, China has resorted to industrial espionage, deploying cyber theft on a massive scale.

Scholars have been writing about possible conflicts between the United States and China over energy supplies for years, with some suggesting that China's growing thirst for oil might bring the two nations to war.[3] But as peak oil supply concerns waned and a potentially more abundant global oil and gas landscape emerged, the war-over-oil thesis was cast aside. In its place, U.S. policy makers began to focus on America's competitiveness in the world of energy technology, including advanced nuclear capacity and 5G. The Trump administration made protection of U.S. technology a priority for the Federal Bureau of Investigation (FBI). Highly publicized cases against Chinese espionage attempts to gain

American secrets for self-driving vehicles and nanoscale electronics hit newspaper headlines in 2019-2020.

Throughout the 2000s, I traveled to China at least once a year with my academic colleagues for an ongoing dialogue regarding global energy security. The meetings followed a similar pattern. The director of the Chinese center hosting us would make welcoming remarks and set the stage by outlining China's perceptions of U.S. foreign policy (mostly explaining how U.S. Middle East policies were "destabilizing" to peace). The Chinese leader would then emphasize China's desire to have constructive discussion with the United States. Ambassador Edward Djerejian, former U.S. ambassador to Israel and Syria and director of the James A. Baker III Institute for Public Policy where I worked, would make corresponding remarks about U.S. foreign policy goals, often focusing on conflict resolution in the Middle East and the U.S. interest in having China take a more constructive global diplomatic role. The Chinese delegates to the meetings often had a narrow script. We tended to be more spontaneously responsive to what they were saying. Eventually, the dialogue would come around to oil. That would be my cue to bring up my point that China's oil imports were going to rise significantly; that its strategic interests were therefore going to begin to mirror those of the United States; and that support for Iran would soon run counter to China's future strategic and economic interests. Once in a blue moon, some Chinese scholar with strong English-language skills would pull me aside someplace where we were less apt to be tape-recorded and explain that he or she agreed with my assessment. But most of the time, the rhetorical response was that U.S. sanctions and the U.S. invasion of Iraq were creating any and all problems for global energy security, not Iran's foreign policy or its support for regional terrorism.

One year, the meetings took place at CICR, the China Institute for Contemporary International Relations, a think tank that was an offshoot of the Chinese military intelligence agency and that operates directly under the State Council—in other words, a place where I had to be escorted to use the ladies' room. The discussion turned to differences in the theories of American and Chinese analysts about U.S.-Chinese bilateral relations. The conversation was more open than in the past, as it came at a time when China had been liberalizing speech and promoting more freedom in published writings by experts. I decided to break out of our usual themes and throw out a more controversial idea. "Some U.S. analysts believe that China's Middle East policy is intended to fuel conflicts that tie up the U.S. military," I began. Such a policy could create two advantages for China, I explained. First, the conflicts bogged the U.S. military down in the Persian Gulf and made it harder for the U.S. Pentagon to focus on China's core concern, northeast Asia. And second, it was expensive, forcing the United States into larger deficits and allowing China to fund U.S. debt, limiting U.S. freedom of movement vis-à-vis China. A young Chinese man at the meeting was emboldened by my comments. He blurted out that it *was* China's policy, and that it was a pretty brilliant strategy that was working. Ambassador Djerejian, a skilled and experienced diplomat, smoothed things over with some well-timed humor, but the more lasting impression from the young man's impetuousness was unmistakable. It spoke to the possibility that strategies that weakened the United States relative to China would be worth any insecurity created for China's oil supply. The reality of Chinese nationalism is now more unmistakable. But even two decades ago, in 1999, the U.S. bombing of China's embassy in Serbia, for example, led to rioters ransacking McDonald's and Kentucky Fried Chicken franchises in Beijing.

This Chinese strategy to support so-called rogue nations in the Middle East appeared to work for a while. The United States got bogged down in multiple conflicts in the Middle East in the 1990s and into the 2000s, and the U.S. economy became vulnerable to the rise in military bills, its growing deficit, and the financial fallout from oil price shocks. By the time the financial crisis of 2009 hit, the U.S. trade deficit had ballooned to over $677 billion, or almost 5 percent of GDP, because of the high cost of oil imports and the rising trade imbalance with China. China held $2 trillion in U.S. debt.

But by the 2010s, the situation began to shift. American energy abundance has rapidly turned the United States into a major exporter of oil and natural gas and is now cushioning the U.S. economy from oil supply disruptions. By contrast, China's efforts to invest in oil resources abroad to replace declining domestic production has had less success. As I laid out in an article in *Foreign Affairs* in 2018, from 1998 to 2014, China spent upwards of $160 billion on oil and gas assets in such troubled oil states as Venezuela, Sudan, Iran, and Iraq. The investment is expected to reap less than two million barrels a day by 2028.[4] That compares with the $14 billion Saudi Arabia spent to add two million barrels a day of capacity in the previous decade. China's domestic oil industry has also fared poorly, leaving the country increasingly dependent on rising imports from the Middle East and Russia. China's crude oil imports now average more than thirteen million barrels a day. That's up from just five hundred thousand in 1997 and substantially more than the U.S oil purchases from abroad, which have leveled off at six million barrels a day, mostly from Canada and Mexico. U.S. crude oil imports were offset on a trade basis by exports of about three million barrels a day of U.S. domestically produced crude oil to Asia and Europe prior to the COVID crisis.

Chinese oil imports are expected to rise to over twenty million barrels a day in the next decade. More than a fifth of the eighteen million barrels a day of Middle East oil that traverses the Strait of Hormuz goes to China. In the 2010s, Beijing started to realize what a large problem this was going to be. In its twelfth five-year energy plan, which extended from 2010 to 2015, China's policy makers noted a "profound adjustment in energy supply patterns" resulting from the shale oil and gas boom in the United States and Canada. The plan characterized China's energy outlook as "grim."[5] China's thirst for oil would continue to grow, making it more vulnerable to conflicts in the Middle East or to any supply cutbacks by the Organization of Petroleum Exporting Countries (OPEC), just at the time the United States would be less vulnerable because it would have enough domestically produced oil to meet its own internal demand.

Now OPEC, and oil in general, is China's problem, not America's problem. This new reality has forced China to change its thinking not only about its own policies toward the Middle East but also about whether it could count on the United States to guarantee the free flow of oil to Chinese shores. America's own oil wealth is leading to speculation inside China that the United States might become less willing over time to use its military to quell disturbances in the Middle East that might disrupt the flow of oil. That sentiment looked increasingly justified in light of the Trump administration's lackluster reaction when Saudi Arabia's oil industry suffered a major attack in 2019, presumably from Iran. In what was read at the time as a spontaneous reversal of the Carter Doctrine, which proclaimed that the protection of Middle East oil flows was a vital interest of the United States, President Donald Trump told the press in the immediate aftermath that while the United States was prepared to go to war, it would like to avoid it.[6] At the time of the incident, the U.S. response included sending a small contingent of U.S. troops and additional missile batteries to use in protecting the Saudi facilities from future attacks. The effort seemed to pale in comparison to the massive response seen in the buildup of U.S. troops when Iraq invaded Kuwait in 1990. The circumspect U.S. reaction even prompted U.S. allies to reevaluate their policy options and opt for a less confrontational approach to regional conflicts and a reopening of dialogue with Iran.[7]

As it became clear to the new leadership in Beijing that China's attempts to develop stronger ties with oil-producing nations were going to fall short of improving China's energy security (one could argue that they made it worse, as supplies from key countries China targeted, including Iran, Venezuela, and Sudan, have faced disruptions), Chinese president Xi Jinping made a strategic pivot. China is now making a giant bet on clean energy and digital technologies.

In 2017, China represented 45 percent of the global total of investment in renewable energy.[8] China's National Energy Administration has announced plans to spend more than $360 billion by 2020 on alternative energy.[9] China's president Xi Jinping has made new energy technology a signature element in his China 2025 industrial vision, now renamed in light of the U.S.-China trade war. China unveiled a national R & D initiative in 2016. Premier Li Kequiang presented the National People's Congress (NPC) with a challenge to support Chinese achievement in critical industries, including clean energy, cybersecurity, space, and data analytics. According to the China scholar Liz Economy, Li mentioned the term "innovation" more than sixty-one times during his speech.[10] She notes that innovation is central to Xi Jinping's "notion of rejuvenation" of the great Chinese nation. In China's national science development program (2006-2020), the need for indigenous innovation is specifically mentioned as a national priority.

In trying to reverse the energy advantage that the United States currently holds compared to China, China hopes to achieve multiple geopolitical gains. First and foremost, China aims to dominate the global clean energy market. Doing so could give it economic and strategic advantages over the United States. The market for clean energy is expected to reach over $2.6 trillion in the coming decade and will be an important sector for major global economies.[11]

By taking the lead in green energy, China also hopes to position itself to be a leading global economic power, potentially overtaking the United States as a preferred economic trading partner. China's green energy initiative offers trading partners the opportunity to lessen their dependence on oil and natural gas, including the oil and natural gas coming from the United States. It also has the benefit of allowing China to break into important sectors like the automobile and military exports industry previously dominated by other global powers. In 2019, new research from the Stockholm International Peace Research Institute (SIPRI) suggested that China was quickly becoming one of the world's largest exporters of military equipment, ranking second after the United States, with large state giants that specialize primarily in a particular sector such as aircraft and avionics.[12] China's North Industries Group Corporation (NORINCO) is now the world's largest producer of land systems. Its export sales ranked eighth globally at $17.2 billion for the period 2015–2017.

If China's green export strategy succeeds, it will not only improve China's energy security and make it less exposed to U.S.-controlled sea-lanes and energy exports, it could help China replace the United States in important multinational institutions and in many regional alliances and trading relationships. By withdrawing from the Paris climate accords and favoring growth in its oil and gas industry over energy innovation, the Trump administration facilitated China's strategy and potentially put the U.S. strategic and economic future at risk.

THE CHINESE GOVERNMENT'S EXTENSIVE ROLE

China's new energy initiative is receiving extensive political and economic support, backed by a combination of restrictions, targets, and subsidies. In 1999, the country embarked on a Clean Vehicle Action Program that called for 10 percent of all taxis and 20 percent of all buses in twelve cities to run on alternative fuels. The program started with natural gas and liquefied petroleum gas, but by 2001 emphasis shifted to electrified vehicles, which were labeled as one of China's key "science and technology projects" and benefited from the National High Tech R&D program.[13] China's eleventh Five Year Plan devoted $7 billion to clean vehicle research. By the twelfth Five Year Plan, new-energy vehicles were one of seven emerging strategic industries, with government support of over $15 billion. Government subsidies for the vehicles also came from local and provincial governments.

Over the past decade or so, China has supported electric car development and production in a variety of ways. The federal and local subsidies have been sizable. To generate sales of electric vehicles initially, the Chinese central government and city governments offered generous cash subsidies of as much as $8,475 a vehicle, with other estimates suggesting total subsidies could amount to as much as $24,000 to $29,000 per vehicle in some regions.[14] The central government also used several other creative policy mechanisms to drive sales, including mandates that encouraged state entities to purchase a large percentage of new-energy vehicles in their ongoing fleet purchasing. At the local level, cities exempted new-energy vehicles from city traffic restrictions, creating a major incentive for individuals to consider EV purchases. Chinese citizens wanting a car in certain major cities such as Beijing and Shanghai could increase their chances of getting a car by buying a new-energy vehicle, which gets preferential treatment in the country's local government license-plate lottery system that limits how many people can get a new car in any given year.

Initially, these policies seem to be paying off. The country has more than four thousand new-energy vehicle models in development. In 2015, China surpassed the United States in electric car sales, both on an annual basis and in cumulative EV sales. There are more than 1.2 million electric vehicles on the road in China today, and Chinese-made EVs accounted for 96 percent of all EVs built and sold in China in 2017.[15] The government hopes to increase that number to over five million in the coming years. But the policy has been an expensive one, and big subsidies have fostered corruption in some corners of the Chinese auto industry; at least five Chinese firms have been fined for filing for $150 million in subsidies, padding vehicle sales numbers.[16]

When the Chinese economy started to falter in 2019 as the trade war with the United States began to take its toll, Chinese car sales stalled. It was in this context that the government decided to take a new approach to clean energy vehicles. It announced it would cut back its consumer subsidies for electric cars and focus on its carbon credit program for automobile manufacturers with targeted EV output rates, giving domestic carmakers an advantage over Western automakers who are still selling a high volume of gasoline-powered cars in China. The shift would allow China to penalize foreign cars without being accused of relying on unfair trade practices and subsidies to support its domestic industry. It is assumed that Chinese EV carmakers will be able to meet carbon target levels easily, leaving foreign carmakers at a possible disadvantage. Tesla, which is now producing five hundred thousand cars a year in China, is an exception; it lobbied for and is receiving subsidies from the Chinese government for its cars to be produced at a new factory near Shanghai. Under China's carbon credit system, automobile manufacturers must earn carbon emission credits for roughly 12 percent of their sales. To the extent that foreign carmakers cannot meet that target, they will need to buy credits from local Chinese EV manufacturers, essentially transferring capital from foreign companies to local EV firms.

With the removal of consumer incentives, sales of new-energy vehicles fell by 4 percent compared to the previous year; sales of electric vehicles fell only 1 percent, but declined more substantially toward the end of 2019.[17] Chinese authorities said privately that government funds would be better utilized in expanding charging infrastructure, but as the decline in sales gained momentum toward the end of 2019, Miao Wei, head of the Chinese Ministry of Industry and Information Technology (MIIT) calmed markets by saying no additional subsidies would be removed in 2020. MIIT's plan for electric vehicles called for EVs to reach 25 percent of all light-duty vehicle sales by 2025.[18]

Chinese leaders plan to shift support for EVs by encouraging the installation of charging stations. According to the China EV Charging Infrastructure Promotion Association, China already had 1.174 million charging stations at the end of 2019, operated by eight new Chinese charging companies.[19] China also has battery-swapping stations, where drivers can replace discharged batteries on certain brands of cars. China has shifted to other means of supporting national champions that are less apt to get in the crosshairs of international trade rules, such as land access and credits to state enterprises, which are increasingly taking over from or partnering with private firms.

Moving forward, China is considering stricter regulation that would permanently shift its economy away from gasoline- and diesel-powered vehicles by mandate, instead of by financial incentive. A recent Chinese study on "China's Timeline for Phasing Out Traditional ICE-Vehicles" from the China Oil Consumption Cap Plan and Policy Research Project, published by respected Chinese think tank iCET in May 2019, noted that importing 70.9 percent of the total oil used in the country poses "a potential threat to China's national energy security," and that vehicles accounted for 42 percent of total consumption. China's Hainan province has already announced a ban on sales of combustion engine vehicles by 2030. The report recommends a phased reduction in the number of such vehicles, with bans starting first in the wealthier major urban areas that can most easily absorb the higher investment needed to shift to advanced vehicles without jeopardizing economic development, such as Beijing, Shanghai, and Shenzhen, and regions undertaking pilot programs like Hainan and Xion'an.

In a second phase, cities that are leading in new-energy vehicle promotion and cities with industrial clusters would be targeted to reduce oil-fueled vehicles. China first began its foray into clean vehicles to curb air pollution back in 1999, when it introduced the Clean Vehicles Action plan for twelve demonstration cities.[20] The program set targets for alternative fuel vehicles, including subsidies for buyers of natural gas vehicles. In recent years, China has imposed restrictions on diesel fuel use for heavy trucks servicing specific ports in Northern China and Tianjin, among other locations, prompting a shift to LNG as a fuel for freight trucks. In addition, fuel-pricing policies that allowed China's national oil companies to benefit from selling expensive pipeline natural gas imports into transportation markets promoted the development of a large fleet of LNG heavy-duty trucks in China's freight industry. In its thirteenth five-year plan for natural gas development, China set a target of ten million natural gas vehicles, about twice the current number in the country as of 2016.[21]

China has also tapped the benefit of turning over fleet vehicles to new technology, taking advantage of high turnover rates for work vehicles. China is now the world's largest purveyor of electric buses (e-buses). China has already electrified 18 percent of its total bus fleet nationwide and has mandated that all new buses be emissions-free by 2030. As of 2019, of the 425,000 e-buses operating worldwide, 421,000 were in China.[22] Bloomberg New Energy finance projects that China's municipal e-bus fleet will hit 600,000 by 2025. The United States is home to only 300 e-buses, notwithstanding California's recent mandate requiring that all new buses be emissions-free by 2029. Europe has a weaker mandate but promotes zero-emissions buses as well. BYD, China's e-bus powerhouse, is aiming to expand its e-bus sales to Europe. Reflecting China's strategy to have local governments support new-vehicle industries, Shenzhen, the home of BYD, is the global leader in e-bus fleets, with 16,000 e-buses in operation.[23] Shenzhen local government reportedly provided BYD with $435 million in subsidies in its early years, from 2010 to 2015.[24] To help BYD, the government also banned electric buses from using the type of battery produced by foreign competitors Samsung and LG Chem. The country approved construction of a factory by America's Tesla, which has open-sourced its technology.

China's push into electric vehicles has convinced Beijing of the need to lock up lithium supply chains vital for that industry. Chinese companies have purchased stakes in lithium mines in Australia, Mexico, Chile, Argentina, and Ireland.[25] But before raw lithium can be used in industrial battery making, it needs to be heavily processed. China's lithium production represents more than 60 percent of all the lithium produced worldwide.[26] Chinese companies are now among the world's largest processors of lithium, and the Chinese city of Xinyu, whose lithium factories produced the sought-after carbonite for China's nuclear warheads, is a major supply chain center for the global EV industry.

China has also taken steps to reduce its dependence on foreign lithium sources by increasing its recycling capabilities, a strategy that could give Chinese firms a long-term commercial advantage over competitors. China's National Natural Science Foundation is funding recovery science for rare metals, and China's National People's Congress hosted a session in 2019 to highlight the need to invigorate China's self-sufficiency in lithium through domestic recycling. Since then, the Ministry of Industry and Information Technology has begun piloting a lithium battery recycling initiative, which now includes more than 3,204 recycling stations operated by auto companies.[27] New regulations have been implemented to ensure that Chinese electric vehicle manufacturers are required to create the networks whereby old batteries are collected, stored, and transported for recycling. A network will include traceable platforms that track materials from automakers to car scrappage companies to utilization and recycling enterprises.[28] GEM, a Chinese company that started out as a scrap collector and now is a major cathode manufacturer, raised $500 million in capital to develop its recycling abilities and has announced it will construct facilities for recycling car batteries and metals.[29] Other companies leading the effort include Hunan Brunp Recycling Technology, a subsidiary of Chinese lithium-ion battery leader CATL.

Beyond lithium, China has made a concerted effort to exploit its position as a leading supplier and processor of the rare earth minerals needed for green energy technologies.[30] The sector has long been designated a "strategic" industry in which foreign participation inside China is banned. In 2014, China's MIIT ordered China's rare earth processing industry to integrate and restructure, forming six large state enterprise groups, with mining quotas allocated to just the six officially sanctioned state ventures. The vast majority of China's domestic reserves—more than 80 percent—are found at the Baiyun Obo mine in inner Mongolia. China is also a major importer of rare earth minerals and was forced to start stockpiling materials following a dispute with Myanmar, which was a major Chinese supplier of rare earth carbonites. It is often misconceived that China controls the vast majority of the world's reserves of rare earth minerals, but this is not the case. China is home to roughly one-third of current global rare earth reserves, with other deposits found in North America, Australia, Southeast Asia, Central Asia, and Africa. But, significantly, mining is not the most relevant metric. China is now home to more than 85 percent of the world's rare earth ore-processing capacity and is a key supplier to the American technology sector.[31] In response to the difficult U.S.-China trade talks in 2018–2019, a push has begun to construct new rare earth processing plants inside the United States to ensure more secure supplies for U.S. industrial and military needs.[32] The United States has a national defense stockpile of vital materials and, in 2018, barred U.S. defense companies from relying on Chinese imported rare earth magnets. Still, at present, the U.S. commercial sector could suffer from any sudden cutoff of access to Chinese rare earth processing, leading to renewed interest in diversifying supply chains.

Beyond the exposure to competition for access to rare earth minerals processing, another significant area of China's clean energy initiative that has obvious dual-use military applications is in the areas of artificial intelligence and automation. When it comes to artificial intelligence (AI) development, China's move to assure a lead could be material to U.S. national interests. In China's AI development plan, it is noted that AI is a strategic technology linked both to economic competitiveness and to national security.[33] Drones are an emerging technology area of competition between the United States and China and one that can be expected to rely heavily on AI and autonomous capability in the future. Both China and the United States are working on stealth drone technology. Surveillance technology is equipped with computer-vision machine learning related to technologies used in self-driving cars.

That self-driving technology is part of the battlefield in the U.S.-China rivalry is highlighted by the U.S. Federal Bureau of Investigation's (FBI) focus on the threat of Chinese attempts to steal self-driving technology. In February 2020, FBI director Christopher Wray laid out how China's willingness to use a wide range of methods and techniques to steal U.S. technological know-how "stands out as the greatest long-term threat to our nation's information and intellectual property, and to our economic vitality."[34] The director noted that China was targeting a wide range of sectors, from defense to academia to agriculture to technology companies, and said the FBI had more than a thousand ongoing investigations across the United States. Among the most prominent FBI cases has been the arrest of two Chinese employees of Apple on charges that they were attempting to steal confidential materials regarding driverless car technology for Xiopeng Motors, a Chinese start-up with backing from China's e-commerce giant Alibaba Group and Foxconn, a manufacturing contractor to Apple in China.

Important Chinese agencies, including China's Ministry of Industry and Information Technology (MIIT), the National Development and Reform

Commission (NDRC), and the Ministry of Science and Technology (MST), have designated smart connected vehicles as targeted technology, and the NDRC has also published a draft strategy for "Innovation and Development of Intelligent Vehicles."[35] Plans specify that industrial investment funds and science funds will target the technology and call on commercial banks to increase financial support as well.[36] Several of China's major technology champions, such as ZTE, Huawei, and Baidu, are pursuing demonstrations of self-driving cars using 5G networks. China's giant e-commerce firm Alibaba and social media firm Tengxu are also active in self-driving technology. Baidu completed China's first 5G-based autonomous driving road test in the new economic development zone of Xiongan in 2018. Since then, it has received forty licenses to test driverless passenger cars in Beijing. The company says its self-driving cars have driven millions of miles in twenty-three Chinese cities.[37] Plans include a smartphone app that will include a robo-taxi service; its roadmap includes future geo-fenced highways and urban roads.[38] But Baidu is not alone. Chinese firm WeRide is piloting robo-taxi services in Guangzhou, while Huawei is partnering with several car firms, including Audi, GAC Group, Beijing New Energy Auto, and Changan Automobile, to launch self-driving car networks.[39] Silicon Valley start-up Pony.ai—founded by the famous Chinese coders James Peng and Tiancheng Lou, who previously worked for Google and Baidu—created a second headquarters in Guangzhou to test its robo-taxi service, PonyPilot.[40]

GROUND ZERO: SEMICONDUCTOR CHIP MANUFACTURING

China's push to self-driving technology is inextricably linked to its efforts to achieve self-sufficiency in semiconductor chip manufacturing, currently dominated by U.S. firms, because processing technology is a key aspect of the self-driving industry. China allocated $20 billion in 2014 to build a national semiconductor industry, including extending resources for state-backed chipmaker Yangtze.[41] In 2019, unhappy with the progress being made, China launched a second fund that has targeted corporate acquisitions and mergers with Taiwan's semiconductor industry. It has also stepped up efforts to recruit talent from Taiwan.[42]

China's focused efforts to get a 5G network launched more quickly than the United States and other democratic competitors, such as India, Japan, and South Korea, could help it attract self-driving industry to its shores by being the first to offer an irresistible opportunity to operate at scale. To do so, the Chinese government is offering cheap equipment and virtually free airwaves.[43] China's 5G operators are expected to pay less for base stations. China already has more than 350,000 5G-operable base stations deployed, more than ten times as many as the United States.[44] In the United States and India, telecommunications companies have to pay billions for access for airwaves, and permitting and engineering can also be more expensive. Getting 5G installed quickly is material to other successes because its speedier transmission of big data enables so many other technologies, such as factory automation through the Internet of Things and self-driving vehicles. If its products could be more quickly brought to market at scale, that might give China a leg up on digital technology exports.

In addition to self-driving cars, Chinese private-sector entrepreneurs may also inadvertently (or purposefully) be bringing China a future military advantage. China's lack of infrastructure for credit cards and consumer lending in comparison with the United States has made mobile phone payments backed by facial recognition software so ubiquitous in China that military strategists believe that technology can enable it to leapfrog AI surveillance capabilities. The Chinese private company SenseTime is a world leader in computerized-vision technology, and Da-Jiang Innovations (DJI) is one of the world's largest exporters of consumer drones. DJI is updating its products to incorporate machine learning; however, it currently depends on American semiconductor content. Ziyan, a Chinese military drone manufacturer, exports products that allow for targeted precision strikes using missiles or machine guns.

DIGITAL MILITARY APPLICATIONS

Beyond drones and autonomous vehicles (AVs), China is also developing a large fleet of low-cost, long-range, unmanned submarines not only for reconnaissance but also as a possible asymmetric challenger to U.S. aircraft carriers. Advancements in networks of undersea sensors are also helping China better detect U.S. submarines and other underwater assets. China's military R & D has a specific focus on autonomous and swarming unmanned systems for vehicles and boats to use in asymmetric warfare techniques. China demonstrated a record-breaking formation of 1,374 rotary-wing aerial AVs in Xian in 2018.[45]

Various Chinese and American commentators have noted that China is promoting strong cooperation between Chinese commercial companies and the Chinese military. China's thirteenth Five-Year Plan states that the Chinese government aims to "encourage the flow of factors such as technology, personnel, capital and information between the economic and defense sectors" and to strengthen the "coordination between the military and civilian sectors in sharing of advanced technologies, industries, products and infrastructure."[46] Article 7 of China's National Intelligence Law authorizes the government to compel cooperation between China's private companies and its government. Well-known firms Baidu, Alibaba, Tencent, iFLytek, and SenseTime[47] have officially been characterized as national champions, raising their stature vis-à-vis state-run enterprises.[48] The tight relationship, while advantageous to Chinese AI firms, can also be tenuous, as seen with the sudden arrests of wealthy Chinese entrepreneurs.[49] Popular venture capitalist and social media celebrity Xue Biqun (Charles Xue) was detained in 2013 "for suspected involvement in prostitution" as Xi's government moved against popular bloggers who used their platforms to advocate for political openness.

The relationship between the U.S. military and Silicon Valley is a much more fraught one than its Chinese counterpart, colored by the country's uneasy interactions with the tech industry over privacy. Apple famously refused to unlock an iPhone to assist the FBI with an investigation against gun violence by a suspected terror sympathizer, arguing that it was a matter of protecting civil liberties. In 2018, Google, a company that once had the motto "Don't Be Evil," opted not to renew a contract with the Pentagon's AI Maven project after employees protested that their work could be used to develop advanced weaponry.[50] The Pentagon's Silicon Valley office had initial difficulties getting established, especially when it came to getting different companies to work together.[51]

The comparison between the tech-government relationship in China and in the United States raises tough questions about the institutional framework for innovation and whether the free-market system is inherently advantageous. In the debate over innovation in the United States, it is often said that free markets will deliver the winners and that government intervention in markets is not necessary and, in certain circumstances, even deleterious to productivity and invention. But as discussed in chapter 1, the Darwinian view that the best technology will rise to the top is not always correct.

SANS AMERICAN CAPITAL, CHINESE BACKING
FOR AMERICAN INNOVATIONS

Sadly, some promising U.S. technologies that have failed to find financial back-ing in the United States have wound up in China. One revealing case is that of the American firm Applied Materials, which believed that an innovative techno-logical element of its plasma television production could be useful in reducing the cost of producing solar panels. The company approached the U.S. Depart-ment of Energy seeking support for the idea but were discouraged from pursuing it. In its later venturing with China, the company suggested that their Chinese partners might want to test out the possibility of licensing the technology for the development of solar panel manufacturing, which had been targeted for Chinese government support at the time. The breakthroughs emanating from the deal allowed China to outcompete U.S. solar manufacturers. A similar story exists for 3D car manufacturer Divergent 3D, whose founder was unable to raise sufficient capital in the United States but found a willing investor in the Chinese gov-ernment, which not only funded the construction of a production venture but offered the company's founder a position at a Chinese university. These examples represent a pattern seen often in recent years in which U.S. start-ups and inno-vation companies have turned to China as a source of more patient capital than the limited U.S. private-sector venture capital world. China is also famous for its ability to scale implementation of new products and services.

Even the American success story Tesla, the pivotal U.S. electric car company, illustrates the allure China can create for American technology. Under fire from investors and labor, Tesla's stock was plunging in 2019 amid concerns about its growth prospects and flagging demand for its cars in the United States because of ongoing production problems. However, the company's stock and prospects turned around precipitously after it opened its first manufacturing plant in Shanghai and it was announced that Tesla would qualify for Chinese government subsidies.

China is also more willing to try things and to provide state support for pie-in-the-sky innovation. For example, the Chinese firm Shangdong Pavenergy is producing a type of plastic-covered solar panels it believes could be used to pave roads, allowing China to generate solar energy from its highways. China even has the ambition for its solar roads to including wireless capacity to charge EVs. The first experimental solar road was built near a substation in Shandong province. The experiment has a long way to go, but it shows the willingness of Chinese firms to deploy almost anything. State-owned road builder Qilu Transportation is willing to take a flyer.

At a Chinese technology conference I attended while researching this book, one American-educated Chinese entrepreneur explained to me the benefits of the Chinese system compared to the U.S. laissez-faire approach. She told me how she had launched her energy-efficiency technology firm in Washington State, but uncertainty about changing regulations and tax incentives, permitting difficulties for new technologies, and the uphill nature of selling a new product in mature markets like the United States caused her great difficulty in getting established. When, after several years of struggle, the Chinese government offered to relocate her business back to China, she jumped at the chance. She said that clear government mandates and incentives made her business take off, and she was happy to have come back to China despite her happy times in America. Her story reminded me of an op-ed I had read years before by columnist Thomas Friedman, writing on Chinese versus U.S. energy policy in 2009:

> One-party autocracy certainly has its drawbacks. But when it is led by a reasonably enlightened group of people, as China is today, it can also have great advantages. That one party can just impose the politically difficult but critically important policies needed to move a society forward in the 21st century. It is not an accident that China is committed to overtaking us in electric cars, solar power, energy efficiency, batteries, nuclear power and wind power. China's leaders understand that in a world of exploding populations and rising emerging-market middle classes, demand for clean power and energy efficiency is going to soar. Beijing wants to make sure it owns that industry and is ordering the policies to do that, including boosting gasoline prices, from the top down.[52]

I remember, when Tom Friedman's opinion piece appeared in 2009, thinking how simplistic it was. I am not sure if I was more agitated by Friedman's calling an authoritarian regime "enlightened" or by the idea that he believed China was going to overtake Silicon Valley because they wrote it down in a five-year plan. For me the question was whether, in a place where rampant official corruption meant that merit did not always determine economic winners and younger-generation innovators did not have free access to information or freedom of speech, it was possible to create an innovation ecosystem that could beat the American system where any eighteen-year-old could invent something in his garage and, if it worked, potentially attract investors. Now, I get it. Not all of America is like the television show *Shark Tank*, and it can actually be hard to raise money in the United States, especially given the student debt crisis. But here's the thing: In China, a system so built on repression has rigidities that threaten its success. And that brings me to the rest of the story about my conversation with the energy-efficiency entrepreneur.

I tend to be paranoid about conversations that take place "spontaneously" in countries known for repression, so I might have assumed that my entrepreneur friend had come to explain to me her happiness in China because she was planted to do so by some crazed public relations specialist within China's intelligence apparatus. But then an unusual thing happened. My friend began to rethink her position out loud. At first she was explaining to me how convenient it was to be a working mother in China compared to the United States. She could order whatever she needed for her family online and, unlike in the United States, did not need to be home to accept a delivery. Her groceries would arrive at her housing complex, and the security guard there would bring them inside her home and put them in the refrigerator for her. He even policed the community. When a neighbor took a bicycle from her yard, he went and moved it back to her garage without any trouble for her, because it was clear to him from the community surveillance system that it was her possession. It was on this last point that her confidence in her new life began to break down, because (I am just guessing here) it must have become clear from the look on my face that I myself would not want a member of the Communist Party whose job was to keep me under surveillance to bring my groceries into my house every day.

In China, the personal credit system is not a commercial endeavor based solely on how well you pay your bills. It is a social rating system that includes your personal associations, your community volunteering, and in fact, your social behavior. This social credit system via the National Credit Information Sharing Platform is supported by the big tech companies that my entrepreneur friend was describing, delivering all her purchases to her doorstep seamlessly. Alipay, the credit vehicle used by many Chinese to buy items from the internet, is involved in this system. If you borrowed someone's bicycle without their permission in China, and certainly if you stole it, your credit rating might be damaged.

I am guessing that if you attended an unsanctioned protest in China, face recognition software would be used to give you a credit demerit or worse. You would be labeled a "trust breaker" and could be penalized in a range of ways, including being denied promotions at work or the right to own a house.[53]

As my friend was sharing the benefits of her security guard for the digital retail economy, the tenor of our conversation became much more two-sided. She suddenly confided that she missed Seattle and that she actually liked going to the supermarket in America. I offered some comforting observations about how we American scholars know that democracy is a messy system of governing (some political scientists actually use that phrase), but then added carefully that it has many lifestyle advantages, including the right to privacy and well-developed legal rights for individuals to hold businesses and government accountable via the courts. We talked confidentially for a little while about privacy and the impact of state corruption in China. When we got to the subject of local food contamination, she reminded me to be careful about where I ate, saying that her family only ate fish in places they knew and where they could see the fish live before they ate it. Before we parted, she confided that maybe she had made a mistake moving back to China. All the surveillance made her feel anxious, she said, even though she would never do anything "wrong." It made me remember the counsel of a researcher from China who was visiting my university and looking at some data together with me on my laptop. He told me to make sure to always put a piece of tape over my camera hole.

These manifestations of China's authoritarian system of government highlight the fact that such a system is replacing human initiative, accountability, and transparency with repression as the counteragent to corruption, inefficiency, and inequality. It is a weakness that China must overcome in stimulating an innovative technology culture, and it is one that gives the United States an edge to transcend China's massive spending on digital R & D. More than 1.6 million Chinese die prematurely from the ill effects of air pollution each year.[54] China's aging population is expected to peak in 2029, eventually hindering workforce development and creating potentially crippling problems related to elder care and massive pension obligations.[55] The entrenchment of Chinese state enterprise is another barrier to start-up culture, which has begun to slow in the face of ongoing trade disputes with the United States.

The conflict between freedom and innovation and China's repressive government system started to come to a head in 2019, when a highly visible number of famous Chinese entrepreneurs began to be forced into retirement by Chinese authorities, amid an economic downturn propelled by the U.S.-China trade war and later reinforced by the outbreak of the new coronavirus. Among the high-profile executives to step down in 2019 were Jack Ma, founder of Alibaba, and Pony Ma, founder of internet giant Tencent, as well as Liu Chuanzhi, founder of computer manufacturer Lenovo, and Robin Li Yanhong, cofounder of Baidu.[56] Tencent's performance took a beating in 2018 after regulators stopped approvals for new online games. The retirements are further evidence that the Chinese Communist Party wants to ensure that the private sector and individual entrepreneurs do not become an alternative center of power to its authoritarian structure.[57]

REPRESSION HITS THE CHINESE PRIVATE SECTOR

At the time Xi Jinping formally became president in 2013, private firms accounted for more than half of all investment in China and about 75 percent of economic activity. In 2017, a new national intelligence law was initiated that required companies and individuals to "support and cooperate in national intelligence work."[58] Communist Party loyalists have become more visible players inside private firms or on their boards, and state-owned enterprises appear to be playing a resurgent role after years of retrenchment.[59]

The United States faces tough choices on how to confront the technology challenge from China. In the week following the signing of the phase one trade agreement between the United States and China, which increased U.S. sales of raw materials to China, U.S. Secretary of State Mike Pompeo told executives from Silicon Valley that the United States is "facing a challenge from China that demands every fiber of your innovative skill and your innovative spirit." He added, "We need to make sure that our companies don't do deals that strengthen a competitor's military or tighten the regime's grip of repression in part of that country. We need to make sure American technology doesn't power a truly Orwellian surveillance state."[60] The articulated threat is not just in the military sphere. It is also in the competition for allied security networks and trading partners.

Kurt Campbell and Jake Sullivan smartly point out in a seminal *Foreign Affairs* article that China may become a stronger ideological challenger than the Soviet

Union, not because there will be a resurgence of Communism, but because Beijing is exerting "a pull towards autocracy."[61] They suggest that the example of China's system, which is skillfully combining authoritarianism and digital surveillance, could lead to an erosion of democratic governance across the world in a manner that would harm U.S. interests and alliance systems. Campbell and Sullivan warn: "China's fusion of authoritarian capitalism and digital surveillance may prove more durable and attractive than Marxism, and its support for autocrats and democratic backsliders will challenge American values and provide China cover for its own egregious practices."[62] The 2019 U.S. National Intelligence Strategy specifically acknowledges this problem: "Without common ethical standards and shared interests to govern these developments, they have the potential to pose significant threats to U.S. interests and security."[63]

Beijing has been promoting its "digital Silk Road" that will likely include construction of passageways to expand information exchange with its Belt and Road Initiative trading partners. As part of this program, China not only sells its information hardware but actively extends its own preferences for censorship beyond its own borders. China has tried to extend its censorship over WeChat outside of China, for example. It also shares technical knowledge and experience in surveillance and political repression with like-minded foreign leaders. And the fiber-optic cables that China might install in other countries could give it access to data such as sensitive government information if it clamps or bends the fibers in a way that creates physical conditions that could be tapped at a later point allow data to leak out and thereby be transferred to a surreptitiously installed receiver. This risk would make it more difficult for the United States to share confidential information with any allied countries that might be attached to Chinese digital Silk Road infrastructure. Several countries, including U.S. allies from the developing world, have agreed to cooperate with China on an interconnected digital Silk Road. This could be a problem down the road if those countries are connected with Chinese infrastructure.

This threat—that China might export its authoritarian practices, either as technological enablers within its commercial products or philosophically through its global leadership along with its dominant digital products—is going to become the defining economic and foreign policy challenge for the United States. It is no exaggeration to suggest that the level of success of U.S. economic competition, standards, and regulations for the deployment of digital energy technologies could influence America's ability to sustain its current leading position in the world. If the United States fails to compete effectively against a barrage of Chinese digital exports, China, not the United States, might come to define the scope of their use. The advent of artificial intelligence, lidar and other kinds of sensors, automated vehicles, drones, and computer-assisted household electric and appliance systems comes with an ethical and moral component that will define our human future. The technologies themselves are agnostic as to the appropriate ways of using them. The United States needs to lead on what is acceptable, not only at home but internationally. Failure to do so will degrade the global world in which we must exist.

CHINA'S DOMINANT STAKE IN GLOBAL LOGISTICS

The U.S. Navy plays a preeminent role in protecting the free flow of oil via the sea-lanes, especially in vital routes from the Middle East to oil-consuming regions. Its dominance of the world's oceans gives it a preeminent role in facilitating global trade by protecting global seaborne commerce and otherwise maintaining order at sea. China has limited global naval capabilities and is not expected to rival the United States in naval power for years to come. But China has made substantial infrastructure investments that will be important in the clean energy economy, including key investments in mining and ports. Its Belt and Road Initiative (BRI) has allowed China to improve its ability to influence global supply chains for its new cleantech economy. Through this initiative, China is investing across multiple logistics sectors, including energy infrastructure, warehousing, trucking, railway, ports, and marine carriers. Chinese technology companies have laid more than 59,488 kilometers of undersea cable involved in ninety-eight projects in the Indo-Pacific, South Pacific, and Atlantic Ocean regions. Chinese firms now participate in about a fifth of all undersea cable projects, up from single digits just a few years ago.[64] Moreover, China's five biggest shipping carriers control 18 percent of all container shipping, and two-thirds of the world's top fifty container ports have some degree of Chinese investment.[65] The Chinese have invested in ports in Gwadar, Pakistan; Colombo, Sri Lanka; and Chittagong, Bangladesh; as well as ports in East Africa and Malaysia. Maritime equipment and high-tech shipping are targeted in China 2025 for policy support, including subsidies and preferential finance. The question has been raised whether China's active strategic initiatives in logistics could affect U.S. access to critical supply chains.

Beyond ports, through BRI, China is injecting itself into the energy indus-try of dozens of countries, suggesting it will spur regional development and promote "five connectivities" defined as "policy coordination, connectivity of infrastructure and facilities, unimpeded trade, financial integration, and close people-to-people ties."[66] The International Monetary Fund (IMF) has warned that the ambitious scale of China's BRI poses financial risks to countries that are not judicious in their use of Chinese financing, noting cases in which Chinese-funded megaprojects have been accompanied by faulty construction, distressed national debt levels, and cronyism.[67] Ecuador's oil-for-infrastructure deal that financed the troubled Coca Codo Sinclair dam is one case in point.[68] The deal, which mirrors many Chinese infrastructure projects around the world, has embroiled Quito in perilous debt and a major national corruption scandal. In Pakistan, the IMF bailout discussions centered around China's $62 billion in infrastructure and energy projects, equivalent to one-fifth of Pakistan's GDP.[69]

Ironically, therefore, the United States has almost as much at stake from an economically failing China as one that is aggressively rising.[70] An economically failing China could potentially be more repressive, have a greater need to exter-nalize its problems by diverting failing state enterprises to foreign venturing, and potentially lose its capacity to counterbalance the financial crises it creates in other countries. As we look to the future of U.S.-China rivalry and energy geo-politics, both risks need to be considered.

All in all, the United States must simultaneously engage China on common global interests such as climate change while investing more heavily in meeting the competitive and security challenges that could come from its industrial pol-icy, especially where digital energy technology is concerned. China's past willing-ness to confer with California and U.S. federal officials on climate change and air pollution policy measures offers a possibility to work in parallel to advance rules for digital energy technologies that promote lower emissions, even as differences will remain on how personal data from those technologies is managed inside China or inside the United States. Moreover, even in the face of stricter U.S. enforcement of intellectual property rights on digital products and more strin-gent American restrictions on Chinese investment in sensitive, dual-use tech-nologies, the United States could work together with China on scientific efforts related to nonsensitive technologies, such as carbon sequestration and direct air capture, that do not have security applications. In the following chapters, I go into more detail about the disruptive digital energy technologies on the cusp of widespread use and how to utilize them to tackle congestion, air pollution, and greenhouse gas emissions in urban settings. I then return to the opportunities for the United States, China, and other countries to engage in parallel efforts to ensure that these technologies can achieve their environmental potential, even as nations differ on how much state-run surveillance and data privacy are optimum for society's broader goals.

CHAPTER 4

Meet the Jetsons

Revolutionary Transport Via Automation and Data

I t's funny the things we remember from elementary school. My third-grade teacher used to assign us to read independently in class using cardboard cards from a "reading laboratory kit" put out by Science Research Associates, a small Chicago-based educational testing publishing company. I don't remember anything about the content of the many essays on these SRA reading comprehension tests, except for one particular item. It was a nonfiction article about how someday we would not have to steer our cars because the car would be guided by radar from the road. For decades afterward, I wondered what the author of that particular SRA card might have been referring to and why it never happened.

Ironically, I found the answer to that question when I was researching this book. Apparently, the first concept "self-driving" car was exhibited at the 1939 World's Fair in New York. General Motors had a Futurama exhibit that included a miniature landscape under a glass dome that included superhighways filled with radio-guided cars. Like many of the more amazing items predicted for the 1960s at the fair, radar-operated cars did not come to be. The smart-road concept was kicked about for several decades. The General Motors Firebird III concept car was designed to have a receiver in the front that could pick up a radio signal from an electric cable in a roadway. The smart-road concept was based on the idea that a smart highway system could be developed that would have something akin to airport control towers every twenty miles or so to control traffic flow. Scientists also experimented with magnetic systems. That line of inquiry died out as it was ultimately impractical. Eventually, the self-driving crowd moved to cars equipped with video cameras. A German scientist succeeded in sending such a car down the Autobahn from Munich to Denmark in the 1990s.[1]

It was also a German roboticist who put self-driving cars on the map in the United States. According to his biography, Sebastion Thrun programmed his first driving simulator at the age of twelve. In 1995, Thrun came to the United States to work in robotics at Carnegie Mellon University. Carnegie Mellon had already had some success in the field of driving and automation. About that time, Dean Pomerleau was driving around Pittsburgh in his minivan, trying to use artificial intelligence to keep track of thousands of normal driving decisions and using the data thus collected to formulate replicable, computerized rules for operation. In 1996, a version of the car basically steered itself across the United States, while two researchers manned the throttle and brakes.

At about the same time, Congress authorized the Pentagon to try to build a fleet of autonomous ground combat vehicles. The project was not very successful in its early years. In 2002, the Defense Advanced Research Project Agency (DARPA) issued a grand challenge. It would give $1 million to any team that constructed a car that could drive a 142-mile course through the Mojave Desert with no human intervention and no crashing. The course would extend from California to Nevada and include hairpin turns and GPS markers.[2] None of the fifteen finalists made it past the first ten miles. A Berkeley student named Anthony Levandowski entered the race at his mother's suggestion. Apparently, he had spent hours as a child playing with remote control cars. Levandowski's team's entry, a self-driving motorcycle that had worked well in a short qualifying match, failed to get much past the starting line.

DARPA was not discouraged from its mission. It immediately upped the prize money to $2 million and set a new date for a second round. Thrun, now at Stanford, entered with a Volkswagen Touareg prepared with machine learning. Thrun and his student Mike Monemerlo drove the car down desert roads to teach it how to identify the flat part of the road, as opposed to the road's bumpy shoulder, and to read ahead by analyzing what flat terrain looked like from a distance.[3] The car, nicknamed Stanley, won the race, beating out cars designed at Carnegie Mellon whose team had laser-scanned the Mojave and used satellite data to identify obstacles along the route. Thrun and Levandowski eventually wound up at Google and then moved on.

The task of teaching a computer-assisted car with sensors, automated steering, and a big-data digital map to follow is an enormous undertaking that involves several digital technologies. Your current car may already have a camera embedded to help you back up. Cameras read everything from lane lines to speed signs and traffic lights. Improved vision for your car will help the vehicle navigate better, eventually without your steering it. Car radars are also being improved so your car knows where the other vehicles are, regardless of whether it is foggy, rainy, or snowy. Tesla vehicles have an autopilot feature that allows drivers to switch lanes hands-free simply by flicking their turn signal. When you visit the company's headquarters, sometimes your host will command a Tesla vehicle to drive by itself from the Tesla corporate parking area to the company's front valet portico, just to show you it can.

Then there is the spinning bubble you can see on the roof of experimental self-driving cars. That is the car's lidar (light detection and ranging technology) system. The lidar system sends out millions of laser beams every second and, like a giant bat, measures how long it takes for them to bounce back. The data generated this way are used to build three-dimensional maps, which programmers hope will be more accurate than radar or two-dimensional photos. The maps created with lidar help the car use machine learning to verify its instantaneous sensor readings so it knows exactly where it is, down to the centimeter. It is more precise than the current GPS-generated Google maps on your phone.

There is no question that automated vehicle technology is going to revolutionize how we think about mobility and e-commerce. The possibility of a seamless network of electrified robo-taxis, self-driving delivery vehicles, and public transit linked to smartphone applications might seem like science fiction, but the COVID-19 pandemic crisis in 2020 gave a flavor of what is to come. In China's pandemic epicenter of Wuhan, unmanned, autonomous electric vehicles, monitored remotely from a computer screen in a different location, were used to deliver hospital supplies, to disinfect isolation areas, and to deliver meals to quarantined people. In the United States, the National Highway Safety Administration granted temporary approval to Silicon Valley firm Nuro to use battery-powered robot vehicles to deliver groceries for Walmart in Houston. As in China, the Nuro vehicles can be monitored and controlled remotely by a human operator at a computer in a different location.

A transportation system that revolves around digital advances like autonomous vehicles and ride hailing could sharply reduce oil use and eliminate carbon emissions, but that is by no means a given. How we utilize smart transportation solutions and self-driving vehicles could be a major influence on whether congestion, air pollution, and greenhouse gases can be tackled in the urban setting. Both China and the United States have a common interest in seeing this technology get off the ground from a sustainability point of view. But competition, rather than collaboration, is likely to characterize the sector, because autonomous technology and the artificial intelligence and computational science that support it have dual-use military applications and could also subject users to hostile cyber manipulation if its security firewalls are penetrable. Still, there is room for countries to compare best practices for environmental regulation to ensure that autonomy contributes to carbon mitigation, instead of driving increased emissions.

EARLY PILOTS OF SELF-DRIVING

To get a sense of the magnitude of both the technology and its remaining challenges, I visited my colleague Ellen Hughes-Cromwell at the University of Michigan's Mcity. Mcity, which sits behind a giant chain-link fence shrouded in a green covering like a private tennis court, looks like a badly implemented Hollywood set of a highway leading to a small cardboard-cutout town front. Some of the world's largest car companies come here to test their pilot vehicles on a course that has all the tricks of the trade: a shady stretch designed to confuse the car's sensors, the same way a tree-lined street might on a sunny day; a four-way-stop-sign intersection, where the car has to predict who gets to go first; and scrub brush along the side of a highway, where the correct exit ramp must be selected. When the University of Michigan team describes how many hours of driving it takes for a car to learn this simple test track, I am struck with the impossibility of training a car to go on any road, at any time, anywhere in the United States. I have so many questions. My Subaru front camera eye sometimes does not work in heavy rain, for example. And then there is snow, which covers the highway lane lines used for computerized lane assist. What if someone hacks my trip and sends me, and everyone else on the road, like ISIS lone wolves into pedestrians?

To ensure adequate testing so that such problems do not arise, leading companies are operating prototypes that operate in limited, predetermined areas and routes, starting first with drivers who can intercede when a problem arises and then transitioning to full driverless autonomy. Vehicle fleets are being purpose-built to service specific, limited commercial tasks. Imagine a self-driving car that can deliver a pizza to your curbside if you live within a particular set of streets. Waymo vehicles can already do that, based on a project that began following an initiative imagined by an ambitious television producer of the Discovery Channel show *Prototype This!* In 2008, Google's Levandowski and his team, answering a request from *Prototype This!*, retrofitted a Prius to do the job. Eight police cruisers from the California Highway Patrol escorted the car from San Francisco over the Bay Bridge to Treasure Island before it got stuck against a concrete wall. More recently, the supermarket chain Kroger has been testing home delivery of groceries via automated vehicles in Arizona.

The California's Department of Motor Vehicles requires companies actively testing self-driving cars on public roads to report the number of miles those vehicles have traveled and how many times the human drivers sitting in the cars during testing were forced to grab the wheel to ensure safe operation of the vehicle, known in the autonomy business as "disengagements." Although experts question the validity of counting disengagements as a measure of the technology's maturity, the leading company, Waymo, an Alphabet Inc. spin-off subsidiary, logged 1.2 million miles in California in 2018 and reported a disengagement rate of one per 11,017 miles.[4] Alphabet is the parent company of Google, and the car uses Google software. The company operates the majority of its fleet in Arizona, where subscribers are already being whisked around in driverless robo-taxis (with no human test driver) to positive firsthand testimonials. In Chandler, Arizona, a small city outside Phoenix, Waymo vehicles can be ordered up almost instantaneously by smartphone, much as ride hailing works in cities around the world. The company announced in 2020 that it will repurpose a former American Axle and Manufacturing facility in Detroit to open the world's first autonomous vehicle factory, benefiting from an $8 million incentive from the Michigan Economic Development Corporation.[5] The next closest competing company, GM Cruise, logged 447,621 miles in 2018 in the city of San Francisco and required about twice as many disengagements.[6]

Analysts say that robo-cars like the ones shuttling people around in Arizona are likely to be deployed by ride-hailing firms within the next five years in a few cities around the country, at first probably in geo-fenced areas whose boundaries would be defined by a virtual operating perimeter that can be easily mapped out and controlled. Eventually, robo-cars might be utilized by big brand-name companies like Starbucks to bring you to their storefront for free. Walmart has already piloted a program in which customers place an grocery order online and a Waymo self-driving vehicle brings them to the store to pick up their goods.[7] Depending on where you live, that might be sufficient to convince you not to own a personal automobile.

Las Vegas's Innovation District is offering a self-driving shuttle bus on a 0.6-mile route in the downtown area. Next up for the city will be a test run for an autonomous taxi called Robotaxi. The Boston-based start-up Optimus Ride is testing an autonomous shuttle bus service on closed-loop, private roads in the new high-tech development at the Brooklyn Navy Yard in New York City. The company also plans to offer autonomous ride hailing to a retirement community in northern California. A U.S. government–funded program in Columbus, Ohio, is providing an autonomous shuttle van program in an area of South Linden.

Theoretically, robo-taxis that can be hailed from a smartphone could obviate the need for personal car ownership in urbanized locations and optimize vehicle size to the purpose of the trip. General Motors is betting on that with its plans to create a ride-hailing company that will use its own self-driving cars. It has unveiled its autonomous shuttle vehicle, Origin, that will seat four and eventually be part of the company's Cruise ride-sharing service. The self-driving vehicles used will include GM's new, low-cost Ultium battery, which has a range of four hundred miles on a single charge.[8]

In today's market, consumers often buy the largest car they might need for a family vacation and use it for all purposes, regardless of whether a smaller car might be advantageous for shorter trips or where parking is limited. In a digital shared-ride system, more fuel-efficient vehicles, including electric and hydrogen vehicles, might become the preferred-choice winners for short trips. In this case, a transition to alternative fuels could be accomplished with the construction of fewer fueling stations. Additionally, self-driving vans and buses that could be hailed digitally could service custom routing, replacing inefficient city buses and provide mobility to communities now underserved by public bus systems. Batteries and wireless fast chargers could facilitate rapid bus systems to go electric and reduce inner-city pollution from diesel fuel. These ideas are not fiction: Momentum Dynamics has already installed a two-hundred-kilowatt wireless charger in Washington State that charges an electric bus during the vehicle's routine stops along the route, and UberPool already offers cheap door-to-door shared service for riders traveling along similar routes.

THE IDEALIZED AUTONOMOUS VEHICLE SYSTEM

Ride-hailing services have become so ubiquitous in many cities that it is often forgotten that the first one was founded as a smartphone app to increase carpooling.

Launched in 2007, the app Zimride matched riders for commuter or other kinds of carpooling trips, initially marketing to schools and large companies. The service became so popular that in 2012, its founders launched an innovation—an app called Lyft that used an algorithm to match users with "unused" readily available cars and peer-to-peer drivers to "reduce the cost of transportation."[9] The service had the extra benefit of allowing riders to tap faster carpool lanes around San Francisco and caught on quickly. Uber, which began as a limousine service hailing app in San Francisco, followed with its own peer-to-peer driver service in early 2013. The business of using computer algorithms to match riders and available drivers in the most cost-effective, optimized manner went global. Now Major brands include not only Lyft and Uber, but Didi Chuxing in China, Ola in India, and Grab in Southeast Asia. Micro-transit companies use the same technology to sell rides in vans and small buses for the same kind of app-based, demand-responsive, curb-to-curb services around urban and suburban areas.

Futurists at car companies such as Ford and BMW envision that cities will be equipped with a complex network of intelligent vehicle, public transit, and road systems that integrate ride hailing in smart, self-driving cars with public trains, subways, and buses that charge wirelessly from solar energy installations backed up by battery storage. In the same way that drivers now use smartphone apps like WAZE to share information about traffic conditions, driverless cars will someday connect wirelessly with other vehicles, roadside infrastructure, the police, and data stored in the cloud in a seamless system of machine learning by fleets of vehicles.

Ford Motor Company chairman Bill Ford endorsed this new mobility business concept in a 2011 TED talk, and the company created a new division called Ford Smart Mobility to develop and commercialize mobility services. Ford is also investing $1 billion in the automated vehicle company ARGO AI and aiming to put its first hybrid electric AV on the road by 2021, followed soon thereafter by an all-electric AV.[10] The company has been working with multiple cities, including London and Miami, and aspires to create ride-hailing businesses and delivery service companies in limited geo-fenced areas. Navigant Research estimates that the global market for smart city solutions and services will rise from about $40 billion in 2017 to $94 billion by 2026.[11] Passengers will access this smart mobility system with automatic payment systems via smartphone apps, which will calculate the shortest route from their current position to their planned destination, much the way routing software can currently display on your screen a map of best options for trip planning. As longtime transportation guru Samuel Schwartz said in his book *No One at the Wheel*, "When AVs become the norm, the reverberations will make app-based rides on demand seem like a minor blip on the transportation landscape."[12]

In this ideal world, each autonomous car on the road would communicate with every other and then connect to smart traffic management systems to ensure efficient traffic flow patterns that would, by computerized design and operation, avoid congestion and accidents. Researchers Fagnant and Kockelman studied this possibility of ride sharing with AVs in cities through a simulation and found that fewer cars would be needed to make the same number of trips. Their calculation was that one ride-sharing AV could replace up to eleven human-driven vehicles on the road in today's cities.[13] Smart traffic fleets of AVs would reduce the need for stop-and-go braking and acceleration, which currently accounts for a high proportion of energy use in vehicles. City congestion has a large influence on fuel consumption. In the United States, for example, traffic in 2014 caused upwards of 3.1 billion gallons of wasted fuel, Texas A & M's Transportation Institute calculates.[14] Moreover, fewer accidents would mean that vehicles could be lighter, lowering the amount of fuel that is needed for propulsion. In other words, self-driving cars could significantly reduce the amount of oil we need to get around.

In its study "Digitization & Energy," the International Energy Agency found that improved efficiency through such automation and ride-sharing systems had the potential to cut transport oil use in half. But its also warn that without efficiency gains from the technology, oil use could rise as automation facilitates more travel miles.[15] A 2016 empirical study on the entry of ride-hailing firm Uber into new cities found that ride-hailing services led to significant reductions in overall congestion, travel times, and fuel use.[16] But ride hailing is considered a risk to public transit; in Boston, researchers found that 42 percent of ride-hailing customers said they would have taken the MBTA subway if ride hailing had not been available.[17]

Recent work by University of California, Davis, researcher Alan Jenn has found that the environmental benefit of electrifying vehicles used for ride hailing was three times that of electrifying privately owned personal automobiles, given the higher average number of miles driven by a ride-hailing driver compared to an average household driver.[18] Jenn notes that in California, the number of Chevrolet Bolt vehicles rented by Uber and Lyft drivers skyrocketed under GM's business model that leases the cars to drivers who save on ownership and fuel costs. Parking policies that favor EVs in some European cities, such as Amsterdam and Madrid, have incentivized ride-sharing drivers to shift to EVs.[19] Scholars from Boston University found that if U.S. automated ride-hailing fleets shifted more definitively to electrification, greenhouse gas emissions could be reduced quite substantially, potentially by 50 percent or more, even under baseline projections for decarbonization of the mix of fuels used for power generation in the United States.[20]

California is out in front on the issue, with discussions about how to regulate tailpipe emissions for autonomous ride-hailing fleets. The California Public Utilities Commission (CPUC) is the agency responsible for regulating autonomous vehicles for use by fleet services, such as ride-hailing companies. In California, at least five carriers have permits to carry passengers in autonomous vehicles: Zoox, AutoX, Pony.ai, Waymo, and Aurora Innovation. The CPUC has solicited input from stakeholders for its process of developing new rules to oversee autonomous ride hailing and will need to align its regulations with clean miles standards for ride-hailing fleets to be imposed by the California Air Resources Board (CARB).[21] The board concluded in a 2019 study that the ride-hailing fleet operating in the state emitted 50 percent more emissions than the average of the total statewide passenger-vehicle fleet, despite having a larger percentage of fuel-efficient vehicles.[22] Fewer than 1 percent of ride-hailing vehicles in the state were electric in 2018. The higher emissions rates were found to be a function of lower traveling speeds and cruising periods when drivers have no passengers to carry. The study was completed to allow the board to determine a baseline of greenhouse gas emissions for ride-hailing firms, which will be called upon to submit an emissions reduction plan by 2022 to meet emissions reduction requirements.[23] The standard would be a good model for regulating autonomous vehicle fleets.

Widespread deployment of autonomous vehicle technology will take time. It takes millions of man-hours to map the routes that AVs might travel in an effort to promote machine learning so that the vehicle software can adapt to changing road conditions. To achieve the kind of real-time systems operations needed for an entire city section operating with coordinated autonomous traffic comprised of robo-vehicles would likely require an upgrade to fifth-generation (5G) mobile wireless technologies. 5G will be able to process data as much as twenty times faster than current Long-Term Evolution (LTE) information technology systems. With 5G, machines will be able to respond in three milliseconds, seven milliseconds faster than the human mind. Existing cell phone towers will have to be supplemented with a large number of smaller stations enabled for peer-to-peer communication (P2P) at a lower millimeter wave band level of the radio spectrum. This is technologically more challenging because radio waves above twenty gigahertz (GHz) do not travel well through solid materials like walls. This means a denser network of transmission and reception equipment will have to be installed to allow the network of data to operate smoothly. 5G networks are still in their infancy, and experts project that the switchover to 5G will take at least a decade.[24]

GAME CHANGER: DRIVERLESS TRUCKING

Despite the obvious benefits to convenience, autonomous vehicles are not universally popular, and already a few unhappy assailants with knives, guns, rocks and lead pipes have attacked Waymo vehicles in Arizona. The bigger problem will come once the driverless vehicles start taking people's jobs. McKinsey Global Institute says that more than 1.5 million jobs could be lost as automated heavy trucks enter the marketplace by 2027. The Teamsters Union in the United States does not have a proactive position against self-driving trucks, but six hundred thousand drivers are union members. At the end of 2018, Tesla founder Elon Musk unveiled a long-haul electric truck that will have Tesla's autonomous technology and the capacity to drive convoy style—that is, with a lead human driver setting the steering, acceleration, and braking of a line of self-driving trucks, using technology that will synchronize movements like a virtual train. This practice, called platooning, reduces the natural drag created by the wind shear between vehicles, enhancing energy efficiency. Volvo and Daimler are already testing self-driving trucks in Europe by. In 2016, Uber tested a fully automated truck carrying two thousand cases of Budweiser beer on the windy highway from Fort Collins, Colorado, to Colorado Springs. China is competing with a start-up called TuSimple, which aims to launch autonomous semis by 2020.

Utilization of big data and computerized logistics planning is already allowing trucking delivery firms like UPS to eliminate miles traveled by organizing package deliveries using route-planning programs assisted by artificial intelligence.[25] Packages are scanned and stacked into trucks on the basis of delivery locations to minimize drive times; drivers are no longer left to select routes at random but now follow digital routing based on GPS-assisted calculations for the fastest arrival times. United Parcel Services Inc. (UPS) reported that upgrading its operations to this computer-assisted system eliminated one hundred million miles of vehicle travel in its first year of use in 2017. Logistics experts from McKinsey & Co. estimate that the use of such systems will eliminate about 20 to 25 percent of all fuel used in on-road freight. If dedicated lanes for autonomous trucks were established, the fuel savings could be even higher; platooning of large vehicles would create additional efficiencies of between 10 and 20 percent by reducing wind shear between trucks as well as braking and acceleration.[26] Figure 4.1 shows the potential oil savings that could result from the widespread use of computer-assisted logistics efficiency programming for freight trucking.

Researchers from the Massachusetts Institute of Technology (MIT) have found that online shopping and dedicated truck lanes could go a long way to reducing the amount of oil used in the freight sector.[27] As online shopping replaces personal trips to the mall, the number of trips it takes to get goods to the consumer could fall and with it, fuel consumption. Dedicated lanes for self-driving trucks can contribute as well by lowering congestion, leading to less wasted fuel, according to research from Georgia Tech. As the online retail industry progresses to automation and the use of consumer big data to ferret out purchasing patterns, shipment patterns may also change to include more seasonal pop-up stores walkable to urban consumers, changing the nature of the

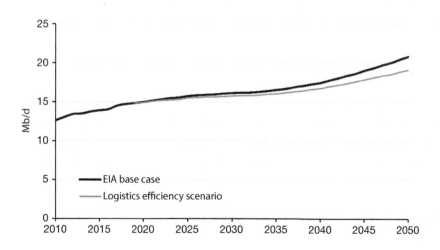

4.1 Worldwide oil demand from heavy-duty truck freight transportation

distribution center business. However, should retailers like Amazon choose to keep goods in roving warehouses on trucks that can deliver goods almost instantaneously, then all the benefits of saved fuel and reduced congestion could go out the window. In this case, automation could dramatically increase oil demand, wiping out the environmental and energy security advantages of the technology.

My research on freight scenarios with Arizona professor Daniel Scheitrum shows that these travel efficiency technologies, if taken in combination with alternative fuels, can have a large effect on oil demand compared with a business-as-usual scenario. We tested the sensitivity of oil demand by demonstrating what a full shift of commercial freight away from oil-based fuels would look like and found that it could contribute significantly to a peaking of oil demand. The possibility that companies could launch self-driving trucking delivery services with alternative fuels is not a pipedream. In 2019, Amazon.com Inc. ordered one hundred thousand electric vans from U.S. start-up Rivian. UPS followed with its own announcement that it was ordering ten thousand electric delivery trucks from the UK firm Arrival Ltd. Both companies intend to test autonomous trucks for delivery.

Electric mobility was one of twenty-five policy and technology measures recommended to reduce air pollution by the United Nations 2018 Environment Report.[28] The effect of full electrification of the global commercial truck fleet would be dramatic, even if personal automobiles remained gasoline fueled. While the effort to electrify trucks is just beginning, natural gas trucks are more pervasive, with close to eighteen million natural gas trucks operating worldwide. In recent years, China has made a large push to convert freight fleets to natural gas, with the number of natural gas trucks rising from 60,000 in 2000 to more than 1.5 million today. The technology for electrification of larger commercial fleets is moving fastest for buses. Global electric bus sales increased by 32 percent in 2018, according to Bloomberg New Energy Finance. China is the largest producer of electric buses, with close to 20 percent of its buses currently electrified. The European Union has a target of 75 percent of new bus sales in European cities to be electric by 2030. New York City has pledged to achieve a 100 percent electric bus fleet by 2040. Shanghai will achieve 100 percent electrified buses by 2020.

ROBO-TAXIS VERSUS PUBLIC TRANSIT

How companies will choose to deploy their automated vehicles is already becoming a matter of public interest, and not just because a few early adopters have caused traffic deaths. Preliminary studies on the autonomous vehicle's close cousin, ride hailing, indicate that all those quick trips in an Uber or Lyft gasoline-fueled vehicle are not as eco-friendly as the companies would like you to believe. Researchers at Berkeley found that a third of San Francisco riders surveyed were using ride-sharing services instead of public transportation, rather than to supplement it.[29] A survey of ride-sharing customers in the Boston area found similar results.[30]

Technology developers such as Apple, Google, and Tesla have major programs to disrupt the transportation sector and have done a good job conveying how their products can contribute to solving some of the world's largest problems, including climate change, urban mobility, and energy security. But it is the social context and application of digital technology that will determine how the host of revolutionary products and services will shape our future. It remains to be seen if the same innovations that are being postulated as modern solutions to society's ills could actually make those problems worse or add some new ones we cannot currently imagine. As driverless cars become more ubiquitous, policy makers will need to be diligent to ensure that the way they are integrated into urban landscapes is a constructive one that lessens fuel use and congestion. Some cities, such as New York and London, are already experimenting with pricing the use of streets and public spaces in specific congested parts of the city to influence driving patterns and discourage excessive fuel consumption and emissions. Eventually, carbon intensity fees or required AV integration with public transit goals may be adopted.

The final tech frontier in removing congestion might come from the drone sector, with companies testing autonomous aircraft that could transport customers above street traffic from one rooftop landing pad to another. Electric vertical takeoff and landing aircraft (eVTOLs) are not just science fiction. Air taxis are being tested in real time, and more than seventy major companies, including Airbus and Boeing as well as Uber, have products in development.[31] Uber Elevate has announced plans to offer air taxi services in Dallas, Los Angeles, and Melbourne by 2023. Volocopter GmbH of Germany was scheduled to open a landing facility in Singapore for test flights in late 2019. In China, drone start-up Ehang says its autonomous passenger drones will be operating in Guangzhou in 2020 with three or four regular routes. While the future might not hold a Jetsons-like world of flying cars, local air travel might change considerably.

Finally, there is the possibility, seemingly remote at present given terrorism concerns, that drones will revolutionize home goods delivery. In the United

States, strict rules that sharply limit how far a drone can travel would make drones as a chief means of delivery impossible; defunct San Francisco start-up TacoCopter's now banned plan to bring Mexican food to your home by drone is a case in point. Still, that has not stopped the big tech companies from thinking about it. Amazon Prime is boasting a possible Prime Air delivery service that it claims will help make half of its package deliveries net zero carbon by 2030. Imagine, say, a helicopter drone bringing your groceries from the roof of a local Whole Foods to your doorstep in suburbia.[32] Jeff Bezos, Amazon's CEO, has a page on the company's website with a demonstration video. Google's Wing division has also expressed the aim of using drones to improve its carbon footprint. And, believe it or not, there is some evidence that a drone delivery would save oil and thereby emissions. One study found that in the California market, use of an electric drone to deliver a one-pound package would shave off half the carbon emissions when compared to a diesel truck.[33] Eventually, some system of air clearance and registration for large delivery companies might make drone delivery an everyday occurrence. If it did, the influence on traffic patterns and oil use could be significant.

The bottom line is that autonomous vehicles are already on the horizon and quickly finding markets. The COVID-19 pandemic proved the utility of having small vehicles that could complete discrete tasks without a human driver, first in China and then in the United States. The benefit of a robo-car delivery outweighed the perceived risk of the vehicle's autonomous operations' being monitored by computer from afar. It is not hard to imagine an uptick in deliveries by self-driving vehicles. In turn, the more people get used to receiving their pizza or groceries from a robo-vehicle, the more confidence they will have about riding in one or having them on local streets. Then it's a hop, skip, and a jump to geo-fenced urban streets where ride-hailing fleets are autonomous. To get the environmental benefits of this new technology, however, will take performance standards, such as the clean miles greenhouse gas emissions standard now planned for California.

But autonomous vehicles are just the tip of the iceberg in the digital energy revolution. A host of other digital applications for power generation, household energy, and manufacturing will have more consequential impacts on the kind of energy we use and how we use it, in some cases changing us from passive users of energy to prosumers, potentially trading energy in both directions as consumers and producer-sellers.

CHAPTER 5

Alexa

Beam Me Up Clean Energy

oogle X headquarters looks like a giant warehouse-style art gallery to which someone has added some temporary walls and doors. To the left of the front desk is a hall with a collection of the latest Google inventions. A bright white Waymo autonomous vehicle sits like a sculpture with exhibit signage. A sample of the parachute fabric for the balloons that will someday bring internet across the globe sits in a glass case, together with the giant stuffed animal slippers that were worn so the team's feet would not tear the delicate fabric when working with it. A model of a flying wind turbine hangs from the ceiling by invisible wire, much the way airplanes are displayed at the Smithsonian Museum in Washington, D.C.

Google X has an innovation procedure. Employees are encouraged to submit their wildest ideas on "bad idea day." It is common for thousands of ideas to be brought forward. A committee of X planning executives, called space cowboys (in a reference to the term "moon shot," which is now used routinely in Silicon Valley to mean an ambitious, innovative project), narrow the ideas down to just a handful. One or two teams with winning ideas are then challenged to spend six months planning out their vision.

It's a bit of a gimmick, I find myself thinking, to keep morale up in the grind of coding and business development, like buying lottery tickets on the New Jersey shore. But it's hard not to imagine how a good idea could scale exponentially, with the infinite financial backing of the mothership. As I walk around with Adi Aron-Gilat, X's strategic development leader, she points out teams meeting in makeshift conference rooms, relaxing in game rooms, and getting snacks in the cafeteria. It seems like a college dorm. We are not the only group there for a tour. I feel like I want to sit and play video games in the recreation room. Workers can also break for the onsite yoga class. It reminds me of a Montessori preschool, the kind that was popular back when millennials were three years old.

My daughter once remarked she thought the ride-sharing firm Lyft was ironic because, having moved away from home, millennials were paying perfect strangers who were baby boomers (i.e., the age of their parents) to drive them around in a car pool to their various activities as if they were attending after-school extracurricular programs. As a baby boomer myself, I find it hard to believe that this organization, and others like it, are going to transform the way we live. But the more I see the endless things we will be able to do with different kinds of smart devices and robots, the more optimistic I am that we could, in fact, use a lot less oil in our daily lives. Big changes are coming in a variety of sectors beyond transportation that will disrupt how we get our energy and where we need to use it. One of the biggest changes will be in how we make things.

THREE-DIMENSIONAL PRINTING

As countries reconsider how to shrink their reliance on global supply chains to preserve jobs, reduce risk, and bolster national security for vital goods, such as medical supplies and heavy machinery, more governments and companies are turning to advanced manufacturing technologies such as three-dimensional printing as a solution. Over the past year, the benefits of 3D printing have become more visible. For example, 3D printing provided a ready solution to the shortage of medical equipment during the early days of the COVID-19 pandemic in the United States. As a manufacturing technique, it was already experiencing rising interest from the U.S. military, aerospace, and the oil-drilling services industry. Now, in the aftermath of major disruptions to global trade from COVID-19-related shutdowns and the geopolitical fallout of the U.S.-China trade war, 3D printing and other advanced manufacturing techniques are likely to gain momentum. Eventually, 3D printing could revolutionize car manufacturing.

But one of the least understood unintended consequences of a world with smaller, restricted supply chains and an increase in the use of digitally enhanced manufacturing techniques is that global oil use for shipping and moving goods could fall significantly. The United States is only now just beginning to think through what advanced manufacturing will mean for its global competitiveness, but it could make a meaningful contribution to ensuring that the U.S. economy remains among the world's most important innovators and suppliers. It can also better ensure that American consumers can be the master of their own destiny when it comes to everything from medical equipment to consumer goods.

As to the oil-related effect, think about this. If I am printing my own stuff like toys and sneakers at home on my 3D printer, think of all the goods made in China or Indonesia that are not going to be wrapped in plastic (made from oil) and shipped to my house (in boats and trucks that run on oil). The material I start with to print out my "thing" might be oil based, but larger items might be graphene based. Graphene is a strong, flat cyclic carbon structure, likely to be sourced from coal derivatives. The potential of advanced manufacturing to dramatically shrink the oil-thirsty global supply chains is huge. Maybe in the future, when I am tired of my "thing," some home recycling system could reduce it back to its base material and then I could 3D-print it into something else.

I took a group of tech-savvy energy people to watch a 3D printer at Carbon 3D of Redwood City, California, make an Adidas sneaker. In additive manufacturing, such as 3D printing, products are produced by layering materials, one layer at a time, to match a precise computerized design of the dimensions of a three-dimensional object. The process differs from traditional manufacturing in which machinery is used to cut down a block of material to get to the right shape. Think about building up a sculpture by adding pieces of clay versus sculpting down a block of marble to get to the same shape. The latter involves cutting away and discarding a lot of wasted material. Carbon's sneakers are sculpted, in effect, by precisely applying light and oxygen to a pool of resins and elastomers to build up foamy-looking lattices that will be shaped by design software to become a useful object. That's the technical science-oriented description. Now let me tell you what it looks like to a layperson. You are standing in front of a machine that looks like a coffee-making vending machine about three feet wide and four feet tall. Like a coffee machine, it has a small square opening with a plastic window that opens and closes and a platform (think where you put your coffee cup down). On the computer screen, the technician shows us a picture of a fancy sneaker sole that looks like something Spider-Man would wear. It is not quite solid but more like a hardened spongy mesh. He pushes a button, and goop starts seeping up from the base of the area behind the plastic window (think coffee pouring up from the bottom instead of down from a spigot). But it is seeping into a shape, and after about three minutes it is clear that the shape is the bottom of the Adidas sneaker. Our group is amazed. We ask when we can buy the sneakers commercially. They say there will be up to three million on the market within two years.

Adidas's 3D-printed custom shoes are the tip of the iceberg for a new kind of retail strategy of customized design. The shift would end the practice of manufacturing clothes and other small items in regions with low-cost labor and then shipping them all around the world. The intermediate step of storing goods in intermediary warehouses or transshipment terminal hubs would be eliminated, and production would be moved closer to the end-use consumer. In Adidas's new production planning, barrels of raw elastomer materials will be shipped to manufacturing points closer to market. But one can imagine a day when consumers will design their own sneakers on-screen at home and schedule a delivery from a nearby "printing" facility. In the emerging on-demand culture, products will not be shipped from Southeast Asia to the United States. Rather, production and delivery will likely go micro and local, much like today's same-day deliveries of groceries or basic staples by Amazon or Walmart.

THREE-DIMENSIONAL PRINTING AND PEAK OIL DEMAND

The potential of additive manufacturing like 3D printing to influence the peaking of oil demand is not yet as well studied as that of electric cars, but it could wind up being a bigger threat to the oil industry than other, better-known digital trends. To date, additive manufacturing has focused on complex machines such as engines because it is currently expensive and best applied to customized parts. But some day, the technology will be cheaper and more widely dispersed, and it will reshape how companies manage their production, with sizable implications for energy use and supply chain management.

Today's manufacturers depend on complex supply chains in which component parts are made cheaply in different countries around the world and then shipped to an industrial plant for assembly before being shipped to the final user. All this shipping of parts around the world is oil intensive. Assembly plants are not necessarily located in the country of final sale either, adding freight to ship products to their final sales market. For example, popular American cars are often assembled in Mexico with engine parts from Brazil. Transmissions and other electrical and mechanical auto parts can be made as far away as Hungary, China, and Thailand.

Advanced manufacturing could change all that, both by lessening the number of parts that need to be transported for assembly and by eliminating some or all of the distance those parts have to travel. In addition, equipment manufactured using additive methods will be lighter, requiring less energy to operate. Already, 3D-printed plane engines are being made with fewer components and at the point of assembly, thus reducing dependence on distant supply chains. These 3D-printed engines and equipment will be lighter as well, requiring less energy to operate. For example, airplane manufacturer Cessna is launching a new plane with a 3D-printed engine. Previous Cessna plane engines had 855 parts; shifting to 3D printing will reduce that number to twelve. The new engine will be 5 percent lighter and 20 percent more fuel efficient, in addition to having 10 percent more operating power. Engine design has also been accelerated. What used to take eight to ten years is now, via 3D-printing design, a two-year process.[1]

Additive manufacturing offers multiple benefits, including fewer assembly steps, greater customization, and minimized waste. Metals manufacturers are showing the most interest in 3D printing to lower production costs and shorten lead times for manufacturing metal products, including nickel, nickel alloys, and other high-value metals. The technology is of particular interest for high-cost items made in small production batches, including for maintenance departments in need of on-demand spare parts. For metals industries, 3D printing reduces the number of steps compared to traditional metal production. After the metal is produced using conventional smelting and casting processes, the next step is converting it to a powder or wire. The 3D printer then prints the metal component by melting the powder or wire to the desired shape. Conventional milling, stamping, and processing of large sheets of metal create extensive waste material, whereas 3D printers only melt exactly the amount of metal powder or wire needed to manufacture the product. Use of 3D printing avoids the expense of building milling and refining facilities and can be located at or near the end products' final destination. Figure 5.1 shows the difference in manufacturing steps using 3D printing versus traditional manufacturing.

Right now, the barrier to 3D printing is the high cost of the printers and metal powders, but as producers of the powders improve their yield rates, these costs can be expected to come down. McKinsey & Company consultants expect 3D printing to expand from aerospace and medical applications to oil and gas, automotive, robotics, and consumer products fairly rapidly.[2]

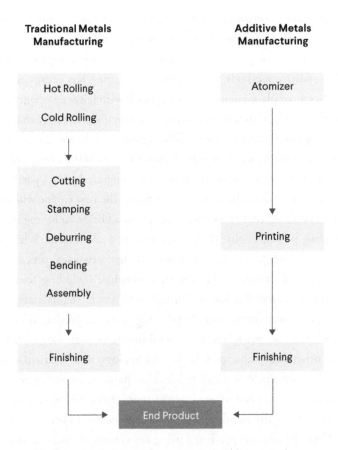

5.1 Traditional metals manufacturing versus additive metals manufacturing

Creating raw materials—elastomers, graphene, and metals powders—will boost electricity use. Fabricating aerospace parts using additive methods right now requires high-intensity lasers or electron beams and a powerful cooler. But the raw material inputs into 3D printing will be much more compact than final goods, meaning that greater quantities can be transported in a single load because a far greater mass of raw materials will fit in one shipping container as compared to final products and their packaging. This will reduce the total number of shipments that will need to be made on top of the lower number of parts for assembly and transport. Less waste also reduces the energy needed for disposal processes.

One study suggests that the widespread use of additive manufacturing in the aerospace and construction industries could reduce energy demand globally in those sectors by as much as 27 percent.[3] Using a modeling study involving the development of the Airbus A320 with or without additive manufacturing, the researchers found that eliminating the need for an intermediate manufacturing step could reduce the oil used to transport materials by more than half. Reducing the weight of construction materials through 3D printing provided similar savings.

The momentum to adopt advanced manufacturing techniques is likely to receive a boost from the rise of populism and trade protection globally. The Trump administration's trade policy accelerated the push for countries, especially the United States and China, to reduce their dependence on globalized supply chains in favor of bringing industry back to domestic markets and shifting to regional supply chains from more dispersed, globalized suppliers. Economic and strategic drivers are providing impetus for the shift to shorter supply chains. In a shrinking pool of jobs globally due to increased automation, countries have added incentives to protect jobs at home and in bordering countries. As trade relations deteriorated during the recent trade war, China and the United States began reevaluating the security of supply chains for strategic materials and other important manufacturing inputs, such as rare earth metals and lithium, with an eye to reducing potential exposure to disruption.[4]

REVOLUTIONARY ELECTRICITY TECHNOLOGIES

The dramatic change in the way I might design my own customized goods will be matched by the radically different choices I might have for organizing electricity in my home. You probably only think about your electricity when a storm knocks it out or perhaps when you get your monthly bill. But someday soon, your Echo Dot or Alexa will be taking verbal instructions from you about the temperature of your house or when to turn appliances off and on to lower your electric bill. You might also have a small battery storage device in your house to take advantage of a community push to renewable energy. That is already happening in Adelaide, Australia, where power brownouts were common and the government is turning to renewables to try to remedy electricity shortages.

Today's electricity grid is built around a large-scale centralized generation system designed more than a century ago. Large power plants produce electricity, which is then transmitted over long-distance transmission lines to places where demand is highly concentrated in cities and industrial centers. This infrastructure, as discussed in chapter 2, is designed for electricity to flow in one direction, from power station to customers.

Grid operators face a unique challenge in the current system. They must ensure that the amount of electricity flowing into the electrical transmission system from generating companies is an exact match for the demand for electricity from end users. The grid's supply-demand balance at the established frequency must be maintained properly at all times to avoid overload or reverse power surges that can create a possible explosion or power outage. Undersupply can lead to drops in voltage or brownouts, curtailing service. Utilities manage this electricity load challenge by using pricing and contracting methods that incentivize large users such as manufacturing plants to lower their electricity use for a brief period of time. This is called an "interruptible" load program and is often how utilities deal with sudden increases in demand, such as during a heat wave. Utilities can also carry extra generation capacity or system upgrades that allow them to provide a few hours of peak generation during unusual events. These costs are passed on to consumers in higher electricity bills.

In certain parts of the world, such as Southeast Asia and Africa, lack of population density in remote rural areas means that it is very expensive to bring electrification to each home by means of the large-scale electricity systems that are used in populated areas. Wires lose a certain percentage of the electricity being transmitted the farther it has to travel along a transmission line, and without a critical mass of users in one location, it can be prohibitively expensive to lay wires and sell electricity across a vast area with only a few customers. As a result, many poor communities remain without modern energy services like grid-based electricity. In fact, just under a billion people around the world still lack access to electricity. Even in a wealthy, developed country like Australia, providing stable electricity to remote parts of South Australia have proven challenging.

Now, digital innovation is revolutionizing new business models for electricity generation and distribution at the local level. One concept is to aggregate home systems, including rooftop solar, electric cars, and home battery storage, into a virtual power plant so that anyone involved in the system, including individual home or auto owners, can feed generated electricity to the grid. One of the first large-scale tests of this kind of project is located in South Australia, which was looking for innovative solutions to an electricity generation shortfall and frequent brownouts.

The South Australian government partnered with Tesla Energy to combine individual rooftop solar generation panels paired with in-home battery storage power packs into one seamless integrated system in South Adelaide. Key to the system's operation are smart inverters, which convert solar energy's direct current into the alternating current used in households and most modern applications. Traditional inverter technology cut off at a predefined voltage threshold and disconnect from the grid. They cannot adjust to sudden surges or dips in electricity. In the case of wind and solar energy, which are inherently variable according to time of day and weather changes, a different kind of inverter is needed that can adjust to the inevitable spikes and lulls in solar and wind production. Smart inverters are able to use software-assisted programming to manage precise control of grid variations and consistently supply power to the grid, supporting continuous voltage even in the face of changing conditions such as cloud cover for solar energy.

Often in the middle of a very sunny day, when the sun is brightest, housetop solar panels can produce more electricity than needed. Household battery systems allow homeowners to store that electricity to use later when the sun is not available. In the Tesla Energy South Australia system, some portion of the excess energy not used by a member household can be automatically sold back to the grid and controlled centrally by South Australian government grid operators. When grid conditions are stressed, surplus capacity from household batteries are tapped via an intermediary company and provided to the grid as if from a centralized power station—hence the term "virtual power plant." The system changes electricity consumers into electricity "prosumers" who both use and produce electricity for the overall system.

At a broader system level, automated home storage can be used to facilitate the adoption of a higher percentage of renewable energy and lessen the amount of fossil fuel backup "peaking" generation needed to support balancing supply and demand. As more solar and wind energy becomes available, the chances of its offering more electricity at a particular time of day than is needed rises without a way to balance the market. For solar energy, the job of an independent system operator (ISO) in competitive electricity markets is to ensure that a surge in electricity supply does not overpower the system, literally and figuratively. To do this, the system operator must find a way to adjust any oversupply at midday, when solar is at its peak, or in the evening, when demand is low but wind availability tends to be highest. Managing this oversupply is called curtailment, when either renewable producers are forced to turn down supplies because of lack of demand or when they pay a buyer (called negative pricing) to use the excess.[5] Storage systems can help alleviate curtailment by finding a place to keep the electricity for use when demand might be higher. When solar is not available due to cloud cover or wind intermittently slows down, sudden shortfalls can be overcome by drawing on batteries or by calling upon other power plants, such as natural gas peaking units, to quickly increase alternative supplies to the grid.

Household battery storage systems can replace diesel generators that are often used for backup when electricity from the grid is cut off by storms or brownouts caused by sudden surges in demand. Storage systems can respond more quickly and precisely than diesel generators to dispatch signals during a contingency event. The faster electricity supply and demand can be brought into exact equilibrium, the lower the chances of a brownout or explosion and the less demand curtailment is needed for customers whose contracts provide for interruptible supplies. Homeowners with rooftop solar will be able to use home storage to make or save money as well, when the opportunity arises. This can be facilitated by using electricity from storage devices during high-cost peak hours, typically at the end of the workday, and programming optional electricity use, like charging a car or running a washing machine, for times of day when electricity rates are lowest, like overnight or in the early morning.

To incentivize these kinds of decentralized, small-scale systems, often referred to as distributed energy resources (DERs) or mini-grids, in the United States will require major regulatory and electricity pricing reform. Many states still work under regulatory systems in which utilities can only earn additional revenue by adding large-scale infrastructure and then charging ratepayers more money based on a regulated rate of return mandated by the state public utilities commission. Typically, regulatory regimes do not encourage utilities to work together with small-scale, distributed energy providers as the utilities get no revenues from doing so. If anything, renewable energy can reduce the profitability of large-scale plants that have inflexible fixed operating costs. To the extent that renewables with battery storage siphon off demand at peak times, when utilities could charge a premium for supplemental supply, utilities lose out on higher revenues that might have been possible had renewables with battery storage not been available.

Reforms are needed to encourage utilities to integrate a DER solution where it can best serve to stabilize the grid by relieving location-specific congestion along the electricity distribution system. Utilizing a DER solution could help a utility avoid the higher costs of upgrading existing large-scale infrastructure with expensive equipment just to meet infrequent, temporary peaks in demand, but the current regulatory system only incentivizes the latter. What is needed is a new system in which the financial rewards for installing DER solutions are integrated with a new successful business model for utilities. One such system is under pilot in New York. There, the local utility can now retain a portion of the capital investment savings when a DER solution is used instead of a more expensive capacity expansion. In the New York model, the utility, the DER provider, and ratepayers split the savings in avoided costs that can be achieved by installing a DER solution. Another system could be one in which a utility or intermediary company compensates homeowners, businesses, or landowners through long-term leases for the physical geography (be it a rooftop or land) where a solar system or battery system is installed and then the utility or intermediary company owns the electric power produced by the system.[6] The various assets from these DER systems can then be aggregated as a scheduled power generation source that can be sold to utilities or directly into the grid.

Finally, in the United States, Federal Energy Regulatory Commission practices that apply minimum offer prices for state-supported clean energy resources need to be retired in favor of fully credited systems for pricing energy storage and large-scale renewable energy.

VEHICLE-TO-GRID CHARGING TECHNOLOGY

Someday soon, electric vehicles will be able to play a flexible role as a home storage system, or many parked electric vehicles could serve as a virtual power station in much the same way as home batteries now work in the South Australia pilot. Tesla's Model 3 car aims to have bidirectional charging capability—that is, a car battery that can send stored electricity back into the grid.

Imagine you commute to work in your electric car and plug in from your assigned parking spot. An automated system ensures that your car always has a minimum charge that you have agreed to but then fills up the rest of your charge during times of excess solar energy to optimize as much solar energy as possible. You also agree with the local utility to allow it to tap some percentage of your car battery when it is charged to balance the grid, in the same manner as a virtual power station, if clouds arrive and more energy is needed for a period of time. In effect, all the parked and plugged-in cars are on call to serve as a source of electricity to balance the grid. The fleet of EVs are a fast-responding virtual power station providing electricity services when needed.[7] Your car, in effect, earns you money from the system operator while it is parked doing nothing. The system is called vehicle-to-grid, or V2G. When you drive home, you can use any spare stored electricity to power your home (V2H) and then recharge while you are sleeping using excess wind power that might be available.

At some point, you might not own a car, and your transportation network company provider, such as Uber or Lyft, would be the one to coordinate with the grid operator for when autonomous parked electric cars with charged batteries will be available. This could be easier to organize (fewer parties to contract with and a centralized headquarters where unused vehicles are charged and stored) or harder to organize if the transportation network company AV fleet has less downtime than individually owned vehicles.

Flexible pricing systems for electricity trade and consumption will be needed to facilitate virtual power home storage or V2G systems. In the United States, we remain very far away from this ideal. Most utilities today only earn more revenue if they add more large-scale infrastructure and sell more electricity, because the way they make money is by charging a regulated rate of return on the money they invest in such assets. New incentives are needed for power companies either to partner with distributed energy companies or to invest in small-scale household systems themselves. Progressive utility leaders envision a system in which they might lease a storage device to a residential or business customer and charge for its use, much as cable television companies provide equipment in homes and businesses and then charge for monthly usage. Alternatively, the role of utilities might change to serve as aggregators of electricity supplies coming from many different kinds of electricity-generating and storage assets—both large centralized plants and small-scale distributed networks. Or your utility might simply become the manager of an entire system of automated control and communications systems that manage transactions on behalf of market participants, in the manner of a central clearinghouse. Blockchain technology, which can identify an individual transaction with a digital ID, could permit the secure transfer of electricity in exchange for payment, via secure peer-to-peer financial settlement.

Longer term, excess renewables could be used to power water electrolysis (using an electrolyzer device that splits water into its components, hydrogen and oxygen) to produce hydrogen that could be used to power fuel cell vehicles or be stored and used in stationary fuel cells to generate electricity at a different time of day when renewable energy is not available, especially when seasonal availability is lower. Right now, this technology is expensive compared to fossil energy for most applications, but companies in California and Europe, where carbon is priced, are increasingly investigating renewable green hydrogen as a business. Six of Denmark's largest conglomerates are teaming up to build a large-scale, green hydrogen facility powered by offshore wind by 2023, using a 1.3 gigawatt electrolyzer to make hydrogen by splitting water molecules. Costs for renewable green hydrogen are expected to decline rapidly over the next ten years as more systems are manufactured, lowering component unit costs.

OTHER ALTERNATIVES: TAPPING RADIO FREQUENCIES OR GARBAGE AS FUEL

The ultimate frontier would be if all your devices could just magically charge themselves from thin air. Few people actually think about the physical fuel that is used to generate the electricity when they plug in an appliance. Is that plug bringing you wind energy? Hydroelectric power from a nearby dam? Solar energy? Nuclear power? Coal-fired generation? Or coming from a natural gas peaking plant? Chances are you don't know, and chances are, it is some combination of more than one of these primary energy sources. But what if the energy that charged your phone could come literally from the airwaves? This is a technology now being studied by engineers working on 5G networks. It turns out that energy can be moved through 5G networks, and that might create a unique opportunity. One of the most novel energy technologies being studied today is radio frequency harvesting, which in effect would convert the energy in radio waves transmitted to user devices, wireless networks, and antenna arrays. The equipment to do radio frequency energy harvesting while simultaneously transmitting information signals, referred to as simultaneous wireless information and power transfer (SWIPT), does not yet exist, but 5G providers have the incentive to develop it to reduce the energy needed to fuel expanding information technology networks.[8]

And what if I could sell you a machine that would turn your garbage into electricity or fuel for your vehicle, as in the famous scene in the 1985 Hollywood blockbuster *Back to the Future*? It is not as farfetched as it seems; companies around the world are working on waste-to-energy solutions.

A lot of people in Davis, California, have thought about how to turn waste into something useful. Somewhere down a dirt road, behind a field of cows and a wonderful makeshift butcher shop where you can buy a steak that an agriculture student just butchered as part of their "meat lab" requirement, is a biodigester built to the specifications of a feisty, persistent woman named Ruihong Zhang, a professor of biological and agricultural engineering at the University of California, Davis. I say persistent because a less determined person might have given up, but Zhang and her students have kept adding new layers of sorters and scrapers to her brainchild, a state-of-the-art anaerobic digester that converts twenty thousand tons of waste from local landfills into usable electricity. I know a thing or two about the giant pile of waste in the Davis landfill because I sadly contracted a lice infection at a beach resort in southern California and in the end had to pay to dump our mattress. The mound of garbage as far as the eye can see is nothing short of shocking, like a small mountain range of grimy stuff. Mine was not the only mattress there, among heaps of other decaying household items like couches, chairs, cabinets, and dirty paper refuse. I wondered how many other people had trouble getting rid of some insect infestation in their houses or if people just could not find a useful place for their stuff when they moved on to another town.

Zhang was on a mission because all that decaying garbage produces methane, a potent greenhouse gas that is warming the planet. More than half the things we throw away make it into landfills in the United States. It is a huge problem. Zhang's biodigester is a collection of giant white tanks connected by huge pipes. Her closed-loop technology allows microbes to eat a wider range and greater quantity of organic waste like food scraps, animal waste, and vegetation. The problem is, no matter how well people sort garbage, the occasional bit of plastic wrap or scrap of metal always gets caught in it. That jams the biodigester's feed-in system and makes for expensive delays.

Industrial gas companies like Air Liquide are trying to create a tiny, miniaturized digester system that is less finicky for use at an apartment building or individual house level. It would be great if someday we could just throw stuff into a cross between a compost pile, a trash masher, and a blender, and generate our own electricity. Some companies have placed generators on top of landfills or are collecting the methane that leaks from them and converting it to renewable natural gas that can fuel a truck. My research team at UC Davis created a computer simulation that showed what percentage of the U.S. eighteen-wheeler truck fleet could be powered that way with some incentives from carbon prices.[9]

Mike Hart, a serial entrepreneur who owned a small railroad, has a different solution. His company Sierra Energy is proving up technology to gasify garbage into syngas for generating electricity or making diesel fuel or hydrogen without the need to separate the kinds of garbage. The Pentagon has looked at the technology as a way to dispose of its waste. The U.S. Department of Energy has funded a pilot. But like many technologies, it is hard to prove up and scale fast.

That the way we view waste has to change is a given. An estimated five trillion pieces of plastic are currently stuck in the world's oceans. By 2050, the ocean could have more plastic than fish by weight, according to a report on the problem by the World Economic Forum. With all that plastics pollution, political pressures are mounting for change, with several major economies announcing future bans on single-use plastics. In 2017, China instituted an import ban on twenty-four different types of solid waste, including plastics, textiles and, unsorted wastepaper. The policy has focused industry on seeking new solutions. Europe has targeted all plastic packaging to be recyclable or reusable by 2030. Citi predicts, in its study "Rethinking Single-Use Plastics," that a new battleground might emerge for container suppliers who will be forced to shift away from plastics to packaging made from aluminum, glass, and paper cardboard.[10] WoodMcKenzie Consultants predicts that the market for bioplastics—plastics made from plant materials rather than oil—could grow by 50 percent in the next five years.[11] IKEA, the Swedish furniture retailer, has said it will try to produce all its plastics products from bio-based polymers. Coca-Cola has launched a "Plantbottle" technology that includes 30 percent plant-based materials and aims to get to 100 percent plant-based bottling. So far, it has sold fifty billion Plantbottles. As new ways to manufacture and deliver goods take hold and consumer preferences change, the future of plastic might also adjust itself, with consequential impacts on oil use.

The upshot of all these technologies is that it could become easier than it seems now to break the link between economic activity and oil. Once we can envision a world in which your car can be part of your integrated home electricity system, your garbage can generate electricity for your community, and you can print your own sneakers—eliminating oil that is now used to transport consumer goods—it is easier to imagine the end of the oil era. It is also easy to imagine how the country that has the best system to manufacture and promote these technologies domestically would have a more resilient and diverse energy supply and thereby serve as a model for other countries, creating export opportunities, new jobs, and global prestige. That is China's bet, and Europe's too. Ironically, much of this innovation begins in the United States with American entrepreneurs, but we have failed to create the regulatory and financial conditions that would allow these technologies to be deployed here at massive scale. But suppose the United States mobilized a stimulus package to promote digital technologies and moved forward with regulations that would stimulate their wider use. What would the world look like twenty years from now? How much oil use could be eliminated, and what would that mean for the environment, for geopolitics, and for major oil-producing countries? I address these questions in the following chapters on the geopolitics of the digital energy revolution.

CHAPTER 6

The Energy Future and the Possibility
of Peak Oil Demand

Boom and busts have characterized the oil industry since the 1880s, and I have seen several of them. There is a sort of collective amnesia that suddenly strikes oil people when prices start to rise sharply. They always have an explanation for why this time is the "real" one when oil prices will not go back down. So far, they have never been correct about that permanent rise in prices. In this chapter, I explain why they will not be.

There is usually a trigger to a sharp rise in oil prices, most often a geopolitical event like the 1973 oil crisis or Iraq invading Kuwait. Sometimes a very robust period of economic growth can be a catalyst, because the accompanying rise in industrial operations, movement of goods, and building construction creates such rapid and strong incremental demand for oil that producers cannot drill fast enough to meet the demand.[1] When that happens, oil sellers like to remind you that oil is a finite resource: once you use it up, it is gone.

The idea that we would someday in the future run out of oil has been around for more than a century. When I started writing about oil in the 1980s, it was a common assumption that industrial countries like the United States and the United Kingdom would progressively use up all the oil that was easy to find and produce and would then become increasingly dependent on the vast oil reserves controlled by Middle East countries, such as Saudi Arabia, Iraq, Iran, and Kuwait.

Throughout the 1990s and into the 2000s, many authors penned treatises explaining the thesis that there was not going to be enough oil to satisfy a growing world population. In 1998, just as oil prices were collapsing from a temporary glut caused by a sudden drop in demand in Asia in the wake of the Asian financial crisis, geologist Colin Campbell predicted that global oil production would begin to decline within ten years.[2] His forecast, which turned out to be conspicuously incorrect, was endorsed and elaborated by many respected geologists and commentators, including Princeton geologist Kenneth Deffeyes.[3] They based their theories, commonly referred to as Peak Oil, on the work of a Shell Oil geologist turned professor, Marion King Hubbert. In the mid-1950s, Hubbert used a curve-fitting technique to correctly predict that U.S. oil production would peak by 1970. According to Hubbert's calculations, the technical limitations of producing a finite resource will resemble a bell curve. In other words, there will be an increase in oil production from an oil field until the rate of production reaches its absolute maximum, and then the field will begin to decline naturally as its contents are depleted.

Campbell, Deffeyes, and others applied Hubbert's thesis not just to one field but to all of world oil production. According to Peak Oil theory, as all the older oil fields originally discovered in the 1960s, 1970s, and 1980s reached their peaks, world production would decline, and oil prices would rise—forever. This view of the world oil market gained renewed popularity in the 2000s as oil prices climbed on the back of soaring Chinese demand. Rising prices were explained as evidence of increasing resource depletion across the globe, including the Middle East, and commentators speculated that a looming crisis was on the horizon.[4] Then something amazing happened that has happened many times before. The U.S. oil industry made a technological breakthrough, and all of a sudden there was a surplus of oil again.

The concerns about oil supply "peaking" in the 2000s were coupled with the idea that as more countries industrialized, demand for oil would keep growing. Indeed, world oil demand has been generally rising since the 1960s, albeit with the occasional hiccup during global recessions. In 1965, global oil demand stood at thirty million barrels a day (b/d); at the end of 2019 before COVID hit, it stood at one hundred million b/d. But ironically, just at the point when others have predicted we will run out of oil, now there is debate about whether oil demand could be the thing that peaks.

Standard business-as-usual forecasts suggest that the need for oil to fuel global economic well-being as the world's middle class expands in the developing world will mean that global oil demand continues to its upward path to 2040 and beyond. The most recent International Energy Agency (IEA) reference case scenario suggests the rising consumption of goods in the developing world will drive millions of barrels a day of increases in oil use in trucking, aviation, shipping, and petrochemical manufacturing. International oil companies like ExxonMobil have world energy outlooks that highlight these same trends. In fact, most organizations assume that in the next two decades oil and gas will continue to be the dominant fuels, and fossil fuels more generally will continue to represent 75 percent of primary energy—the energy stored in a source form (coal, oil, biomaterials, wind, or solar) that can be converted into useful end-use energy such as heat, transport fuel, or electricity. ExxonMobil's 2040 World Energy Outlook, for example, projects that the world will reach 1.7 billion cars by 2040, up from 825 million in 2010. ExxonMobil anticipates that energy demand, mainly for oil, in commercial transport will rise 70 percent between 2015 and 2040, based on global economic expansion, with additional demand for oil for heavy-duty trucks of more than three million barrels a day and additional growth in aviation, shipping, and rail of seven million barrels a day between 2015 and 2040.

But, as discussed in previous chapters, the advent of the digital revolution has raised the possibility that world oil demand could peak well before 2040, much as efficiency improvements and stricter government policies have held oil demand in Europe flat over the past decade. This is by no means the consensus view, but it is one that is gaining in acceptance among experts. Even the prospectus for the initial public offering (IPO) of shares in the Saudi state oil firm, Saudi Aramco, included an assessment that global oil demand could peak in the next two decades.[5]

OIL DEMAND HAS FLATTENED IN THE INDUSTRIALIZED WEST

Lending credence to the idea that oil demand may be reaching a limit is the fact that oil demand growth in the OECD countries has been relatively flat, averaging just 0.33 percent year-over-year increases between 2010 and 2019, including sharp declines during the financial crisis in 2008 and 2009.[6] For OECD Europe, with its stricter greenhouse gas emissions targets and mounting regulations, oil demand has fallen to 14 million b/d in 2019, down from 16 million b/d in the peak of winter in 2006. Germany, the continent's largest economy, has seen total oil demand fall from 2.7 million b/d in 2006 to 2.36 in September 2019.[7]

For the European Union as a whole, oil demand has been declining for roughly two decades, even in recent years when economic growth has been notable. By contrast, demand for oil in China and India in 2017 and 2018 continued to rise by 500,000 b/d and 245,000 b/d, respectively.

But as countries like China and India seek to diversify their energy sources and favor digital technologies, there is a question if their patterns of oil use might move closer to those of the developed world. Vehicle ownership remains relatively low in Southeast Asia, leading to speculation that economic growth will drive car purchasing and, with it, oil demand. But there are questions whether Asian economies will converge with the United States' development path.[8] Massive urbanization and increased use of penalties and restrictions on car ownership might start to curb the viability of private car ownership as cities seek smarter designs to combat congestion and air pollution.

As technological advances have taken hold in the transportation and industrial sectors and promoted energy efficiency, the energy intensity of key economies has fallen. Energy intensity is the measure of how much energy it takes to produce a unit of economic output, as defined by GDP. The shift is the proportion of the economy that reflects services also lowers the need for energy as compared to energy-intensive processes such as the manufacturing of cement and steel, for example. Oil use in power generation has also fallen sharply in the United States and Europe with the shift to other energy sources, including renewables and natural gas. In 1980, roughly 18 percent of all electricity produced globally used oil as its fuel. Now oil fuels only 4 percent of global electricity, mainly in Africa and the Middle East, where countries are actively diversifying away from oil use in that sector.[9]

Today, U.S. energy intensity stands at 0.13 tons of oil equivalent (toe) per thousand dollars in GDP, down from 0.32 toe in 1970 and 0.21 toe in 1990. Already, China's energy intensity is also starting to fall, after several decades of expansion through the 1970s and 1980s. China's energy intensity now stands at 0.31 toe per thousand U.S. dollars, about the same as where the United States stood in 1970. By combining remote sensors, communications technology, cloud-based computing, and industrial machinery, businesses will be able to lower the amount of oil needed to undertake the same economic activity. GE calculates that the industrial internet will produce a reduction in energy use equivalent to twelve billion barrels of oil between 2015 and 2030.[10]

The signing of the Paris climate accord in 2015 raised the possibility that governments would aspire to reduce greenhouse gas emissions in their economies by restricting the burning of fossil fuels in an effort to prevent a rise in global average temperatures of more than 2 degrees Celsius compared to preindustrial levels. Scenarios for the energy mix under the full implementation of such targets indicate that a substantial reduction in oil use would take place. The IEA's Sustainable Development Scenario (SDS) projects oil demand to fall to 69 million b/d by 2040, in contrast to the IEA's reference scenario which posits that oil demand will rise to 106 million b/d over the same time period. In 2017, Norwegian oil firm Equinor's 2 degrees "Renewal" scenario, which assumes accelerated clean technology transitions, projected oil use would be 15 percent lower than today at 80 million b/d.[11] Equinor's Renewal scenario describes a combination of stricter regulatory policy, cultural and behavioral developments, and technological innovation, including extensive deployment of renewable energy, household solar, smart grids, electricity storage, and electric vehicles.

A team of scientists led by Adam Brandt of Stanford suggests that energy efficiency improvements and increases in alternative fuels are likely to bring about a global oil production decline by 2070, with alternative fuels beginning to make significant inroads starting in the 2020s.[12] The study identifies stronger efficiency policies and rapid adoption of new transport technologies and alternative fuels as having the potential to bring forward any peak in demand by at least a decade.[13]

I collaborated with several colleagues at the University of California, Davis, and the University of Arizona to build on the Stanford study and evaluate the possibility that oil demand could peak before 2040 irrespective of the Paris accord via widespread adoption of digital technologies that are bringing revolutionary changes to daily life with potentially dramatic consequences for energy savings.[14] Digital technologies utilizing information technology, big data, automation, and electrification are being used to improve vehicle efficiency, fuel switching, and logistics and route planning via automation and ride sharing that induce reductions in overall travel distance. We tested the sensitivity of total global oil demand to changes in vehicle adoption rate by creating a global vehicles sales and stocks spreadsheet model calibrated to align with the more complex International Energy Agency's 2014 mobility model (MoMo).[15] Our spreadsheet model utilizes calculations based on the ASIF method that links travel activity, car stocks technologies and energy intensity, and energy use.[16]

As a first step, we tested what a digital future could mean if it slowed car sales in the developing world. We found that oil demand was highly sensitive to changes in the rate of new purchases of vehicles in the developing world. Car ownership could fall in any number of ways, including increases in remote, online digital work from home or higher reliance on public transportation paired with ride-sharing services. We found, for example, that a 25 percent slower rate of growth in private vehicle ownership in non-OECD countries would reduce oil consumption by 13 percent in 2050. This is a significant finding, because car sales in China and India have been declining over the past two to three years. In April 2019, vehicle sales in China had fallen by 14.6 percent compared to a year earlier, representing the tenth consecutive month of declines. New-energy vehicles (mainly electrics) in China rose in the same time period by 62 percent as China promoted the vehicles through regulation and consumer incentives.[17] Passenger car sales in India also fell by 17 percent in April 2019 compared to a year earlier.[18] Increased use of ride hailing and flagging interest because of economic uncertainty and rising traffic congestion have contributed to a slowing of interest in car ownership in those markets.

The question of what the introduction of autonomous vehicles into urban settings might mean for long-run oil demand involves a great deal of uncertainty. Will autonomous vehicles be electrified or run on gasoline? Will they be owned and operated by individual drivers living in private households or be part of ride-hailing company fleets that integrate with public transit? A group of researchers from the U.S. National Renewable Energy Laboratory (NREL) found a wide range of possible outcomes that could influence final oil use.[19] They tested assumptions to quantify the effects if AVs encouraged algorithmic-assisted carpooling and reduced travel miles through optimized route planning and found this could reduce oil demand by up to 75 percent for passengers traveling in AVs versus conventional vehicles. However, their findings also suggested that reductions in the inconvenience of driving time could alternatively lead to more frequent and farther travel, depending on geographic and policy context, pushing oil demand up. In a further example, other researchers found that ride hailing added a cumulative increase of six hundred extra miles traveled in New York City between 2013 and 2017 before surcharges were put into place.[20]

Within this context, we tested a 30 percent increase in vehicle miles traveled (VMT) globally and found that it would result in a 12 percent increase in projected global oil consumption for 2050 compared to business as usual. By contrast, a 50 percent reduction in VMT would yield a 20 percent decrease in oil use in 2050. In combination with other digital effects, such as some electrification of vehicles and efficiency gains in freight, this would likely be sufficient to peak oil demand.

We then expanded our sensitivity analysis to include a broader range of outcomes from the adoption of digital technologies. We examined the outcome of a 20 percent drop in passenger car vehicle miles traveled as automation takes effect combined with big-data-assisted productivity gains in transportation logistics that improve fuel efficiency in road freight, air, and shipping by 20 percent.[21] This combination would produce a 34 percent reduction in 2050 global oil consumption and a near-term peaking of oil demand in the 2030s. We found that automation's impact on the number of miles traveled is a critical input to oil demand outcomes. While digital technologies have the potential to eliminate oil use in a variety of ways, it could also take things in the opposite direction. If digital technologies like self-driving cars are fueled by gasoline, and if they increase vehicle miles traveled, they could actually increase oil use. For example, if ride-hailing drivers are cruising roads looking for passengers, that might use more fuel than if each of their passengers used their own cars to take a single trip. Households might be more inclined to send their cars on errands if they could do so without driving themselves. Self-driving vehicles could also increase the attractiveness of living far from work. Figure 6.1 illustrates the large range of outcomes in final oil demand growth or decline that could come about, depending on different scenarios for how ride-hailing and self-driving scenarios play out.

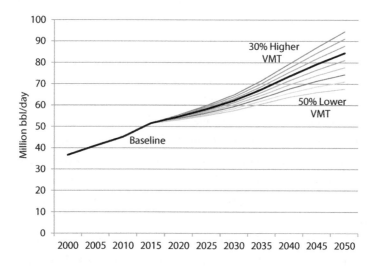

6.1 Oil consumption sensitivity to VMT

BANS ON GASOLINE CAR SALES

Thus, the question of whether the cars of the future will run on gasoline is highly material. In this regard, policy could be as important as technology. Several countries around the globe, notably France, the UK, and China, have announced plans to ban sales of new cars with internal combustion engines (ICE) that burn gasoline or diesel fuel by 2040 or earlier. Several major cities, including London, Barcelona, Copenhagen, and Seattle, have also announced an intent to impose bans on ICE engine vehicles within city limits by 2030 while California has proposed a statewide ban by 2035. National ICE bans could be phased in, starting with key cities, as has been proposed in China. Alternatively, countries might need to have a proactive policy to shift car manufacturing away from gasoline and diesel vehicles.[22] The experience of diesel car bans in Europe is instructive.[23] Car manufacturers have adjusted their manufacturing and sales strategies to reflect restrictions on diesel-fueled cars in twenty-four major European cities. Demand for diesel cars has also dropped precipitously as car owners worry that repair servicing, spare parts, and fueling stations will become increasingly hard to find. In Germany and the UK, sales of diesel cars have continued to drop, and the prices for used diesel cars are falling.[24]

In fact, car culture has become so unpopular in certain locations that some cities are trying to remove cars altogether. In Europe, a handful of cities have converted roads in the heart of their tourist areas for the exclusive use of bicyclists and pedestrians. Hamburg was the first city to announce that it will be free of private car use by 2034. Norway's capital, Oslo, has already restricted cars from the downtown area, in addition to an existing car-free waterfront promenade and central station. Similarly, Madrid has limited the number of cars that can enter its downtown from the outskirts on any given day and is looking at closing part of its center to cars.[25] In fact, over thirty-two European cities are studying car-free zones.[26] London's congestion pricing plan is generally considered a success, reducing traffic by a quarter and personal vehicle use by 40 percent.

Figure 6.2 highlights the cities, regions, and countries that have made announcements regarding future restrictions on the sales of ICE vehicles in the next two decades. Many of the proposed bans have yet to be elaborated, so not

When Bans Go Into Effect

By 2025	By 2030			By 2040
• Athens	• Amsterdam	• Heidelberg	• Netherlands*	• British Columbia
• Costa Rica	• Auckland	• Iceland*	• Quito	• China* (expected)
• Hamburg	• Barcelona	• India*	• Seattle	• France*
• Madrid	• Brussels	• Ireland*	• Sweden*	• Oxford
• Mexico City	• Cape Town	• Israel†	• Vancouver	• Scotland*
• Norway*	• Copenhagen	• London		• Sri Lanka
• Paris	• Denmark*	• Los Angeles		• United Kingdom*
• Rome	• Hainan	• Milan		

* Ban applies only to new vehicles
† Ban applies only to imported vehicles

6.2 Bans on internal combustion engines by 2040
Source: Council on Foreign Relations

much is known about how they will be implemented and what will replace gasoline or diesel cars. If it were up to the tech industry, the solution would be large numbers of electrified, automated ride-hailing fleets efficiently coordinated to keep congestion to a minimum, complemented by rooftop drone shuttles. These solutions will, no doubt, be implemented. However, it seems more likely that strengthened public transportation will need to play a large role if ICE car bans proliferate, given the large numbers of people whose transportation will need to be provided for. Urban density that promotes accessibility—that is, neighborhoods where walking and biking can accomplish the bulk of everyday activities—may also replace extended commuter transit networks as more of the world's population moves to urban regions as expected.

The idea that an entire country would literally ban today's car technology sounds extreme. But, in fact, it is a surprisingly slow and gradual way to force a technology shift. That is because cars have a shelf life of fifteen years or longer. If you are thinking that might vary by country, you would be correct. But older vehicles discarded in wealthy nations like the United States are often resold in the developing world, extending their life by many years before scrappage. It is not uncommon for Americans to keep a car for ten years. Take, for example, my son, who tends to be hard on a car. He found that his beat-up pickup truck was as much a status symbol in Texas as having a sports car. Statistics bear out his experience. The average life of a pickup truck in America is 13.6 years, according to U.S. Department of Transportation statistics.[27] The number of years that people keep a car matters because the ICE bans being proposed are on new car sales; in other words, no new gasoline cars can be made and sold after a certain year. No one is proposing repossessing your or my existing gasoline car. Governments are telling car companies the last model year they can use a gasoline engine. From that time forward, say 2040, I can keep my existing gasoline car, but if I buy a new car, it cannot run on gasoline. Think of it this way. If the president of the United States announced he was giving a free electric car to every American with a registered vehicle, but you could only qualify if your car was at the end of its life—as Chuck Schumer, the senator from New York, did when he proposed in 2019 to give a tax credit to low-income families with aging vehicles to purchase an electric car—it would take fifteen years before the last gasoline car was turned in for an EV.

My colleagues Lew Fulton and Zane McDonald from University of California, Davis, and I wanted to see how much oil use could be eliminated by banning new sales of ICE engine cars. When you hear the phrase "ICE ban," it sounds big. We decided to set up a computer simulation to see just how big it could be. We developed a global vehicles and stock model and calibrated it to align with the modeling framework of the International Energy Agency (IEA). Our tool was not as complex as the IEA's Mobility Model (MoMo), but it was informed by the same relationships of population, new vehicle technologies, average car stocks by technology, energy efficiency per kind of car, and representative levels of travel activity (VMT).[28] We created scenarios that would let us test how much gasoline, diesel, electricity, hydrogen, or biofuels might be used in any given year between now and 2065.

As part of the exercise, we constructed a business-as-usual baseline scenario that builds off the IEA's published ETP (2017) Reference Technology Scenario, also called the four-degree scenario (4DS), which takes into account policies that are expected or about to be enacted.[29] We then constructed a straightforward ICE ban scenario. To simplify the calculation, we assumed that total sales of vehicles would remain the same as in the baseline. It is possible that with self-driving robo-taxis, the number of cars might shrink, as discussed. But for simplicity's sake, we calculated the change assuming there would still be the same number of cars, with the same level of engine efficiency, traveling the same distance as in the baseline. We assumed that plug-in hybrid cars would be exempt from the ICE ban, because that seems likely. To make reasonable projections, we established a glide path for automobile manufacturers (OEMs) to begin to adjust their product lines as early as 2030 in anticipation of the bans. This makes sense not only based on patterns already seen in bans on diesel engine cars in Europe, but also because so many carmakers have already announced plans to increase rollouts of electric and plug-in hybrid cars.

Table 6.1 shows the results if ICE bans (new car sales) are implemented in the EU, India, and China, three major markets that have indicated a willingness to impose such bans. The results are disappointing for those hoping a ban would lower oil use dramatically. By 2050, only 5.5 million barrels a day of oil are eliminated. Were the bans to be expanded to the entire world, the level of oil use eliminated rises to 15 million b/d over a twenty-year period. In terms of ICE automobiles eliminated by 2040, about sixty million vehicles would be replaced in China and OECD Europe. If the rest of the world were to follow with a target date of 2045 for a global ban on new ICE car sales, we estimate that 160 million

TABLE 6.1   ICE ban: oil use implications

	Transportation oil demand (mboe/d)		Oil displacement (mboe/d)	
Year	BAU	ICE sales ban (OECD, China, India)	BAU	ICE sales ban (OECD, China, India)
2015	49.8	49.8	49.8	0.0
2040	57.7	54.3	57.7	3.4
2050	56.7	51.5	56.7	5.2

BAU = business as usual; mboe/d = thousand barrels of oil equivalent per day

ICE vehicles would be eliminated. In the latter case, our calculations indicate, a transition to electric vehicles worldwide could near completion by 2060.

Policies could be added to an ICE ban target that might speed the process of shifting the car fleet. The Obama administration program of "cash for clunkers," which gave car owners a subsidy for trading in older vehicles, is often cited as a way to get car owners to trade up to more sustainable new vehicles.[30] In an example of this kind of program, U.S. senator Chuck Schumer proposed in 2019 a federal government program in which lower-income Americans with cars eight years or more old would receive cash vouchers to purchase an electric plug-in, plug-in hybrid, or fuel cell car.[31] A study by the Brookings Institution questioned the practice, however, arguing it was an expensive way to get cars off the road that would soon by retired anyway.[32]

REDUCED OIL USE FROM SHRINKING TRADE AND FREIGHT

When thinking about the future of global oil use, there is a tendency to focus on cars, but those who do not believe that oil use could peak most often cite areas of growth related to freight, including marine and aviation fuel, and rising plastics use. For example, OPEC's forecasts for rising oil demand rely heavily on these sectors to project that the need for oil will continue to rise in the coming decades. OPEC estimates that freight, including movement by truck, ship, rail, and air, represents roughly 40 percent of the 58 million b/d of oil used in the transportation sector and expects strong growth to come from the movement of goods as the global economy grows. Eighty percent of the world's goods move by ship.[33] OPEC forecasts that this waterborne movement of goods will increase between now and 2040 by 700,000 b/d to average 5.4 million b/d. They expect aviation fuel demand to increase by an additional 2.3 million b/d to 8.9 million b/d by 2040. And OPEC has made clear that it is betting on plastics to keep oil use rising. OPEC's projections are that plastics manufacturing will require an additional 3.1 million b/d of oil by 2040.[34]

The 2020 coronavirus outbreak demonstrated how quickly demand for shipping and aviation could change. In the first half of 2020, in the wake of the rapid spread of coronavirus globally, there was a dramatic lowering of oil use in global aviation and marine shipping. The drop came on top of a significant shrinkage in global trade in 2019 as a result of the U.S.-China trade war. Air travel has seen similar sudden jolts from terrorism and other pandemics like SARS. In the aftermath of the September 11, 2001 terrorist attacks, for example, global travel declined significantly and did not start rebounding until 2004.[35]

But it is equally possible that a more permanent disruption to oil use in freight and travel could come from structural trends. The combination of the trade war and coronavirus showed leaders around the world how vulnerable their economies were to shocks to global supply chains. As a result, a trendline back to promoting national industries could gain momentum in the 2020s, fueled by the shock to the global economy from China's economic slowdown in the wake of the coronavirus crisis. Moreover, proliferation of advanced manufacturing techniques such as 3D printing could accelerate the trend away from global supply chains by streamlining the number of parts to complex products like engines and heavy machinery and centralizing the production process in fewer locations. As discussed in chapter 5, the rise of 3D printing could reduce the demand for oil used in shipping of parts and components in manufactured products.

One unintended consequence of the 2020 coronavirus outbreak is that many global companies began to increase their use of videoconferencing to replace global travel and employees were given the option to telecommute. While it is too early to tell how lasting these trends might be, it is entirely possible that they will increase the proclivity to meet by internet, structurally reducing some oil use in future transportation patterns. As companies get more comfortable with teleconferencing technology and internet meeting programs, demand for travel may flatten or even decline, rather than increasing as previously forecast. Any increased tendency to meet by videoconferencing would be supported by climate activism, which has started to focus on travel shunning by influential celebrities and concerned citizens alike.

McKinsey & Co. also posits other conditions that might contribute to a peaking in oil demand. While OPEC, in addition to the International Energy Agency and other corporate forecasts, see the petrochemicals sector, and particularly plastics, as a key area for growth in oil use globally, McKinsey's study suggest that petrochemical demand for oil might wane over time as more countries impose regulations forcing recycling and efficiency gains are made in packaging. Already, environmentally conscious markets like Germany and Japan have seen a decline in per capita plastics demand. McKinsey estimates that a 20 percent recycling rate could prove possible, up from only 8 percent currently.[36] Plastics made from biomaterials and efficiency gains could eliminate another 5 to 10 percent of demand. McKinsey estimates that these trends could shave 2.5 million barrels a day from oil demand out to 2050, compared to business as usual. Figure 6.3 shows a breakdown of McKinsey & Co.'s scenarios for long-term plastics demand.

So far, the launch of digital technologies, especially automation, has been erratic and unpredictable, rendering the timing and extent of its ultimate impact on oil demand trends somewhat unclear. But although there are many uncertainties regarding when or whether oil demand will actually peak in the coming decade or two, the prospects that an oil demand peak might be inevitable is already bringing dramatic changes to the oil sector. Private oil companies, in an effort to continue to attract investors and capital, are adjusting their value proposition. Rather than seeking to increase oil reserves and future production capability, companies are instead focused on reducing costs and improving profit margins. In a future world where oil demand may not be growing, companies will need to be prepared to compete for dwindling market demand in a potentially lower oil price environment.

As companies focus on finding and producing oil at much lower costs, they will turn to enabling technologies. In its 2015 Technology Outlook, UK oil producer BP noted that the use of digital technologies, including improved subsurface imaging and automation, could lead to a 25 percent reduction in the cost of producing oil and gas by 2050. That estimate now seems conservative. Cornerstone Macro estimates that automated drilling alone will reduce costs by 15 percent, while a whole host of future technologies, including artificial intelligence, data analytics, predictive maintenance, and automated and remote operations and management, will reduce capital requirements for oil and gas development by 30 percent and operating costs by up to 50 percent.[37] These technologies will enable companies to speed up drilling, create operational efficiencies, and reduce workforce requirements.

GLOBAL OIL SUPPLY: FROM SCARCITY TO ABUNDANCE

In a world where oil will be able to be produced faster, cheaper, and easier, historical fears of oil scarcity have given way to the prospects of oil supply abundance. In her book *Windfall*, Meghan O'Sullivan writes, "Whereas, particularly in the last thirty years, energy scarcity and the fear of energy shortages have shaped the relationship between energy and international affairs, abundance, not

Summary potential: $70bn value pool from $200bn investment

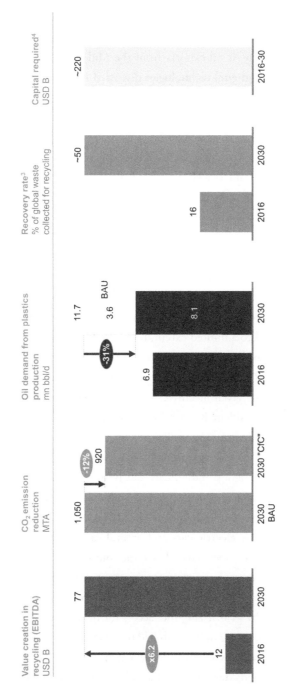

6.3 McKinsey & Company long term plastics scenarios

Source: McKinsey Plastic Stream Model

scarcity, will be the defining feature of the coming years."[38] Geopolitical upsets can still be on the horizon to return the world to oil supply anxiety, but if prices do rise temporarily (say, if oil exports from the Middle East or elsewhere are disrupted), the host of digital technologies discussed in earlier chapters will be available to consumers to respond.

Back in 1973, when oil became scarce in the United States, everyone's car ran on gasoline, homes were heated with oil, electricity was generated using oil, and factories needed oil to operate machinery. Oil permeated every aspect of daily life. Shortages meant blackouts, stranded commuters, and no heat. Texans donned bumper stickers that read "Let them freeze," in reference to New Englanders lacking heating fuel. America's economy was thrown into recession. The oil historian Daniel Yergin dramatically declared, in his book *Global Insecurity*, "Energy stringency could pose a serious challenge to the fundamental stability and functioning of America's economic, political and social system."[39] At that time of oil insecurity forty years ago, fewer alternatives to oil existed. Demand was reduced mostly by cutting down on economic activity. Neighborhood carpooling was embraced to a limited extent, but it could only be arranged by calling a personal friend or business associate on the home telephone to coordinate. Americans were asked to adjust the thermostat in their homes and to drive less. Industry was eventually given incentives to install more energy-efficient equipment. In early 1981, President Ronald Reagan deregulated the price of natural gas, propelling more substitution for oil.

Today, unlike in 1973, when few energy-saving technologies were sitting on the shelf awaiting a stimulus, individuals and businesses have multiple digital tools available to fashion a response if oil were suddenly in short supply. A major global oil supply crisis would undoubtedly accelerate the adoption of alternative fuel vehicles such as electric cars and natural gas or other alternative fuel trucks. It would also give impetus to ride-hailing companies to partner with public transit authorities or governments to manage rationing of fuel. Ride-hailing firms have already imagined a partnership in which governments could stretch limited fuel supplies by prioritizing fuel access for drivers who provide pooled rides. Unlike the 1970s, when individuals had to personally seek out carpool buddies, automated algorithms would seamlessly match riders with greater efficiency to reduce fuel use. Goods delivery could also be optimized via big-data analytics, reducing the number of trips consumers would need to make to the grocery store or mall. Banking and other kinds of retail services would move increasingly online. Commuters and business travelers could use the internet to telecommute to business meetings. Some of these patterns have already emerged in the wake of the COVID-19 pandemic. Manufacturers could install 3D printers to shorten supply chains, thereby obviating oil-based shipping by truck, ship, and rail. In a word, the leverage that oil exporters have dangled over Western consumers like a sword of Damocles for decades would begin to dissipate as it became more starkly clear that we could eliminate even more oil from our lives, if only we had the will to do so.

The realization that we have the technological wherewithal to reduce our oil use is a powerful antidote to the petro-power that has defined the twentieth century. Game theory research shows that developing substitute technologies, even if they are expensive and risky, has immediate value,[40] because it creates a motivation for oil producers to sell as much oil as possible before the substitute technology can be put in place. I contend that we have already reached that state of affairs. The very possibility that digital technologies *could* create a peak in oil demand is already influencing decision making in the world of oil. Moreover, unlike a theoretical backstop technology, the digital technologies that could reduce the need for oil exist and are already in commercial use. That puts oil producers, like the members of the Organization of Petroleum Exporting Countries (OPEC) in a bind. Promoting too high a price for oil now might stimulate an earlier demise to oil's revenue-generating potential later. If OPEC can no longer rest assured that future resource scarcity will bring financial rewards down the road, it must rethink its entire present strategy. In a world where it could eventually lose market share to the application of digital technology, does it make sense for OPEC to delay developing its vast oil reserves for a future timeframe? Doing so runs the risk that a certain percentage of reserves could become "stranded"—that is, severely devalued or obsolete based on changing market conditions.

New York University climate scientist Martin Hoffert famously introduced the concept that burning all of the world's known fossil fuels would raise global temperatures so precipitously that it would be like returning to the time of the dinosaurs.[41] I heard Hoffert give this talk the first time he broached the idea. It was a compelling but largely theoretical exercise to try to demonstrate that we needed to do something about global warming. Seven years later, another group of scientists took Hoffert's thesis to the next level. They asked the question, what proportion of the world's proven reserves of fossil fuels could be used and still keep the rise in global temperatures to a 2 degrees Celsius limit? The answer was somewhat shocking: no more than half of the world's remaining stores of fossil fuels should be produced.[42] In the two weeks following the publication of this science article, the stocks of sixty-five U.S. oil and gas companies shed close to 3 percent of their value.[43]

The whiff of uncertainty about future oil demand, whether due to a global climate agreement or to a rapid shift to digital technologies, has ushered in new thinking among the world's largest private oil companies. They are actively withdrawing from high-cost oil reserves that take decades to produce in favor of producing cheaper legacy assets that can be brought to market more quickly. When companies believed that rising oil demand was going to support higher prices, they were willing to engage in risky billion-dollar oil exploration and production projects in far-flung regions like the Russian Arctic and the Caspian Sea. Those projects take many years to develop and implement, and profitable returns depend on payouts of oil production that can be sold for several decades. In a world where oil demand is peaking, rising oil production and sales growth might not be possible for all players. Thus, companies have to decide whether it makes sense to look for more oil, rather than developing and selling the inventory of oil reserves they have already found while market conditions are still favorable.

A SHORTER INVESTMENT CYCLE FOR OIL

In the 1970s, 1980s, and 1990s, it was common company practice in the global oil industry to try to find as much oil as possible, add the new reserves to corporate balance sheets, and thereby improve the performance of stock prices and earnings. Companies might not invest to produce newfound oil right away; instead, projections about the oil price would determine the potential profitability of greenlighting a project at a particular juncture. The decision to wait, often made during times of temporary economic contraction or excess market supplies, was referred to as "warehousing." Companies would evaluate the many projects that could be brought to final decision investment (FDI) and select only the best handful for funding in any given year. In the early 2000s, companies also bought back their own stock shares instead of investing more capital in exploration. Private company opportunities were limited by the fact that many foreign countries opted to produce their reserves themselves, without recourse to foreign assistance and investment dollars, or to delay their own FDI in hopes that an eventual rebound in oil prices would bring more profits for capacity expansion.

But in recent years, as the U.S. shale boom has taken hold and the prospects for long-term demand have weakened, the largest private oil companies have begun to favor investment in fields that can be brought on line quickly, in one to three years, instead of megaprojects that might take seven to ten years before the first oil is produced. The major oil companies withdrew from $2.5 billion in Arctic exploration leases in the mid-2010s, for example. By 2019, ExxonMobil and Chevron Corporation, long proponents of long-lead-time megaproject investments in Russia, the Middle East, and Venezuela, announced a pivot to spending a higher percentage of their capital on shorter-cycled, onshore oil resources in the United States, Canada, and to a lesser extent, Argentina. In March 2019, as OPEC was coming under pressure from oil market surpluses, the two American majors announced they would be targeting Texas's Permian Basin for a new round of capital investment. The move by U.S. producers highlighted the competitive threat such investment might mean for OPEC. In ExxonMobil's case, it suggested that the company would be able to produce new oil from the Permian at a cost of $15 a barrel, considerably below the break-even point for some of the smaller U.S. independent oil companies operating in the Texas shale, and well below the $50 to $80 a barrel oil price levels many of OPEC's members need to meet fiscal budget requirements.[44]

The change in the patterns of investment by the oil majors and the flexible nature of capital deployment in the U.S. shale industry have influenced the boom-and-bust cycle that has characterized oil price movements over past several decades. The oil boom-and-bust cycle has been closely linked to expansion and contraction of global GDP. Periods of strong economic growth bring an upward trend in oil use and, with it, rising prices. Over past decades, the price effects of global demand growth were amplified by the relatively long time it took for new oil fields to be brought on line. Economists noted this trend in a highly cited 2004 paper that demonstrated how existing available aboveground oil inventories and very limited underground reserves that could be immediately produced, such as spare capacity in Saudi Arabia and Kuwait, were not sufficient to prevent oil price spikes as oil demand shot higher during periods of strong economic growth in the 2000s.[45] Higher oil prices do eventually stimulate oil companies to drill for more oil and to invest in new extraction technology, but historically it could take between seven and ten years for new projects to be completed and provide supplemental oil to meet higher demand.[46]

With changed patterns of investment by the private oil companies to favor those that allow for faster implementation, the cycle time from first investment to first oil production has shortened considerably. Equipment design standardization and new project management techniques have allowed companies to reduce the investment cycle time to two to four years for larger offshore projects and three to nine months for shale oil and gas. Since the 2010s, sudden increases in oil prices have quickly unleashed higher volumes of oil from U.S. shale plays, leaving peaks in prices more short-lived compared to historical trends, when rising oil prices during economic expansions could last in excess of five years (figure 6.4). Brent oil prices rose to $81 a barrel in November 2018 amid strength in the U.S. and global economy, up from a low of $30 a barrel seen in 2016 as new oil production from the United States reached new highs. Prices were already easing again in 2019 based on optimistic forecasts for U.S. production combined with concerns about economic slowdown in China. They collapsed dramatically in the start of 2020 as the spread of coronavirus put a damper on global economic growth. Extremely low oil prices and brimming oil inventories in March and April 2020 forced a large shut-in of U.S. shale production, demonstrating the market responsiveness of U.S. shale supply in both directions. The comparison between shorter boom-bust cycles in recent years and those of prior decades, when they were more extended, is shown in figure 6.4.

Even before the COVID-19 pandemic took a bite out of global oil demand, the ability of shale producers to bring on new oil production quickly to respond to price increases was a major challenge for OPEC, which had previously cooperated to jointly cut oil production to defend higher price targets. In 2019, for example, Wall Street analysts like Citi and Cornerstone Macro forecast that U.S. producers could fill most of the expected increase in oil demand for the coming five years, opening the prospect that OPEC would lose up to 3 million b/d of market share to U.S. producers at a $65 oil price. By 2020, OPEC began to consider that lower oil prices might be in its long-run interests to curb U.S. production growth.

The prospects that oil demand might peak in the coming decades render these more immediate challenges even weightier, because any lost market share might become increasingly hard to get back if the overall pie of demand were to shrink. By analogy, one can think of the American game of musical chairs. If during the

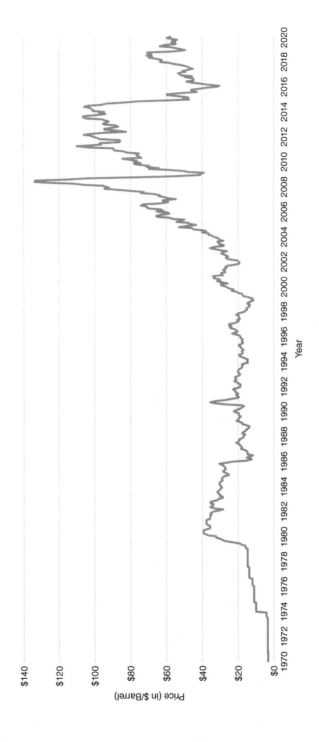

6.4 West Texas Intermediate (WTI) historical crude oil spot price (1970–2020)

game, chairs are added each time the music stops, then participants can easily find a chair because there are more chairs than players. But in the traditional game, where a chair is taken away during each round, it gets harder and harder to be the one who gets to sit down in one of the remaining chairs when the music stops and not be left with no seat and thereby knocked out of the game. In the future oil musical chairs competition, oil producers are assuming that the players with the lowest cost of production will win a remaining chair.

OPEC's RESPONSE TO A LOW OIL DEMAND SCENARIO

Several of OPEC's largest members in terms of production capacity—Saudi Arabia, Kuwait, the United Arab Emirates, and Iraq—have such low-cost production, under $10 a barrel, they are assuming that they will be the last ones standing in any future competition for shrinking end-user oil purchases. These Middle East producers might be tempted to continue to hold back production to keep prices high to sustain national budgets at home, figuring U.S. shale production will eventually peak and sputter out, as production discovered in the 1970s in Alaska and the UK North Sea is currently doing. But it is early days for drilling technology innovation related to digital applications, and new ideas on how to utilize more data, automation, lasers, and CO_2 injection hold promise to improve oil recovery rates, not only in the United States but in other unconventional oil fields around the world.

Thus, for OPEC, the benefit of high oil prices brings more risk in a world of possible peak oil demand if those prices facilitate higher-cost oil producers like the U.S. shale industry, Brazil, and even Russia to quickly monetize their remaining under-the-ground assets first, at the expense of future Arab Gulf production. Indeed, scientists Christophe McGlade and Paul Elkins concluded that upwards of 260 billion barrels of Middle East oil reserves are the most likely to become stranded in a global agreement to limit carbon emissions.[47] This has led to at least a theoretical impetus for OPEC's Mideast members to consider hastening their own efforts to get as much of their oil out of the ground as possible to prevent a larger stranding of their reserves.[48]

Whether OPEC keeps trying to hold prices up in the face of shrinking market share amid a shorter, more frequent oil boom-and-bust cycle or tries to push out more oil to monetize as many reserves as possible, the end result will likely be hard for petrostates to navigate on a budgetary basis. That will bring geopolitical drawbacks that are already starting to manifest themselves in global discourse. The possibility that lofty oil revenues might dry up over time has already destabilized some of the weaker ruling political institutions within OPEC countries, prompting consolidation of power and increased repression. Some petrostates, like Russia and Iran, have turned to hard power means to replace the geopolitical power previously attained through their oil stature. These early responses bode ill for the future geopolitical shifts likely to come if peak oil demand were to make itself more apparent.

Oil-linked debt troubles are already reverberating across the Middle East, Latin America, and Africa, and any worsening in the long-term outlook for oil is likely to accelerate that trend. The United States and China have a common interest in working together to ensure a soft landing for oil producers, but it is not clear whether economic rivalry and other kinds of security tensions will get in the way of constructive engagement on the issue. In the case of America, Middle East and Latin American oil economies are particularly intertwined with Western financial markets and the U.S. dollar. Any pinch in capital flows from the wealthiest oil states could create instability in the global financial system, at the same time potentially burdening the United States with defense or humanitarian duties as internal political conditions worsen in major states. China, as the world's largest oil importer, may welcome a larger global oil surplus, but it must also be concerned about a looming sovereign debt crisis among oil producers. Not only is China the major debt holder for numerous troubled oil and gas states, but it would also have to worry about financial troubles leading to cutoffs of oil dedicated to go to China, much as it has lost any hope of promised imports from Venezuela, whose oil industry has been decimated by years of mismanagement and corruption.

In the midst of the spring 2020 oil demand shock, when more than a third of global oil demand was curtailed practically overnight as a result of the coronavirus lockdowns, the G20 raced to support interventions to stabilize the oil market. The consequences of not doing so appeared very dire at the time, not only for the oil states themselves but also for sovereign credit markets.[49] Now the question moving forward becomes whether that experience laid any groundwork that would allow for international cooperation to create a more orderly, managed retreat of global oil use as a transition to new technologies takes hold in the coming decades. Would the consequences of stranded oil and gas assets transform into a global multilateral issue of high priority for the G20 instead of a problem for only the oil exporters themselves? Might a global economic pact on how to share the world's shrinking oil use even be feasible? Investors are already worrying about how falling oil use would affect global financial markets and whether a soft landing is possible. Still, despite the obvious benefits, international cooperation on the energy transition, especially when it comes to the world's largest oil-exporting states, has so far been lacking.

CHAPTER 7

Energy Investor Dystopia

“Ten years, 252 days and 10 hours from now, we will be in a position where we set off an irreversible chain reaction beyond human control, that will most likely lead to the end of our civilization as we know it. That is unless in that time, permanent and unprecedented changes in all aspects of society have taken place, including a reduction in CO_2 emissions by at least 50 percent,” Greta Thunberg told the UK Houses of Parliament in April 2019.[1] The sixteen-year-old Swedish schoolgirl, who has become the voice for future generations where climate change is concerned, has been publicly chastising world leaders for irresponsible behavior when it comes to carbon emissions and climate change. Thunberg is just one of tens of thousands of student activists who are forcefully advocating that public pension funds, banks, universities, and other institutional investors should fully and unequivocally divest from fossil fuels. The students call on these institutions to use their financial power to inspire social and institutional change. In the United States and Europe, the fossil fuel divestiture movement, which takes a moral stand against providing investment capital to fossil fuel producers, has become one of the signature campaigns of climate change activism.

In parallel to the divestment movement, central banks and large institutional investors are increasingly focused on what climate change will mean for global financial markets and large investor holdings in fossil fuel companies and the sovereign debt of oil-producing nations. The Bank of England, Bank of Canada, European Central Bank, and Norwegian Government Pension Fund Global have warned of the potential financial system risks that could emerge from the underestimation of the risk of climate change and its related costs in valuation of publicly listed corporations. U.S. regulator Rostin Behnam, one of five directors of the Commodity Futures Trading Commission, which oversees financial markets in grain, oil, and complex derivatives, told the *New York Times* last year: "If climate change causes more volatile and frequent and extreme weather events, you're going to have a scenario where these large providers of financial products—mortgages, home insurance, pensions—cannot shift risk away from their portfolios. It's abundantly clear that climate change poses financial risk to the stability of the financial system."[2]

Prior to the start of the COVID-19 crisis, investors and credit analysts were working on the assumption that most fossil fuel companies will be able to recover adequate payback on capital expenditure in the ten- to twenty-year time frame that is typically represented in calculations of return-on-investment analysis. But increasingly, stock prices of the largest energy companies are starting to reflect the possibility that the commercial net worth of carbon-intensive assets, operations, and products, including coal mines, proven oil and gas reserves, and related processing facilities, could become obsolete or nonperforming (i.e., become stranded assets) as a result of wider use of energy-saving technologies and a regulated transition to cleaner energy sources. That Apple, Tesla, and Google have surpassed ExxonMobil as among the highest valued companies on the New York Stock Exchange is indicative of changing perceptions about the role technology will play in the future economy and the difficulty that companies like ExxonMobil have had in recent years maintaining a value proposition to investors. Increasing commodity price volatility for oil and gas in recent years has raised questions as to whether the major oil companies will be able to sustain dividend payments to investors, who look to the companies to manage price swings and deliver consistent returns. Some companies, like Royal Dutch Shell, were forced to cut dividend payments during the COVID-19-related oil price drop in 2020.

The possibility that investors will anticipate the risk of a peak in oil demand poses several challenges to both global financial market stability and a secure energy supply. One risk is that investors will begin to deny capital to publicly traded oil companies and sovereign oil producers, even though the world will only be able to implement a gradual shift in energy infrastructure. That could be a problem because economies will need traditional fossil energy to continue to operate the vast stock of existing power stations, vehicles, and manufacturing plants for years to come, as discussed in chapter 2. If financial markets anticipate a shift too soon, sufficient finance might not be available to sustain adequate levels of the oil and gas needed during a transitional period. In this case, energy price volatility and economic discontinuities could develop if oil begins to disappear at a faster rate than cleaner energy savings and replacement technologies are able to go forward at a sufficient scale to keep economies humming.

Such a mismatch between the decapitalization of fossil fuels and the deployment rate of new cleaner energy could affect individual countries differently, depending on their policies toward energy innovation and deployment strategy and their dependence on imported oil. The current edge of the United States in having abundant oil and gas supplies could change, for example, if private investors, who currently support the U.S. oil and gas industry, no longer step up to the plate to finance future U.S. reserve development and production adequately to meet demand. At the same time, in a world where oil and gas supplies might decline faster than cleantech products can be deployed, countries that are providers and manufacturers of cleantech products will have an advantage in global markets over those countries that do not have strong clean energy industries. In such a world, the United States could be disadvantaged relative to China and Europe if it fails to promote digital and clean energy as part of its broader future economy.

Equities of the largest oil and gas firms listed on formal stock exchanges have already underperformed the index of all equities for several years, despite steady growth in global demand for oil and gas. To the extent that large oil companies diversify their future investments to include digital energy technologies, renewable energy, and carbon sequestration technologies, those firms might lower the chances of being hit with a sudden, further cascading collapse in stock valuation or a debilitating reduction in access to bond and credit markets. The problem could be harder to solve for sovereign states whose national budgets are highly dependent on oil and gas export revenues. It remains unclear how markets will allocate which sovereign prolific oil and gas reserves might become stranded. The timeline for such an eventuality is also uncertain. But a looming sovereign credit problem for poorly managed oil-producing countries is already emerging, creating challenges for multilateral international credit agencies and threatening both the stability of those countries and the smooth functioning of global sovereign credit markets.[3] The situation could pose geopolitical risks for the United States, as well as China and other major powers, if not adequately managed.

DEFINING FINANCIAL CLIMATE RISKS

There are several ways climate risk might affect the financial performance of stocks and bonds of oil and gas companies and sovereign credit markets. The first is related to the physical risks of climate change. Certain kinds of oil and gas production and transportation infrastructure are highly susceptible to disruption or damage by severe weather and time-consuming to repair. For example, the high concentration of oil refining in coastal regions leaves it vulnerable to severe storms and sea-level rise. Such vulnerability might make it harder for oil and gas firms to maintain necessary access to insurance markets.[4]

A second way is via regulatory or legal liability risk. New court rulings or laws can influence outcomes by creating a stigmatization effect. Investors have to worry that higher carbon taxes or other regulations might soon come to oil's doorstep. A court ruling against a firm or passage of environmental legislation could change cash flow expectations for fossil fuel businesses overnight. Such climate risks could be prospective, when a company suddenly faces rising mitigation costs based on climate-related events in the future, or retrospectively, when a firm becomes subject to court-ordered damages, such as compensation to plaintiffs. The oil industry currently faces a large number of court actions under multiple principles of law. So far, courts have turned down the remedy sought by several major U.S. cities seeking funding to abate or mitigate damages to public property and infrastructure from climate change. Rulings against plaintiffs have argued that the court should not infringe on foreign policy decisions that are the purview of political branches of the federal government.[5] So far, in the United States, duty-of-care lawsuits that would hold oil companies accountable for physical damages caused by climate change have been ruled outside the role of the judiciary.[6]

Finally, there is energy transition risk: that less oil will be used in the future because new technologies enhance competition from cleaner alternative sources of fuel and promote energy efficiency, thereby reducing the need for oil, or because regulatory policies force a shift away from oil. Transition risk could materialize either by sharply lowering the price of oil, thereby lowering valuations of firm assets or revenues, or by ultimately stranding assets to become unusable, leaving them with no residual value at all. In 2016, the *Economist* published a report on the potential of stranded oil and gas reserves that discussed efforts by investors to get oil companies to disclose how they planned to address transition risk.[7] The report came on the heels of banking estimates that the value of fossil fuel reserves that might go unproduced could be as high as $100 trillion.[8]

There is science behind the idea that not all the proven oil and gas reserves in the world can be burned if governments are to ensure that global warming does not exceed 2 degrees Celsius above preindustrial levels. In one highly cited scientific paper, it was estimated that as much as half of all oil, gas, and coal could become stranded by a global climate framework.[9] A subsequent scientific study found that Canada's oil sands, Arctic oil resources, and more than 260 billion barrels of Middle East oil reserves were among the most likely assets to become stranded.[10] But the jump from that science to the strategic calculation of investors has been slow to materialize.

One academic study has suggested that investor inertia comes from the practice by large institutional investors of making investment allocation decisions based on historical metrics that tend to assess future risks like climate change poorly.[11] Alternatively, investors might be taking a signal from evidence that pension fund divestment is often not effective. One thesis, put forward by authors from Oxford's Smith School of Business, is that the direct impact of divestment campaigns can be limited because divested holdings tend to find their way to investors with a more neutral attitude. The Oxford study concluded, for example, that a three-decades-long divestment campaign against the tobacco industry resulted in only eighty organizations and funds, out of perhaps as many as a thousand relevant institutional investors, divested from tobacco stocks or tobacco debt instruments.[12] Even after big tobacco agreed to pay damages totaling $365 billion in a watershed out-of-court settlement, expansion into new product markets, selling into new geographies in the developing world, and raising prices kept the industry afloat and profitable. The finance professor Brad Barber calculated that the California Public Employees' Retirement System (CalPERS) divestment from tobacco had little effect on the industry but cost CalPERS substantial earnings losses. According to Barber, "from October 2000 to June 2006, a dollar invested in tobacco stocks has grown to $2.77 while a dollar invested in the S&P 500 has decreased to 98 cents. Given CalPERS divested of $365 million of tobacco stocks, it's reasonable to assume the CalPERS portfolio has taken a performance hit of over $650 million."[13]

Many investors also take the view that stranded asset risk, at least for publicly traded companies, is low because firms will be able to produce most of the oil reserves that they currently own before oil demand slips away.[14] This sanguine outlook has not been true for the coal industry. In the United States, for example, the market capitalization of the eleven largest American coal companies fell from $62 billion in 2007 to under $10 billion in 2018, and the list of financial institutions that will no longer provide loans or other financing to coal-mining projects and new thermal coal power generation plants is growing. These developments are taking place despite the fact that a considerable amount of coal is still being used worldwide, especially in the developing world. The situation for oil and gas is somewhat different than for coal because many different fuel sources can substitute for coal burning for electricity and in industry, whereas oil's dominance in the transportation sector is still unparalleled. It is expected that electricity and hydrogen could replace oil in the future, but the timeline for when oil would be fully replaced in vehicles and aircraft is highly uncertain.

In recent years, oil and gas firms have underperformed compared to the overall stock market, and their aggregated market capitalization within the S & P 500, for example, has dropped from 15 percent of the market to just 4.5 percent in 2019.[15] This has raised the question whether investors are starting to shun oil and gas stocks out of concern about climate change transition risk or whether recent volatile oil prices are simply discouraging investor interest in oil companies. An Imperial College study found that in the first four months of 2020, as oil demand was collapsing, stock values of American fossil fuel companies shed 40.5 percent of their value while equities of U.S. clean power companies gained 2 percent. By comparison, the S & P index of major U.S. companies fell about 10 percent over the same period.[16]

The problem of energy firms suddenly losing access to capital is not a small one. Sudden drops in stock and bond prices for U.S. coal firms, for example, have already created severe financial problems for those firms, with many declaring bankruptcy. If investors withdraw from stocks and bonds of certain fossil fuel firms suddenly, as opposed to gradually over time as expected, the consequences could affect energy supply. Both the World Bank and the European Investment bank have sworn off lending to oil and gas projects. Goldman Sachs and a few other banks have also declared they will not fund oil and gas exploration in the Arctic, which is considered environmentally sensitive and a riskier investment.

But even if oil companies continue to find parties willing to fund their industry, the possibility of a global climate pact and peak oil demand increases the possibility that unproduced oil and gas reserves could depreciate in value over time, or even suddenly. Some analysts have argued that biased disclosures of the chances that oil reserves could become stranded because of technological change or government policy are keeping oil and gas asset values artificially high.[17] Regulators worry that a biased and incorrect assessment of transition risk could raise the prospect of an information cascade, in which market participants follow the herd in what seems to be an observable trend regardless of their own knowledge or more accurate information.

The question arises as to what happens if any event or disclosure suddenly unblocks a cascade of sellers. If some market participants realize that a different degree of climate discounting is needed in stock prices and debt for energy companies, what happens if market participants, who do not currently seem to have an interest in arbitraging that valuation difference away, were to enter the market as sellers in a sudden manner? The subsequent repricing of shares could be highly destabilizing not only to the energy companies' future performance and access to capital but also to related financial markets such as the bond market. It could also mean that those firms would no longer be able to provide secure ongoing energy supplies. Where, then, would our energy come from? If private markets did not fund energy development by publicly traded or private companies, then consumers could wind up more dependent on energy funded and produced by governments. That could mean a return to greater reliance on energy supplies from geopolitically risky producers in the Middle East and Russia. It makes more sense to organize an orderly transition whereby such risks could be minimized, but the political appetite to do so has been sorely lacking in the United States at the national level. This is not surprising because, as one would expect, incumbent industries often take political actions to try to defend their market share for as long as possible. History shows that business leaders and workers alike of incumbent technologies fight hard in national political arenas to stave off new technologies that can replace their products.[18]

A PRICE ON CARBON EMISSIONS

One big factor in the uncertainty surrounding transition risk for oil companies is the question of whether, when, and how a levy will be imposed on greenhouse gas emissions via a tax or pollution credit market. To date, more than forty countries worldwide have imposed some kind of price on carbon, either via a tax or a via a cap-and-trade program that requires companies to buy tradable pollution permits for their emissions.[19] But many of these programs are producing carbon prices that are too low to spur deep reductions in carbon pollution. Canada has one of the more ambitious programs, with a national tax on fossil fuels that began at $15 per ton in 2019 and will rise to $38 a ton by 2022. Canada is returning most of the revenue in the form of tax refunds to citizens, offsetting the higher energy costs for the majority of Canadians. Key industries like steel and chemicals will be handled separately under a tradable credits system. Individual provinces can opt out of the Canadian federal plan by advancing their own system. British Columbia and Quebec have taken this option. Although there is no federal carbon price in the United States, California passed a Global Warming Solutions Act in 2006. California has enacted its own cap-and-trade carbon market, but its carbon prices are relatively modest, partly because its initial limit on carbon was set fairly high and also because the system has a ceiling price. California also has a low-carbon fuel standard with a separate credit market that requires fuel manufacturers to decarbonize the composition of their fuel sales slowly over time. China has also begun to initiate carbon-pricing markets and expects to have a nationwide program in the early 2020s.

The disconnect between the price of carbon that might be needed to stimulate substantial reductions in carbon emissions and those currently imposed represents a key risk to stock prices of energy companies. The international oil majors currently use an internal shadow price of carbon in their investment decision making of between $60 and $85 a ton, somewhat in line with expectations that are currently reflected in U.S. stock market valuations.[20] A shadow carbon price is an internal corporate accounting figure that allows companies to incorporate the cost of an additional ton of carbon emissions that will result from some investment. Shadow carbon prices are used across the financial accounting world, from investment and procurement to risk management and strategic long-term planning. As of 2017, more than 1,400 global corporations factored an internal carbon price into business plans and investment decision making.[21] The shadow price of carbon can also represent the implied cost of carbon restrictions on a particular industry, such as regulatory limitations on power plant emissions or efficiency standards for cars. For example, Citi estimated that implementation of the Obama administration's Clean Power Plan in the United States had created a shadow price for carbon in the U.S. power sector of $14 a ton, weighing the costs of compliance and switching to new technologies.

Scientific estimates of the optimal cost of carbon vary, but are generally higher than $80 a ton, leaving deep uncertainty about how to measure the future costs to firms of carbon reductions that will have to be made. Models that calculate the optimal price for carbon are partly based on assumptions about what the future costs of abatement technologies will be and the cost of money. But there is more to calculating the cost of the negative externality of greenhouse gas pollution than just the cost of abatement. There is wide agreement among economists that greenhouse gas pollution, particularly carbon dioxide, represents a quintessential example of a negative externality; that is, the cost of pollution effects is not internalized in the private cost of a good but is instead "externalized" to society as a whole. By allowing high-carbon energy to enter the market without penalty for its adverse effects, coal, oil, and gas are in effect being discounted to their true cost compared to low- or zero-carbon-emitting energy, which does not entail such externality costs. Without an adequate cost of carbon, it has been harder to stimulate green energy investment, which can often be more expensive than running or expanding already installed higher-carbon energy ventures.

Returns on investments in low-carbon energy, or so-called cleantech, have also been uneven in recent years. Through the 2000s, there were highly visible large-scale losses in biofuels investments, such as the Silicon Valley venture capitalist Vinod Khosla's debacle Kior, which declared bankruptcy in late 2014.[22] Investors had sunk $600 million into the venture, which was supposed to turn wood chips into biofuels; at one point, it boasted a $1.5 billion valuation and traded on public stock exchanges. Its revenues never surpassed $2.5 million. Returns in other cleantech ventures of the day were also patchy. Solar panel manufacturing gross internal rate of return (IRR) as of March 31, 2015, was negative at -2.4 percent, for example, as was smart lighting at -3.7 percent, while energy efficiency and management only offered gains of 1.2 percent, according to Cambridge Associates cleantech company performance subsectors benchmark.[23] Several U.S. solar panel manufacturers, including Suniva and Solar World, filed for bankruptcy amid a flood into the market of cheaper Chinese panels. Utility-scale solar purveyors and smart grid and storage ventures fared better with higher returns, but some of the solar companies installing them, like Solar City, have also seen financial setbacks. The relative difficulty of making money in cleantech, even in the face of mounting risks for investors in fossil fuel companies, has prompted proponents of climate policy to argue that carbon pricing is crucial to providing better market design that could lower the risks to energy investing.

ASSESSING THE BROAD COSTS OF CLIMATE CHANGE

Economists and public policy decision makers have long struggled with how to properly account for the known and unknown potential physical damages of climate change. As far back as 1972, the Yale economist William Nordhaus was one of the first people to consider the social cost of carbon (SCC), in his seminal work *Is Growth Obsolete?*, coauthored with James Tobin. Although Nordhaus did not coin the term, he wrote of the cost to society of private polluting behavior and the need to quantify and monetize the damage. The problem with not considering the social cost of pollution, Nordhaus wrote, is we are "treating as free things which are not really free. This practice gives the wrong signals for the directions of economic growth."[24] More recently, Nordhaus has written that "the most important single economic concept in the economics of climate change is the social cost of carbon,"[25] defined as the cost in dollars of the long-term damage done by one ton of carbon dioxide in a given year. The social cost of carbon includes not only all the costs and damages of mitigating and adapting to climate change but also the physical cost to infrastructure and the balancing of costs and benefits between current and future generations.

While the social cost of carbon is intended to be a comprehensive monetary estimate of climate-change-induced damages to agriculture, human health, and property, as well as other climate-related risks, it is problematic to calculate given the range of uncertainties in climate change modeling, economic growth, and the actual risks in a particular year. Economists also debate what long-term discount rate to use for future climate assessments because the cost of money is subject to varying assumptions about the trade-offs between economic activity that produces higher cumulative greenhouse gas emissions today and the need that activity would create for greater reductions in greenhouse gas emissions in the future.[26] In other words, calculations of discount rates are influenced by one's view of the future. Will delays in cutting carbon emissions now force greater reductions in carbon emissions in the future, and how would those greater restrictions curb economic activity down the road compared to the level of economic growth that would be constrained now? Many factors go into such calculations, including assumptions about the costs and availability of carbon-mitigating technologies now and in the future.

Modeling technological change, including the costs of carbon abatement technologies, has been dogged by difficulties with empirical data to use in calibrating modeling techniques.[27] Some modelers assume that improvements in energy efficiency will take place at a historical rate of productivity improvement or in response to changes in energy prices.[28] Others try to calculate technology improvement as a function of R & D investment.[29] It is also popular to study learning curves of other technologies and apply rates of change that are consistent across experience. The problem with this last approach is that if learning-by-doing lowers the cost for low-carbon technologies or fuels and that drives demand away from carbon-intensive fossil fuels, presumably the prices of fossil fuels will also decline, iteratively changing the price-competitive landscape, at least temporarily, and requiring a further lowering of the costs for low-carbon substitutes.[30] This problem is particularly complex to capture in scientific modeling.

The use of the social cost of carbon in the United States finds its roots in an executive order by the Clinton administration in 1993 requiring cost-benefit analysis for federal regulations. Prior to the Clinton order, President Ronald Reagan had also mandated that all regulatory decision making go through a robust cost-benefit analysis that considered the net economic costs of any proposed rule. The cost-benefit analysis in relation to climate change came to a head in 2008, when the George W. Bush administration lost a court case in which they sought to roll back corporate average fuel economy (CAFE) standards. The court ruled that the proposed rollback did not adequately account for the costs of climate change. At the time, different federal agencies used different socials costs of carbon, ranging from $0 to $68 a ton of carbon dioxide (2007 dollars), in their rulemaking procedures.

In an attempt to standardize the social cost of carbon across agencies, the Obama administration in 2009 convened an interagency working group (IWG) to come up with a social cost of carbon that would be used across the federal government.[31] Composed of a dozen federal agencies and departments, including the U.S. Department of Energy and the Treasury Department, along with the U.S. Environmental Protection Agency and the Council of Economic Advisers, the IWG developed a social cost of carbon that could be incorporated into the rulemaking decisions for everything from washing machine efficiency and fuel economy standards to emissions regulations from smokestacks. Its work was based on reconciling three integrated assessment models (IAMs), including modeling by economist William Nordhaus. IAMs are essentially advanced computer models that run thousands of global simulations with hundreds of parameters and variables to determine future scenarios, accounting for global economic growth, future climate impacts, the benefits and damages of increased emissions, and assessed discount rates.

The first social cost of carbon ranged from $21.40 to $44.90 between 2010 and 2050 and assumed a 3 percent discount rate, an assumption that was criticized by external experts. In 2013, the modeling for the social cost of carbon was updated and values increased to $33 to $71 for the same forty-year timeframe. Based on these calculations, the Obama administration used a standardized social cost of carbon of $43 in 2020 for its policies related to CAFE standards, Mercury and Air Toxic Standards for coal plants, and its signature climate change policy, the Clean Power Plan. The Obama social cost of carbon included global damages and was challenged in court. This decision was upheld in 2016 when the U.S. Court of Appeals for the Seventh Circuit ruled that global considerations were appropriate. In 2017, the Trump administration reduced the social cost of carbon used in federal rulemaking to between $1 and $6 a ton in the year 2020 by considering only national damages and increasing the preferred discount rate to 7 percent.[32]

Regardless of how the social cost of carbon is calculated, ultimately the effectiveness of carbon prices will reflect whether they are high enough to stimulate investment in low-carbon fuels or other mitigation technologies. Some economists have argued that, by better tracking the costs that are reflected in business decisions, the shadow price of carbon is a better tool than the social cost of carbon to measure the costs of abatement because it can more quickly adjust to new cost mitigation information.[33]

When scientists consider the charges that will need to be made for carbon, through either a cap-and-trade system or a tax, they consider what technological breakthroughs will be needed to bend the emissions trajectory sharply downward. Most of the models used to calculate this assume that some amount of carbon emissions will be either captured and stored through carbon capture utilization and storage (CCUS) technologies or removed directly from the atmosphere by some sort of geoengineering. The IPCC 1.5 Degree Special Report projected that between 348 and 687 gigatons of CCUS will be needed by the end of the century to achieve necessary reductions in greenhouse gas accumulations in the atmosphere in line with a 1.5 degrees warming pathway.

The costs for CCUS are extremely high to date; hence the concern is that carbon prices would need to be much higher than $80 a ton to move the needle on carbon mitigation. CCUS costs vary based on an existing plant's capacity, coal type, heat rate, and a litany of factors unique to each plant—these are bespoke projects. With limited adoption, robust supply chains have not been established to allow economies of scale. As a result, cost overruns are common, as seen with the canceled coal and CCUS plant in Kemper County, Mississippi, where costs spiraled to $7.5 billion, far exceeding the $2.4 billion cap imposed by the state utility commission.[34] Going forward, more promising technologies are under trial. An Allam-Fetvedt Cycle plant burns natural gas with oxygen and hot CO_2 instead of air to generate electricity. The turbine is turned with a hot CO_2 liquid stream, not steam, and the separation of water and the pure vapor CO_2 at the end of the process allows the CO_2 to be sequestered for use or disposal.[35]

TECHNOLOGICAL INNOVATION FOR NEGATIVE EMISSIONS

Designing systems that create economic value for the captured carbon could help to increase the adoption of carbon capture systems. CCUS has seen an increased focus recently as the energy industry finds use for captured carbon dioxide. Oil companies have long utilized enhanced oil recovery (EOR) to improve wellhead recovery rates. Technically a form of CCUS, EOR is the process of injecting carbon dioxide into the reservoir, which can boost recovery rates by 13.2 percent on average.[36] A U.S. example is the Rangely CO_2-EOR project. Between 1944 and 1986, the oil well produced 1.9 billion barrels; since deployment, EOR recovery has yielded an extra 129 million barrels.[37] The value derived from EOR is equal to the value of the incremental increase in oil production; in addition, there is a $10/ton federal tax credit for carbon utilization, minus the cost of carbon, which further increases its value.[38] Returned CO_2 from EOR is then reinjected into the reservoir for storage. But so far, predictable CCUS revenue streams like EOR have failed to quell investor apprehension.

Carbon emissions released into the atmosphere are cumulative. Some portion of what is emitted stays in the atmosphere for centuries; a smaller portion remains for many thousands of years. As concentration levels rise, scientists warn we could get to the point where so much CO_2 has accumulated in the atmosphere that we will need to achieve "negative" emissions; that is, we will need processes or technologies that remove carbon dioxide from the atmosphere in a permanent way. One such process is pyrolysis of biofuels, whereby a biomaterial, such as algae or crop residues, is heated in the absence of oxygen resulting in a pure form of carbon known as biochar, as well as bio-oil that can be a diesel substitute and syngas that can be used to generate electricity. Biochar can be used as a soil additive, which holds the carbon sequestered in the ground.[39]

Climate modelers have also suggested that adding carbon capture and sequestration technology to biofuels—so-called bioenergy with carbon capture and storage, or BECCS for short—could be a key technology to provide negative emissions, but questions remain about its costs as well as its viability to be implemented at a sufficiently significant scale after 2050.[40] One factor that could constrain the adoption of BECCS is the availability of viable CO_2 storage facilities close enough to biorefining without resorting to large-scale pipelines to bring sequestered carbon to other regions for storage.[41] Other factors have also been cited that might thwart the widespread adoption of BECCS, including insufficient availability of biomass, a lack of sufficient policy incentives in the form of high carbon prices or specific incentives for negative emissions technologies, and concerns about land-use consequences.[42]

Another option for negative emissions is direct air capture, which literally sucks accumulated carbon back out of the air, allowing it to be stored or used in a manner that keeps it from leaking back into the atmosphere. The current state of direct air capture technology, just like large-scale carbon capture and sequestration, is a relatively expensive proposition. Canadian-based Carbon Engineering announced in 2019 that it had raised $68 million for its nascent direct air capture technology from the likes of Bill Gates, Chevron, and Occidental Petroleum.[43] A 2011 scientific study of the technology put its costs prohibitively high at $600 a ton of carbon, but the Swiss firm Climateworks says its costs for direct air capture might dip below $100 a ton of carbon in the coming decade.[44] Carbon Engineering researchers published a study that put direct air capture costs between $94 and $232 a ton.[45]

While it is more controversial, solar radiation management (SMR) appears to be cheap, quick, effective—and imperfect. This technology would entail spraying millions of tons annually of reflective aerosol particles into the lower stratosphere so as to deflect a small fraction of the incoming sunlight and thereby slightly cool the earth, much as a large volcanic eruption does. Mount Pinatubo and countless other eruptions prove that this works, and research, published recently in Environmental Research Letters, contributes to growing confidence that it could be technically feasible and not as cost prohibitive as might be imagined. We estimate that such a program would have start-up costs of about $3.5 billion and would require activity at an average cost of about $2.5 billion a year.[46]

Solar radiation management remains controversial and would not solve all of the problems associated with climate change—most prominently, ocean acidification. Scientists also believe it would be unlikely to return the climate everywhere on earth to the preindustrial temperature baseline. Moreover, the possibility of problematic unintended consequences seems high, and once mature, a sudden termination of the program could result in a disastrous return to higher temperatures. All in all, it sounds like a very bad idea, but one that is getting increased study as other carbon mitigation options remain hard to achieve.

EXISTING CARBON PRICING

Today, more than forty-six countries and twenty-eight subnational jurisdictions, such as cities, states, and provinces, have a tax or price on carbon to help promote the reduction of greenhouse gas emissions. As more countries move in this direction, the United States could find itself disadvantaged in trade compared to other major exporters like Europe, South Korea, and China, which do have carbon pricing. By dropping out of the Paris climate accord, the United States ran a risk that the official global climate working groups linked to global climate negotiations would set energy standards and other carbon-related rules to the detriment of U.S. exports.

The European Union is already considering implementing a carbon border tax that would serve as a fee on goods from non-EU countries that do not have their own carbon tax or form of carbon pricing. By contrast, China, which is expected to fully launch a national carbon market in the early 2020s, is making lower-emitting cars and other products a priority in its future export base, giving it a possible advantage over the United States in global markets.[47] U.S. oil and gas exports abroad could become negatively affected if future customers of fossil fuels focus increasingly on the relative carbon content of fuels. In 2020, the United States did not have strict regulations forcing industry to reduce the leakage of methane from oil and gas operations, except in the state of Colorado. That could mean that U.S. petroleum and natural gas exports could face carbon fees or penalties going forward, compared to suppliers who are using advanced monitoring and methane capture technologies in their operations, depending on the level of leakage that remains customary in U.S. oil and gas production and distribution. Tailpipe carbon emissions standards in key consumer markets could also hinder U.S. vehicle exports. The Chinese government requires that all foreign automakers who want to sell cars in China meet targets that a certain percentage of vehicles sold must be electric. By 2025, foreign companies selling cars in China will have to ensure that at least 7 percent of individual corporate vehicle sales are electric.[48] The European Union has targets for reducing emissions from cars and vans by 31 percent by 2030 and is working to tighten standards for new trucks and buses.

Investor concerns about carbon taxes and the energy transition are putting oil companies are under pressure to adjust their strategies. In January 2020, just ahead of the World Economic Forum in Davos, Switzerland, Blackrock CEO Larry Fink announced that the firm—the world's largest money manager, with nearly $7 trillion in assets under management—was overhauling its investing strategy to make sustainability its hallmark, noting in particular that climate change would be a "defining factor" in companies' long-term performance.[49] Fink's announcement was one of many corporate responses to climate change that became top of the agenda at the international gathering.

In the context of large institutional investors thinking more about how to screen holdings for climate change risks, many oil companies are starting to shift strategies in hopes of preserving access to credit and capital markets. Investors are no longer rewarding oil businesses for adding reserves or maintaining large reserves. The metric for a successful company is shifting away from one that shows strong growth of reserve assets on its balance sheet to one that is succeeding in generating the best possible revenue stream.[50] Companies have tried offering healthier stock dividends and buybacks in hopes of sustaining investor interest, but such a policy could be unsustainable if low oil prices become pervasive over time. To respond to investor calls that they acknowledge the energy transition in their capital-spending strategies, the largest international oil companies have begun to reduce exposure to the energy transition by diversifying capital spending to include renewable energy and biofuels.[51] They are also instituting new programs to lower the emissions from their operations. BP's new chairman made headlines in early 2020 by declaring the company would commit to becoming carbon neutral, both operationally and in its product sales, by

2050. BP and several other major oil companies are now investing in various clean energy ventures such as solar, wind, geothermal, biofuels, and marine energy. In Europe, the largest oil companies are investing in hydrogen and electric fueling infrastructure and battery storage. Total and Shell have also suggested they will purposefully increase the share of natural gas versus oil in their future sales, in an effort to align with the Paris agreement. China's two largest state-owned oil companies have also committed to long-range net-zero-carbon targets.

Although spending on clean energy still represents a very small part of the international oil companies' capital allocations, it is clear that the companies can pivot to address changes in the carbon price and pace of the energy transition. As a result, it remains possible that the most proactive majors will be able to protect cash flows over time by leveraging spending in low- or zero-carbon technologies. The companies are also pursuing carbon sequestration and storage, which could prolong the life of legacy oil and gas reserves. This raises the question whether the exposure for sovereign petrostates is higher than for the international majors. The eight largest majors—ExxonMobil, Chevron, Royal Dutch Shell, BP, Total, ENI, Equinor, and ConocoPhillips—control only about 3 percent of total proven oil reserves. Rather, it is the national oil companies of the Organization of Petroleum Exporting Countries (OPEC) that have the higher risk of asset stranding. OPEC controls 79 percent of global proven reserves, leaving the national oil companies of its members more exposed to peak oil demand.

Some national oil companies, like the oil majors, are actively trying to reduce emissions from their operations and adding investments in renewable energy. Saudi Aramco, for example, has the lowest carbon emissions per barrel of any major oil producer.[52] It is developing a master gas-processing system to virtually eliminate flaring in gas production operations and is investing in carbon capture and use. Saudi Aramco is spending $5 billion on renewable energy, with a target of ten gigawatts by 2023. Kuwait has a target of 15 percent renewable energy by 2030, while the Abu Dhabi national oil company ADNOC is investing in carbon capture, including a capture-and-use project connected to the emirates' steel industry. Russia's state oil and gas firm Gazprom has programs to lower its emissions by improving energy efficiency in its operations and monitoring and preventing methane leakage. The firm is also pursuing renewable energy, including geothermal, wind, solar, and thermoelectric generators, in its power generation business.

But not all national oil companies are preparing for the energy transition, and this increases the possibility that the problem of stranded asset risk could hit markets for sovereign credit harder than for equities in the large international oil companies. In a 2011 study, the World Bank found that only Malaysia had sufficiently used its oil receipts to diversify its economy away from oil.[53] The International Monetary Fund (IMF) reported in 2019 that emerging markets national oil companies' leverage has "nearly doubled" since 2005 while they have been suffering from a decline in profitability. State-owned enterprises represent a large portion of total emerging-market debt securities. The IMF suggests that stranded asset risk could worsen the credit position of sovereign oil states, which are already experiencing rising total government net debt. How these states manage the energy transition could prove material to global credit markets. Petrostates that currently face economic sanctions, such as Iran and Venezuela, could run a higher risk of stranded assets as other oil-producing countries rush ahead to develop remaining reserves first before the world needs less oil.

For some troubled oil producers, the cyclical opportunities to amass fiscal surpluses during times of high oil prices could be fewer and farther between. Their external debt is already on the rise, in many cases due to corruption and mismanagement in their oil sectors. As Venezuela has drifted into a debilitating political and economic crisis, its external debt has risen to more than $156 billion, and stranded asset risk could easily derail any attempt to revive its oil sector, which has been devastated by violence, bureaucratic mismanagement, and sanctions. Other countries, such as Nigeria and Angola, face the prospect that national debt will take a high proportion of retained government revenue in the future.

For the very oil-rich, such as Saudi Arabia and the United Arab Emirates, there is still time to use existing resources to diversify away from their high reliance on oil revenues. Both national oil companies, ADNOC and Saudi Aramco, have used initial public offerings (IPOs) to generate capital to invest in economic diversification. Saudi Arabia's Public Investment Fund (PIF) has invested in growth firms such as Uber, electric car company Lucid Motors, and Magic Leap, a virtual reality start-up, as part of its efforts to decouple future revenue from oil. It has also launched a $1 billion investment vehicle that will tap venture capital and private equity firms focused on small to medium capital enterprises. As for other oil states that are less prepared, international institutions should be preparing to encourage them to begin substantial economic reform. Otherwise, global financial markets could be in for a shock from mounting sovereign debt, failing bond issues, and shrinking foreign reserves. The staggering case of Venezuela's financial collapse is a warning of what could transpire in petrostates with a history of corruption and wasteful spending as statist oil revenues structurally recede.

As financial markets begin to anticipate these economic shifts to the valuations of oil and gas companies and reserves, the risk of stranded oil and gas reserves is emerging as a geopolitical influence. Even if oil prices rise for a brief period of time, economic pressures will continue to mount on petrostates as their ability to amass fiscal surpluses over extended periods in the future looks less feasible. Some governments are intensifying domestic political repression as internal patronage systems to coopt diverse interests of competing stakeholders are no longer sustainable. Others are externalizing domestic political challenges by asserting themselves abroad militarily to maintain geopolitical influence and divert the attention of domestic audiences away from problems at home.

Petrostates will not be the only ones experiencing changed geopolitical circumstances from financial market signals on carbon, climate risk, and stranded assets. The market signal to hasten investment in and installation of new digital and clean energy will alter the geopolitics of major economies like the United States and China, raising the stakes for who best navigates the transition and excels at the development of goods and services in the new energy economy. Threats of oil cutoffs, which once served as a diplomatic lever over large energy-consuming countries, will weaken over time in their effect on states whose technology policy makes them less worried about foreign oil supplies and more reliant on domestically produced renewables and energy-saving digital technologies. Right now, the United States appears to be well positioned to cope with most geopolitical contingencies when it comes to energy geopolitics, but undercurrents of future challenges are on the horizon—both as a threat to the U.S. oil and gas industry's continued success and if the United States does not act to position itself to compete well enough in the new energy economy.

The spring of 2020 might be instructive, as the United States found itself worrying about the ill effects of a total collapse in oil prices. The problem was multifold. Very low oil prices are damaging to the U.S. oil industry, which is now, because of shale, encamped in many U.S. states and thereby economically important. Low oil prices threatened the economic health of important U.S. regional allies and trading partners like Mexico and Colombia, in addition to worsening the situation for fragile states like Iraq and Nigeria, where increased instability could present the U.S. military with new challenges. Finally, low oil prices threatened to add to the number of countries that needed support from the International Monetary Fund, undermining the stability of global sovereign credit markets and, at the same time, increasing borrowing requirements for wealthier petrostates like Saudi Arabia and the United Arab Emirates that might have underpinned credit markets in the past.

With so much at stake, the United States wound up taking a strong diplomatic stance to end the devastating fallout of a brief oil price war that was driving an oil price collapse. The U.S. effort was all the more shocking since typically the United States only wades into global oil markets to thwart an upward oil price shock. In the spring of 2020, the Trump administration successfully twisted arms to get global oil producers to cut oil production in coordination with the G20 states to prevent a meltdown in global emerging-market credit, at least for the spring of 2020, but the U.S. stance opened more questions than it answered about what role America might play if oil markets turned structurally dystopic over a longer period of time. We explore who might be the geopolitical winners and losers in the following chapter.

CHAPTER 8

The Losers

The Changing Geopolitics of Oil

At the Center for Energy and Economic Diversification at the University of Texas Permian Basin, you can rent its newly built, elegant auditorium for $425 for the day. I gave a talk there on the role of the U.S. shale boom in U.S. foreign policy. The acoustics would put Carnegie Hall to shame, but it was unclear how the center plans to organize events that would fill its 125 seats. The men who occupy the drilling sites in the Permian Basin mostly spend their evenings in bars and food joints in Odessa, a dustier city just a mile or two down the road. The social fabric of Odessa is night-and-day different from Midland, where a marble plaque of the Ten Commandments adorns the front of the one upscale local hotel. Buses ship in workers from makeshift trailer homes and motels. Lunch is catered. The day begins early and ends late. Given how much time and effort is spent in the region producing and shipping oil and transporting oil workers and equipment along miles of single-lane, congested roads, it seems as though it would be hard to organize an indoor concert event.

It is hard to explain to leaders from the Middle East just how expansive the Permian Basin is physically. When you fly in by plane, as far as the eye can see is a giant, empty desert whose demarcated squares of bare land are punctuated only by the occasional drilling rig or huge mansion with a swimming pool. This region, just 250 miles wide and 300 miles long, has already turned OPEC on its head. Forecasts are that the Permian Basin alone might be able to achieve a production rate of ten million barrels a day of oil in the coming decade (unless oil prices remain too low to justify drilling), more than any single OPEC country except Saudi Arabia. That success had already put the United States ahead of both Saudi Arabia and Russia when it comes to global oil market share in 2019. This change comes against the backdrop of a changing geopolitical landscape in which Saudi

Arabia and Russia have been forced to cut their oil production and cede markets to U.S. oil to defend their own national oil revenues.

Saudi Arabia and OPEC opted to open the taps in 2014 and 2015, confidently assuming that lower oil prices would stop the growth in drilling activity in the Permian Basin and other prolific U.S. shale areas and potentially stimulate the global economic recovery. I remember pulling aside a member of the Saudi oil industry at a large dinner at an international conference in Europe and trying to explain privately that an oil price drop to $50 a barrel would not be sufficient to stop the growth in U.S. shale oil (his claim over the dessert discussion). He said he was sure of his data and that I was not sufficiently well informed. In 2016, oil prices hit a low of $27 a barrel. U.S. production flickered briefly, some oil companies consolidated through acreage sales, mergers, and takeovers, and ultimately U.S. production continued to rise.

OPEC blinked first because none of its members could ride out the revenue loss that would be entailed in keeping prices low enough for long enough to discourage U.S. drillers. In December 2016, OPEC announced its historic Declaration of Cooperation between OPEC and a group of non-OPEC oil producers, including Russia, to remove 1.8 million barrels a day of crude oil from global supplies for six months, with the possibility of rolling over the agreement in mid-2017 if oil markets were still weak. As of June 2019, Russia announced at the sidelines of a G20 meeting that OPEC plus, as it has been dubbed, would be extending its oil production cuts into 2020 in an effort to keep oil prices from falling, and OPEC met and announced its cuts would extend through the first quarter of 2020. U.S. production reached 10 million b/d at the end of 2017 and more than 12 million b/d by mid-2019. Add in biofuels, natural gas liquids, and refinery processing gains (more refined products are created per barrel than the crude oil that goes into a refinery), and U.S. liquids production was close to 20 percent of world output.

Generally speaking, OPEC's efforts at market management appear to have reduced oil price volatility—that is, the level of statistically measurable variance in the nominal oil price. One recent economic study found that oil price volatility would have been substantially higher between late 2005 and late 2014 without OPEC's intervention. The same study found that between January 2017 and the end of 2019, an OPEC plus oil producer coalition agreement to adopt production cuts reduced oil price volatility to 7 percent, compared to a counterfactual of over 19 percent that might have prevailed without the coalition's actions.[1] But the resilience of the U.S. oil industry could prove a thorny ongoing problem for any oil producer group that wants to restrict competition in energy markets.

U.S. crude oil production could rise again in the coming decade as digital technologies and automation contribute to higher recovery and greater operational efficiency from the shale resources over time. Costs for extracting oil and gas from U.S. shale and other source rock could continue to fall as new technologies, such as automated production platforms, predictive maintenance, and advanced analytics, speed up the drilling process and lower workforce costs. To the extent that these technological developments make oil cheaper, OPEC will have an even bigger challenge if demand continues to fade, given political and environmental pressures to move away from fossil fuel use. Even as the U.S. drilling rig count was falling through 2019, output gains continued. According to Citi, in the five years following the 2014 price fall, the average time it took to drill a well plunged from sixty days to less than thirty days, while the average production per well doubled. That 400 percent increase in efficiency was mostly based on new technology.

INTERNATIONAL OIL PRODUCER COLLUSION REVISITED

That OPEC needed to expand its grouping for defending oil prices to include cooperation with Russia makes sense beyond just the immediate competition from U.S. shale production. There is a giant economics literature debating whether OPEC has sufficient market power to maintain oil prices above the marginal cost of production or to influence short-term price movements. Robert Mabro of the University of Oxford pointed out in the 1990s that the core strategy of OPEC was to utilize a supply plan to steer oil prices toward a target level or, more realistically, toward a target zone.[2] For decades, OPEC has used this mechanism to hold oil prices above the long-term competitive price for oil.

In a freely competitive market, one might have expected the lowest-cost oil supplies to be developed first to the highest degree possible while higher-cost resources would be abandoned until depletion of cheap oil made room for them at a higher price point. Under this kind of competitive structure, Saudi Arabia, Iraq, and the other Gulf producers, whose lowest-cost reserves represent two-thirds of proven world reserves, could have increased their levels of investment and produced a vastly higher amount of oil. Instead, OPEC generally tried to hold oil prices up to maximize revenues over two years. In effect, OPEC had to choose between higher prices or higher market share. They chose the former. The New York University energy economist Dermot Gately noted in a 2004 paper that it was not in OPEC's collective interests to meet rising demand for oil. He calculated that it made no sense for the cartel to add oil supplies into the market because the marginal gain in revenue from more output would be negative.[3] In a growing market, each OPEC member is able to increase output even if any single country's individual percentage market share of the growing OPEC pie remains the same.

Experience has shown OPEC collusion is easier when oil markets are sufficiently undersupplied so that all producers can gain money from making cuts, as opposed to the more usual zero-sum environment where one OPEC member's loss is another's gain. The higher the percentage of the market that OPEC controls, the more pricing power it has. The less oil that can be made available from non-OPEC producers, the better it is for OPEC. In a case where OPEC has a rising share and the need for oil is rising, the elasticity of world demand goes down, giving OPEC more power and influence on prices.[4] Elasticity is the economic measure of how sensitive demand for a good is to relative to other changes in other economic variables such as price or consumer income. In the past, OPEC has been able to take advantage of the fact that the elasticity of demand for oil has been low because there were few substitutes for oil, especially in transport.

But now OPEC is struggling with the lesson of recent years: high oil prices invite energy innovation. Consumers eventually respond to high oil prices by investing in energy-efficient goods, and non-OPEC producers are incentivized to increase investments in higher-cost oil resources and drilling technologies. Both of those eventualities have now taken place, and the pace of progress is increasing exponentially with the advent of digital technologies. In essence, in energy economics terms, the digital revolution has increased the elasticity of oil supply from non-OPEC countries while at the same time, given new technologies that might peak oil use, the elasticity of demand for oil is simultaneously rising. In other words, oil previously had a relatively low price elasticity of demand or was, in economist terms, inelastic. That is even in situations where big price rises occurred, many consumers had little choice but to use the same amount of oil to heat their homes and fuel their cars in the short run. But now, as access to alternative fuels increases and other options to reduce the use of oil through efficient, digitized smart appliances, tele-meetings, and e-commerce expands, consumers can shift away from oil more easily, even in the short run, making oil demand more elastic and thereby more sensitive to price changes.

In the mid-2000s, the IEA estimated that OPEC's share of total world oil supply would rise from 38 percent in 2000 to 48 percent by 2020.[5] In 2019, OPEC's share of total world oil supply had fallen to under 30 percent, threatening its entire enterprise of influencing world oil prices. To regain sufficient market power, especially in light of the changes in the elasticity of both oil supply and demand, it needed to add a major non-OPEC producer to its ranks—hence its changed attitude about cooperation with Russia. Moscow is now a necessity for OPEC, and for Saudi Arabia, if it is going to able to salvage any semblance of influence over the price of oil.

Drilling technology improvements are also working against OPEC. The proportion of oil that can be recovered from resources is rising while the cost of finding and producing the oil is falling. This means that the lower price level OPEC would have to stomach to knock out competing producers is likely to be uncomfortably low for many sovereign national budgets. The cost of finding and developing (F&D) oil escalated steadily in the 2000s as rising prices justified increased drilling activity. Average F & D costs reached $30 a barrel by 2012, up from just $7 a barrel in 2002. Companies responded to this cost inflation by investing more heavily in new technologies with the aim of lowering costs. By 2015, average F & D costs had receded to $15 a barrel, and expectations are that automation, sensors, and other digital technologies will spur further cost savings.

The UK newspaper the *Financial Times* notes in a commentary following OPEC's deal with Russia in mid-2019:

> Five years after oil prices last traded at $100 a barrel, the cartel is stuck in a cycle it cannot get out of. The group has succeeded in propping up the price of oil to $60 a barrel but only through endless rounds of production cuts that have seen its share of the global oil market shrink to the lowest level in almost three decades. . . . Further down the road also lies the prospect that demand for oil could very soon start to fade, complicating OPEC's long term plans.[6]

The COVID-19 crisis, which cratered global oil demand overnight in February, March, and April 2020, rapidly converted the oil abundance problem into a catastrophe. Oil demand receded suddenly as major economies moved into lockdown mode, and oil began to accumulate in storage tanks and floating ships, leaving large oil producers with few options except to throttle back production. At one point in April, it appeared the world might literally run out of places to store oil. At that point, all producers, both within OPEC and in countries with private industry like the United States and Canada, were forced to shut down some of their operations until demand could recover. The experience highlighted the zero-sum geopolitics that could result from disagreement on how production cuts might be shared.

A NEW OIL GEOPOLITICAL ORDER

As the means to eliminate consumer and industrial oil use improve, neither the major oil producers of the Middle East nor Russia have figured out how to manage the geopolitical threat that is now forming against their statist power. The reverberations are already palpable, even though oil demand growth is not expected to disappear consistently for one or more decades.

The first manifestation of the new reality is that the allure of access to large oil fields in risky locales has receded, and with it the diplomatic muscle it gave resource-holding governments. The world's largest international oil companies have focused their capital spending on opportunities outside of OPEC in U.S. onshore shale and deepwater reserves in the U.S. Gulf of Mexico, Brazil, and West Africa. Given the large opportunities in these domains and the future risk of stranded assets and other geopolitical risks, oil companies are less interested in booking large in-place reserves in the Middle East and Russia than in the past, making it harder for oil-producing states to use a stake in oil fields to attract diplomatic support. The age of abundance also means that China's and India's national oil companies are not as actively on the prowl to acquire oil and gas resources as they were in the 2000s. As a result, troubled oil-producing countries like Russia, Iran, and Venezuela will have a harder time using lucrative oil-field investment deals to secure airtight alliances. One upshot is that the United States has started to find it easier to impose oil sanctions against oil-exporting countries when their geopolitical actions bump up against U.S. and allied interests.

For most of the 2000s, under the government of Hugo Chavez and later Nicolas Maduro, Venezuela utilized its vast oil resources to enhance its influence and alliances both regionally and globally. It offered oil loans to spread its influence across the Caribbean and Central and Latin America, to the detriment of U.S. interests, and forged oil ties with China and Russia. For a while, the strategy appeared to be keeping Venezuela afloat, but increased political turmoil and violence in Venezuela in 2018 led to the virtual demise of the country's oil sector. In a sign of how much the energy world has changed, the near-complete loss of Venezuelan oil to global markets failed to rise to the level of a prolonged international crisis. Between January 2018 and June 2019, the global oil market saw a disruption of 2.4 million barrels a day as Venezuelan and Iranian exports disappeared from the market. Oil prices barely flinched.

With Maduro losing the ability to tap oil as a diplomatic lever, the United States became more emboldened and attempted to change the facts on the ground in Venezuela by recognizing the speaker of the democratically elected National Assembly, Juan Guaido, as interim president of Venezuela. The hope was that public demonstrations and a worsening economic outlook would convince the Venezuelan military to abandon its support for ruling strongman Nicolas Maduro. It looked briefly as though Russia and China might give substantial backing to Maduro, who over the years has turned over larger stakes in Venezuelan oil fields to Russian and Chinese firms in exchange for a combination of cash and loans. But ongoing damage to electricity networks vital to oil production, shrinking access to imported lighter petroleum to mix with Venezuela's heavy crude to render it transportable, and mounting Venezuelan financial debt have made the whole Venezuelan affair geopolitically unsustainable even for Moscow and Beijing.

With no oil consumers or oil-field investors desperate for access to the country's oil sector, as might have been the case ten years earlier, Venezuela's situation fell into a political stalemate with no immediate endgame in sight. By early 2019, the problem of Maduro and Venezuela's deteriorating humanitarian situation was off the foreign policy radar screen of most superpower capitals, including Washington. It now is considered a humanitarian crisis requiring foreign aid rather than an energy crisis upending oil consumers. U.S. efforts to use economic sanctions to increase pressure on Maduro and the Venezuelan military to accept a negotiated political transition back to democratic elections has to date not been met with any dramatic pushback from Venezuela's oil customers. Relatively quickly, traders and oil clients fell into line with U.S. restrictions, and Venezuela's oil trade slowly dried up in 2018. The country's oil production fell from 2.2 million barrels a day in early 2017 to 750,000 barrels a day by early 2019. By 2020, it was down almost to zero.

The changing landscape for countries who used to tap their petro-power to influence geopolitical outcomes came into even sharper focus when the United States moved to tighten sanctions against Iranian oil exports in May 2019. In March 2012, after months of behind-the-scenes negotiations, the Obama administration got customers like China, Japan, and South Korea to buy "less" oil from Iran, in compliance with new U.S. sanctions aimed at bringing Iran to the negotiating table on its nuclear program.[7] The effort was an early hint that concern about access to long-term energy export markets could be used to motivate some influential leaders in Iran to push for acceptance of a nuclear deal with the West.[8] Fast-forward to 2019, when the Trump administration announced it was ending temporary waivers initially offered to Iran's key buyers; there was barely a geopolitical peep from major consuming countries, including countries whose oil firms had investments in Iran's oil and gas sector. Europe complied with the request to take purchases of Iranian oil to zero virtually immediately, and France's Total agreed to withdraw from its major South Pars condensate project in Iran. Many Asian allies of the United States also made the needed import adjustments without much fanfare.

No longer able to use access to its oil and gas as an effective lever in geopolitical discourse, Iran shifted to the use of hard power, threatening to interrupt the free passage of oil via the Strait of Hormuz, the vital chokepoint through which a fifth of all crude oil used globally had historically transited. Iran resorted to attacks on regional energy facilities and shipping, ostensibly to make the point that it was still too powerful militarily to ignore. Surprisingly, from the sidelines of a meeting of the Group of Twenty (G20) in Japan in early July 2019, even after several apparent Iranian-sponsored attacks on shipping near the Strait, a drone hit on a Saudi pipeline, and the downing of the U.S. military drone, U.S. president Donald J. Trump stated he felt "no rush" and "no time pressure" to ease tensions with Iran. Even China, whose economy now stands to lose more from oil supply cutoffs from the Middle East than the United States, failed to put Iranian oil at the top of the list for U.S.-Chinese diplomacy.[9]

But perhaps the most telling signpost that the oil world had changed came when, on September 14, 2019, a barrage of missiles and drones hit the highly strategic crude-processing facility at Abqaiq, Saudi Arabia, and facilities at the large Saudi oil field at Khurais, destroying important equipment necessary to treat raw crude oil to remove contaminants before it can be exported or refined. Had the strike been a little larger, it could potentially have knocked out a high percentage of Saudi oil exports for a year or two. The kingdom's policy to maintain high redundancy of equipment and its extraordinary efficiency at quickly bypassing and repairing damaged units saved the day, but the attack failed to stir a lasting oil price risk premium that might have been expected. After a few days' short-lived price rise, price gains evaporated amid perceptions that sufficient oil would come to market to meet demand, even with continuing risks of another major disruption.[10] It was notable at the time that the United States did not engage in the scale of mobilization of its armed forces to the Middle East as it had done in 1990 when Iraq invaded Kuwait, even though it was assumed that Iran—either directly or via proxies—was behind the attacks. While the United States did eventually add to the number of aircraft carriers in place to handle any future aggression by Iran, the combination of the hesitant U.S. response and its circumspection in scale led to commentary that the United States might no longer consider Middle East oil one of its core interests.[11]

Altered geopolitical risk is also evident in the case of Russia and its petro-influence in Europe, where stricter carbon policies and hydrocarbon-saving technologies are increasingly characterizing energy markets. The share of Europe's energy mix moving to renewable energy has soared in recent years to 30 percent of electricity generation, up from 12 percent in 2000. Almost all new power generation capacity installed in Europe in recent years has been renewable power. Renewables also power more than 8 percent of transport energy in Europe, and the European Union expects to reach its target that renewables will constitute a fifth of all energy use by 2020. The rise of renewables, combined with increased access to U.S. and other imported liquefied natural gas (LNG), has meant a weakening in Russia's ability to use its energy supply to Europe as a geopolitical weapon. Russia saw its market share in Europe crater in 2009 to 23 percent, down from 30 percent, as a result of economic slowdown in the aftermath of the financial crisis and rising supplies of renewable energy and cheap imported LNG.[12] Continued natural gas market oversupply has changed the nature of pricing away from long-term oil-linked contracts to pricing linked to the spot market price for natural gas at major trading hubs, like the futures prices at the U.S. benchmark storage area of Henry Hub, or under new hybrid pricing that uses a combination of spot natural gas and other kinds of price indexes like coal or fuel oil. As a result of the greater competition, Russian gas exporter Gazprom had had to move to a flexible pricing strategy and is now focused on maintaining a set share of 33 percent of the European market, even if it means lowering prices.

It might have been imagined that this lessening of Russian monopoly power in European energy markets could facilitate room for improved relations with Moscow. But the changed energy landscape has also contributed to other tendencies, including a more aggressive Russian international posture. Western oil and gas companies have less interest in expensive Russian Arctic resources that have served in the past as a carrot for U.S.-Russia geopolitical resets and created a ready group of commercial interests in getting relations with Russia back on a positive footing. Commercial interests in Germany are still pushing that country forward on the construction of a major new natural gas pipeline called Nordstream-2 which, if completed, will run from Russia to Germany, but generally speaking, there is no push from the commercial sector to get U.S. sanctions against oil and gas investment in Russia lifted. If anything, U.S. sanctions toward companies participating in the Nordstream-2 project slowed the project down.

All this has not moderated Russia's approach to Europe. Instead, Moscow is resorting to military buildups and cyber infiltration into European targets, including information wars and hacked electoral systems. Russia has also made large military inroads into the Middle East via its intervention in Syria, where it now has permanent military bases. Moscow's military position in Syria has enhanced its leverage with Middle East OPEC member countries, who now often cooperate with Russia on oil prices and other matters.

The examples of Russia and Iran offer a more dismal prospect to the consequences of the loss of petro-power by key states via the advent of digital transformations of the energy world. A declining need for oil might lead to more, not less, geopolitical disorder. One possibility is that oil states that were previously powerful will not be willing to go quietly into the night as their oil power diminishes, but rather will assert themselves in different ways. In the case of Russia and Iran, to date, that assertiveness has included increased exercise of hard power through cyber and military means. Another outcome, perhaps even more troubling, would be if powerful oil producers felt the need to destroy the oil sectors of their rivals, in hopes of ensuring that their own oil assets are not the ones that get stranded.

CHANGING TIMES FOR SAUDI PETRO-POWER

All this raises the question of how Saudi Arabia, which is perhaps the most influential oil market player, will react to any lessening of the importance of oil in international discourse. For a country like Saudi Arabia, any loss in the global influence of oil is existential, because the kingdom has one hundred years' worth of oil reserves and a less developed nonpetroleum economic sector. The Saudis have got to be asking themselves, "If our oil no longer mattered, how would we remain geopolitically important?"

Ironically, Saudi Arabia has been able to demonstrate in recent years that its ability to flood the market with oil at the expense of other producers gives it arguably almost as much leverage and importance as when it threatened to cut off oil supply to the world back in the 1970s. That is because countries with higher-cost oil sectors, including the United States, have a goldilocks problem. While a large upward oil price shock might be in no one's economic interests, there is also a bevy of countries for which too low an oil price poses serious problems. Saudi Arabia proved that point in the spring of 2020 when it announced it would respond to the unwillingness of other producers to share equally the burden of throttling back oil production by increasing its own exports. As the prominent oil commentator Ali al-Shihabi wrote in March 2020, Saudi Arabia

> was incurring a substantial cost by maintaining spare capacity that this policy (of keeping oil prices stable) required while generating little in terms of tangible monetary and political return. Indeed, Saudi Arabia was taken for granted by everybody, consumers and producers alike. . . . In effect, everyone took advantage of the kingdom's production policy, which often resulted in less revenue for the kingdom when the price of oil dropped and in a loss of market share when it rose—a lose-lose situation.[13]

As oil prices started to crater and fears of an economic meltdown in multiple petrostates accelerated, all diplomatic roads led back to Riyadh to get it to change course. U.S. congressional leaders weighed in to magnify pressure from the U.S. White House. Russia blinked and agreed to large cuts of its own. U.S. companies announced production cutbacks linked to falling oil prices. A major agreement within OPEC was reached in April, but not before Saudi Arabia had made the point that its interests and its influence were not to be ignored.

Saudi Arabia's influential crown prince, Mohammed bin Salman, has recognized the long-term challenge facing oil and has been smartly pushing to reform the kingdom's economy to be less oil dependent. One idea the crown prince has begun to implement was to sell off a portion of its national oil company, Saudi

Aramco, to private investors and use the proceeds to diversify the Saudi econ-omy beyond oil.[14] In the prospectus for the Saudi Aramco initial public offering, the risk of peak oil demand is specifically mentioned.

Saudi Arabia's new strategy, labeled Vision 2030, can be seen as a direct off-shoot of a changed view about the long-term prospects for oil demand and uncer-tainties about future oil revenues. One element of Vision 2030 is to embrace advances in digital technologies to build a $500 billion city of the future—Neom—that will develop an economy in flying taxis, household robots, entertainment, hospitals, and manufacturing. The city is targeted to be a centerpiece of Saudi efforts to transform the Saudi economy into a diverse, innovative hub that will not rely oil. For now, Saudi Arabia can offer free land and free energy to get businesses to locate there.[15] Saudi Arabia is tapping its sovereign wealth fund as a major tool to accomplish the economic transformation. Not only will the effort diversify the kingdom's economy, but it is also raising Saudi Arabia's importance in financial markets and in the investment world—an effort that will help main-tain Riyadh's global stature. In a testament to the success of the Saudi reform efforts in highlighting Saudi Arabia's eminence, Saudi Arabia hosted the G20 Summit in 2020.

The Saudi state oil firm, Saudi Aramco, is also pushing forward on a diversifi-cation strategy that includes broadening investments globally in petrochemicals, as well as new investments in hydrogen and global natural gas, including a large stake in a U.S. liquified natural gas export terminal. The investments are aimed at improv-ing Saudi Aramco's market position by expanding the integration of its upstream crude oil production with downstream refining and petrochemical investments, as well as entering new hydrocarbon markets in an effort to diversify its revenue streams from heavy reliance on crude oil exports. Saudi Arabia is also turning to renewable energy, natural gas, and nuclear power to generate more electricity to free up crude oil that was previously used to meet local electricity demand.[16]

RUSSIA'S GEOPOLITICAL CALCULUS

The new geopolitical perspectives created by perceptions that oil might become increasingly abundant have also created conditions that have allowed Russia to achieve stronger ties with Saudi Arabia and China that were previously elusive. Common interests in stabilizing oil prices have drawn Russia and Saudi Arabia together in ways that have proved, at least temporarily, inconvenient for the United States. Not only does it mean the United States has to talk to Russia, not just Saudi Arabia and the other Arab Gulf states, about oil prices if they start to overheat or weaken significantly, but it also strengthens Russia's hand as the player filling the vacuum left by America's military disengagement in Iraq and Syria. Russia's greater involvement has changed the equation of the implicit oil-for-security trade-off that characterized U.S.-Saudi relations for decades and has left the entire region, including the problem of Iran's nuclear program, far more complex.

Russia's weakened energy position in Europe has also made it more flexible regarding cooperation with China, again to the disadvantage of the United States—both commercially, for its oil and gas exports, and geopolitically, by more closely aligning two U.S. rivals. Despite years of lingering mistrust, including fears that China would use investment in Russia's oil industry as an excuse to move people across its borders to lay claim to unpopulated territories, Moscow is now more willing to be a partner to Beijing in their shared goal of reorienting the Western-dominated world order. The two countries have paired on naval exercises in the Sea of Japan, the South China Sea, and the Baltic, but longer term, it remains unclear how Moscow will respond to a more expansionist China in the coming years. China, for its part, gains from any progress it can make in laying the groundwork for expanding Chinese influence in the Russian Far East, Central Asia, and the Arctic. Russia's control of the only warmwater Pacific port in its current territory at Vladivostok harkens back to the nineteenth century, when it compelled China to relinquish the region, a regrettable event still active in the Chinese imagination. Russia's less promising oil-related economic fortunes, combined with Western sanctions in the aftermath of its invasion of the Crimea, has forced the Kremlin to turn to China for financial and economic development assistance. For example, Chinese capital now constitutes 45 percent of total foreign investment in the Russian Far East capital city of Khabarovsk.[17]

After almost two decades of stalling, China has also agreed to take increasing amounts of oil and gas by pipeline from Russia, linking the two economies more strongly and reducing China's reliance on imported LNG, including LNG exports from the United States. Clinching China's willingness to commit to Russian supply is the sense that other diverse energy resources are increasingly available, limiting geopolitical risk and weakening Russia's economy, which gives China a stronger stance. The East Siberia–Pacific Ocean (ESPO) crude oil pipeline carried about 600,000 b/d of oil from Russia in early 2019, with the majority (500,000 b/d) going directly to China and the rest shipped by sea from Kozmino port at the end of the line to Japan, South Korea, Malaysia, Singapore, and New Zealand. Russian oil deliveries via the ESPO pipeline are currently paying off a $25 billion Chinese loan to the Russian pipeline firm Transneft and Russian state oil giant Rosneft. China also receives Russian oil via Kazakhstan. The state-run China National Petroleum Corporation (CNPC) has signed a thirty-year agreement for the purchase of natural gas whereby the Power of Siberia pipeline will bring five billion cubic meters (BCM) of Russian gas to China, with lower initial volumes starting by the end of 2020. Russian-Chinese gas trade via the pipeline is expected to increase to 38 BCM by 2025.

Despite growing energy linkages, there is some uneasiness still in Sino-Russian relations as China moves to compete as a supplier of renewable and nuclear energy in competition with Russian oil and gas. China envisions building as many as thirty nuclear plants and numerous wind farms in nine countries along its Belt and Road path by 2030, including in European markets that might otherwise have purchased Russian gas. China is also a major supplier of rooftop solar panels to Europe.

Not long ago, a tightening Chinese-Russian energy relationship might have alarmed other Northeast Asian neighbors like Japan and South Korea, which were also seeking access to Russian oil and gas and found themselves competing with China for supplies from the Middle East as well. But increasingly, digital innovation and the rise of U.S. shale has alleviated such anxieties and put aside the barrage of commentary about how geopolitical rivalries over oil among the United States, China, and Japan would lead to conflict.[18] If anything, the possibility that Saudi Arabia could play less of a role in global energy markets in the future is weakening the long-standing momentum within U.S. foreign policy circles to shore up the U.S. alliance with states in the Persian Gulf region.[19]

OIL'S LAST MAN STANDING

The distinct possibility that great powers like the United States and China will not engage in geopolitical conflict over oil has led to speculation that they will compete over some other resource, such as cobalt or lithium needed for electric car batteries.[20] The argument appears to have gained some credence from recent news reports about China or the United States stockpiling vital materials for defense-related weapons systems in case the trade war cut off access to a critical input. In the new technology economy, the argument goes, Brazil, Chile, Rwanda, Congo, and South Africa will be the crucial countries of the future, behooving the United States and China to court them as they did the oil states in the past.[21]

Still, the idea that wars might be sparked someday by a need for cobalt or gallium is highly speculative. It presupposes that the design of electronic and autonomous weapon systems and civilian products that use the same materials will not change or adapt, that mining companies will not be able to identify more resources as demand and prices increase, that recycling will remain too expensive, and that new nanotechnology materials with the same properties will not be developed in the lab. The experience to date with lithium tells a different story of adjustment and newly developed mines. The 2010 Chinese cutoff of Japan's access to Chinese rare earth metals, including permanent magnets, at first stimulated a jump in prices, but eventually investments were made in new production capacity in Australia, Malaysia, Africa, and elsewhere, and prices collapsed again in a pattern similar to other commodities. Moreover, it is not clear in the new economy if we will reach two billion cars, as predicted, or literally change the way people work, travel, and live in cities. As discussed in chapter 4, the whole model for personal car ownership might change, leaving plenty of metals for batteries used in other applications. It seems much more likely that governments will have to concern themselves with other strains and stresses that might be worsened with climate change, such as shrinking access to clean potable water and arable land for growing food. Already, the world has a hint of the manner in which refugees fleeing disasters could be a key source of future border tensions.

If, over time, as scarcity of oil resources become less of a concern among the great military powers and the importance of alliances with a defined orbit of petrostates declines, the question arises whether the impetus for conflicts among oil-resource-holding countries will worsen or improve. Saudi Arabia appears to have better relations with Russia but worsening relations with Iran, and the possibility of conflicts that would result in destruction of oil and gas infrastructure does not at present seem significantly lower.[22] Some rents from oil will still be possible for years to come, and countries might benefit from the destruction of another producer's oil reserves, reducing the chances that their own available oil would get stranded. One can imagine that Russia would be a big winner if a war between Saudi Arabia and Iran destroyed those countries' ability to export oil, not only temporarily but in a manner that left their reserves inaccessible for a long period of time, just as all oil producers are benefiting from the current massive destruction of Venezuela's oil industry via state neglect, corruption, and internal conflicts. To the extent that Venezuela's industry never recovers, that would reduce the amount of oil under the ground in Saudi Arabia and Russia that might become obsolete and unmonetizable.

In fact, it is likely to be U.S. oil and gas resources that render Russian remaining reserves less valuable, creating a source of tension that could make it harder for the two countries to restore relations to a better footing. In past resets of the U.S.-Russian relationship, access to American know-how and investment in the Russian oil industry has been a major carrot providing incentive and momentum to both sides: the United States needed the oil, and Russia needed to sell it. Now, both the United States and Russia are sellers and to the same markets, which, if demand starts to peak, could intensify competition between them for remaining customers. In this scenario, given an already checkered history of tense bilateral interactions, the chances of rapprochement could be even slimmer now than in the past, unless some multinational system could be put in place to manage how oil producers share the shrinking pie.

Eventually, the lowest-cost oil producers may find that they have an advantage over their more expensive resource compatriots in defending their hydrocarbon assets against energy-saving technologies. The future of Canada's high-cost oil sands reserves seems bleak, while Saudi officials say privately that they are less worried about their reserves getting stranded. Their cost of production is so low, just a few dollars a barrel, that it is clear to them they will be the last one standing when it comes to any shrinkage in demand. That might be true—except their reserve base is so prolific, sometimes estimated at a hundred years of oil left under the ground.

A GLOBAL SYSTEM FOR WINDING DOWN OIL PRODUCTION?

The question whether the shut-in of excess oil will be based on economics of efficiency (e.g., the world will choose the cheapest possible source such as Saudi Arabia as demand retreats) is by no means definitively settled. To date, the fairness of whose oil might or might not be abandoned has not been a topic in global climate negotiations—but it could be. Not all climate change specialists agree with a market-oriented, laissez-faire approach to the question. "The Lofoten Declaration for a Managed Decline of Fossil Fuel Production," signed by six hundred climate science and environmental organizations from seventy-six countries, states that wealthy industrialized nations like Norway should lead in ending fossil fuel production first because they have already benefited the most from burning fossil fuels and are in the best position to diversity away from oil revenue. "This task [to manage the decline in fossil fuel production] should be first addressed by countries, regions, and corporate actors who are best positioned in terms of wealth and capacity to undergo an ambitious transition away from fossil fuel production," the declaration explains. "In particular, leadership must come from countries that are high income, have benefitted from fossil fuel extraction, and that are historically responsible for significant emissions."[23] Oxfam suggested in one report that countries that have a lower standard of living and have the lowest ability to meet their developmental needs without producing their oil should be given priority in the winding down of oil use.[24]

It might seem unrealistic to take such metrics into account, but the reality is there are still poor countries emerging as oil-producing nations today, such as Guyana, Suriname, Mauritania, and Mozambique, all of which have announced major oil and gas finds in the past few years. The revenue from producing this oil and gas could be economically transformative for the populations of these states, yet they will have to worry whether market demand for their potential output will be sustained. That reality is going to be juxtaposed with the political aspirations of progressive climate activists and politicians in the industrialized West to shut down oil production in their home nations. So far, the topic has not been raised in climate negotiations, but as the need to reduce emissions grows, these new oil states are bound to try to argue that their output should be favored over that of other long-standing producers.

Climate activists have suggested that Norway would be one logical country to set itself as an example because it has produced 50 percent of its oil and gas reserves and has a higher percentage of electric vehicles than any other nation. But so far, traditional Norwegian politicians have resisted calls from local civic action groups that Norway be the first nation to voluntarily strand its remaining oil and gas resources.[25] Another would be the United States, where the progressive left wing of the Democratic Party is advocating that the practice of fracking be banned and U.S. drilling on all federal land stopped. Canada's oil sands reserves are already de facto being targeted for shut-in because of their high cost and carbon intensity, which are leading investors and banks to withdraw from continuing to finance the sector.

In light of the international cooperation that came about under U.S. leadership to curtail oil production in 2020 amid the COVID-19 pandemic lockdowns, the possibility that countries could agree to a global system for sharing the remaining budget for oil and gas exporting seems a bit less outlandish than it did before. As discussed in chapter 7, the stakes could be very high for a more chaotic approach that leaves each oil-producing country to fend for itself economically as the need for oil recedes. There is a precedent for financial transfers to lower-income nations from wealthier states to facilitate compliance with a global agreement to lower greenhouse gas emissions. Adding a global production-sharing agreement for oil might obviate some of the larger sovereign credit and geopolitical problems that could arise as oil demand recedes.

Absent a system to share the remaining market for oil as the world transitions to lower demand, oil producers can expect more pressure on their revenues as markets adjust, creating losers among oil producers whose assets are too costly to produce. The possibility that lofty oil prices will not be available in the future to underpin hefty government budgets and handouts could prove destabilizing to weak ruling institutions around the Middle East, prompting some governments to intensify repression. If Middle East governments are unable to deliver on expectations and promises to growing populations for continued economic development, political stability could evaporate. This is already happening in countries like Iraq, where major street protests have been sustained for months and citizens are complaining that corruption and malfeasances continue to leave the public without adequate basic public services. Leaders can no longer believably argue that oil prices are about to recover and usher in a new golden age.

Instead, Middle East populations are increasingly angered by the massive oil revenues that have already been squandered and pessimistic that future revenues from oil will be sustained. This is leading to unrest and instability across the region that could create a vicious cycle in which the domestic and foreign policies of countries in the region become more erratic, more independent of U.S. and Western strategic interests, and less considerate of Western values. In this case, active U.S. participation in the security of the region could become all the more challenging, raising new geopolitical risks that could be harder to resolve.

The new geopolitical realities that could arise as digital energy alters the mix of fuels powering the planet suggest that adjustments will be needed in U.S.

foreign policy. If the United States does not choose to lead in this endeavor, it runs the risk that its global influence and economic standing will diminish and its fate will be determined by other powerful international actors. The U.S. response must acknowledge the changing motivations among the world's largest oil producers and consider where its interests might align with those of China and where they will diverge. To do so means first understanding not only who the winners and losers might be in a shrinking global oil market but also how the greening of the global economy will influence new winners and losers in the future.

CHAPTER 9

Geopolitics of a Greening Economy

Geography was destiny in the geopolitical race for oil, with oil reserves distributed unevenly throughout the world and, with that disparity, geopolitical concerns about access and transport routes. In the new world of clean energy, chances are that ingenuity and industrial capability will play an outsize role, potentially giving a new set of players energy advantages they have previously not enjoyed. The geopolitics of clean energy may be more about technology, patents, and workforce than controlling access to raw materials.[1]

The ability to finance, deploy, and operate electricity infrastructure will also be key in the new clean energy world, with power transmission lines, electricity storage, and dispatch expertise potentially the geo-economic tools of the clean energy future. But capabilities to launch and manage smart electrical grids and 5G autonomous vehicle transportation networks will not just be a matter of which countries can divest from reliance on fossil fuels or win expanding export markets for desirable new technologies. It will also produce a geopolitical race for which countries can defend the integrity of those vital platforms from cyber intrusion and which countries would be best positioned to surreptitiously attack them. In the new geopolitics of clean energy, the powerful nations might be those best able to withstand cyber disruptions to their digital energy and transportation systems or, alternatively, those with the most credible ability to threaten to take down the systems of others.

THE HIGH GEOPOLITICAL STAKES OF DIGITAL ENERGY LEADERSHIP

The United States is finding it increasingly difficult to dominate the emerging geopolitics of green energy. American companies still lead in many of the core digital technologies that will determine the geopolitical winner in clean energy, but Chinese firms are rapidly advancing, with the full backing of the Chinese government. Beijing has committed to a massive industrial program to dominate the market for revolutionary digital energy technologies, especially those with dual-use military applications such as automation, artificial intelligence, and quantum computing. The U.S.-China trade war and then the shutdown of Wuhan province in China at the start of the COVID-19 pandemic laid bare the overreliance of U.S. firms on Chinese materials processing and manufacturing of component parts. Now the United States is scrambling to rectify its vulnerabilities, not the least of which was allowing American utilities to buy Chinese-built electric transformers and other vital equipment that might expose the U.S. electrical grid and future 5G telecommunications networks to diagnostic or other kinds of hidden electronics with malicious capabilities.

As the new wave of digital technology innovation, driven by the convergence of automation, artificial intelligence, quantum computing, and big-data analytics, remakes the world of green energy, it is a vital interest of the United States to maintain its leading role. Leading nations in digital energy will have both military and economic benefits. Superiority in green technologies will also convey geopolitical authority to establish international norms for cyber intrusion and environmental practice. The United States needs to reestablish its ability to lead by example, ensuring that the technologies that dictate the transition to a new digital energy economy promote privacy, individual freedom, and environmental protection. China's emergence as a leading provider of digital hardware and the dominant country with the majority of the world's processing plants for vital minerals and materials for the green revolution creates not only challenges to U.S. security but also the prospect of a world in which surveillance and censorship are normalized to the detriment of Western values and traditions.

Changes in the geostrategic energy landscape as a result of the rising visibility of clean energy technology has already manifested itself in multiple ways. Military threats to the Mideast oil supply, no less potent than in past decades, have failed to stir the same anxiety in the West. The 2020 renewal of the Russian natural gas contract with Ukraine similarly lacked the geopolitical excitement of past renewals. Equally salient now is the need for the United States and its allies to double down to ensure that malevolent actors such as Iran and Russia cannot successfully launch a cyberattack on electric grids, petrochemical complexes, and financial services. It could be argued there is an overstated sense that, given the availability of alternative energy, the security of oil supply chains no longer matters. The reality is that there are more than 1.2 billion oil-burning vehicles on the road globally, compared to just five million electric vehicles. Thus, the idea that the world economy no longer needs to worry about a cutoff of oil supplies is questionable. But the fact that large energy-consuming governments know what they could do if oil were less available is a big change from the 1970s, when there was heightened fear of a lasting economic dislocation.

On the flip side, even though electric cars still do not dominate the roadways, the plan to shift production to renewable energy and plug-in car batteries is creating a mania of sorts about access to the metals and processing facilities needed to produce related equipment. New reports, almost daily, chronicle the metals and rare earth minerals needed to support a low-carbon energy and transportation system. Indeed, the metals requirements for clean energy are substantial. The wind industry, for example, requires 450,000 tons per year of copper, and copper will also be needed for electric vehicle charging stations and car batteries.[2] Cobalt, nickel, and lithium are typically the key metals for car batteries. Political and corporate leaders alike are boning up on where lithium is mined and whether there is a limitation on the production of cobalt. All this has raised the question whether, in the new digital energy age, metals could become the "new" oil.

In a sign of the times, prominent oil wars commentator Michael Klare has recently shifted his attention away from oil to the metals that might be used for clean energy. In his book *The Race for What's Left*, Klare added two chapters on mining's last frontiers, such as cobalt and copper, and the intensifying hunt for rare earth metals and other critical minerals needed to fulfil the electric car supply chain.[3] The number of academic studies analyzing secure access to minerals and rare earth metals is on the rise. Harvard University's 2017 study on the geopolitics of renewable energy, for example, offered the suggestion that cartels could develop around critical materials such as rare earth minerals, lithium, cobalt, and indium and could "exert influence" over parties needing those materials to manufacture elements of the renewable energy system such as batteries, solar panels, and magnets for certain kind of wind technologies.[4]

But the thesis that a geographical limitation to the sources for these inputs will be like the history of cartelization in oil is an imperfect analogy. As demand for the minerals rises, more mines will be developed, and the fact that rare earth minerals are generally geologically abundant will matter more.[5] The environmental engineering professors Andre Manberger and Bengt Johansson analyzed fourteen metals and metalloids critical to electric motors, batteries, and solar tech and found that new mineral revenues could flow to countries not previously associated with the fossil fuel economy, notably Congo, Chile, Cuba, Madagascar, and Zambia.[6] But their analysis also suggested that that not only would recycling and the development of additional mines accelerate in the coming decades if producers try to use market power to increase prices, but that price impacts would likely be short-lived as substitution and alternative supply sources are identified.[7] For example, China's Contemporary Amperex Technology Co. Ltd. (CATL) has been investigating a lithium iron phosphate battery (LFP) system that would bypass the need for the nickel-cobalt aluminum or nickel-manganese-cobalt oxide materials that are typically used as part of the cathode component vital to the electrochemical control process of the charging and discharging of electricity in the battery.[8] In early 2020, American carmaker Tesla was in talks with CATL about using its LFP technology. Also in 2020, General Motors unveiled its own new four-hundred-mile-range soft-stack Ultium battery that will reduce cobalt as an input by 70 percent compared to standard EV batteries.[9]

We have already seen evidence that rare earth metals might be harder to use as geopolitical leverage than oil in the wake of China's rare earth metals dispute with Japan in 2010. That conflict began when Japan detained the captain of a Chinese fishing boat that had collided with two Japanese coast guard vessels inside territorial waters controlled by Japan but claimed by both nations.[10] China reportedly responded to the incident by halting shipments of rare earth minerals to Japan. After a short diplomatic standoff, Japan released the Chinese seaman, but the controversy over rare earth mineral exports from China continued. In 2010, around the same timing as the diplomatic flap with Japan, China imposed quotas limiting its exports of certain rare earth metals, pushing prices up. China's heavy-handed approach stimulated new investments and stockpiling that reduced China's grip on the market and spurred actions by other countries.[11] Japan found major deposits of strategic metals on the seafloor near Minami Tori-shima Island in the Pacific Ocean that could become commercial if shortages were to persist. In 2018, the U.S. Mountain Pass mine, which can meet a significant share of U.S. needs, was reopened, and other mines are planned. The U.S. Department of Defense has banned its vendors from using Chinese-sourced magnets. The U.S. wind industry does not use permanent magnets in its wind turbines, reducing the need for rare earths neodymium, praseodymium, and dysprosium, all used in direct-drive wind turbines.[12]

The myth that China has somehow locked up the materials needed to make electric cars to the detriment of everyone else is not borne out by geography. Lithium, the main component right now for batteries, is mined on six continents. About half the world's reserves are in Chile, predominantly in the arid Atacama Plateau, while a second large reserve is in Cornwall, in the United Kingdom, suggesting there are several countries with developed economies and strong ties to the United States that could be in America's supply chain. There is also the potential for recycling to stretch supply, as well as advances in material science for batteries that might obviate the need for cobalt and other materials that might be more geographically concentrated. Lithium demand could also be tempered by a shift from EVs to fuel cell vehicles, which would use platinum rather than lithium as a major input.[13]

To date, however, much of the lithium-processing capacity is located in China. As the market for electric cars grows, it will take new investments to diversify supply chains for processing and manufacturing. The outbreak of coronavirus that shuttered Chinese processing plants for several weeks is a warning that relying too heavily on one source for processing capacity is problematic. New mines and supply chains for needed metals and minerals have been slow to develop, largely because of the high costs associated with environmental mitigation in the processing of raw materials. But now that the world has seen several examples of how access to Chinese facilities could be cut off—through a deliberate cutoff as during China's diplomatic dispute with Japan, through rising trade tensions such as the U.S.-China trade war, or accidentally by a pandemic—governments are now more likely than ever to intervene to diversify or even re-shore back home how their national industries source the materials for cleantech progress.

Europe, which has some of the world's most aggressive carbon regulatory ambitions, has already responded with a major initiative called the European Battery Alliance (EBA), which is aimed at reducing Europe's dependence on battery cell imports. Part of Europe's $1.1 trillion Green New Deal, which aims to achieve carbon neutrality in the European Union by 2050, the plan includes about $6 billion in investments, mostly from energy and automobile firms but also with public subsidies from the European Union (EU).[14] Cooperation will include ventures between Sweden, Finland, and Portugal on raw materials; between Belgium and Poland on chemicals; between Belgium and Germany on recycling; and major efforts in Germany, France, Italy, and the Czech Republic on battery cell production. Spain and Slovakia will also participate in efforts toward software development and the manufacture of machine tools and battery packs. The EBA has set a target of two hundred gigawatts per year of manufacturing capacity to be available in the EU by 2025.[15] The European Commission has approved more than $3 billion in aid for EBA projects to encourage greater investment in European battery manufacturing and reduce reliance on Chinese companies.[16] New lithium-mining operations are also being tried in Europe, including in Austria and southern Germany.

GLOBAL RELIANCE ON CHINESE SUPPLY CHAINS

Questions remain in the United States about the appropriate level of reliance on Chinese processing facilities that is acceptable for U.S. national security. Part of the debate is fundamentally influenced by one's view of China's long-range trajectory. Will China be a benign but formidable economic rival to the United States? Or will it be a hostile power that must be contained by vigilant U.S. military superiority? The answer to that question is likely to color the geopolitics of energy in the decades to come.

Under the Trump administration, the United States started to crack down on intellectual property theft of vital technologies by Chinese firms and strengthened export controls. One highly visible case is that of the telecommunications equipment giant ZTE, which was briefly banned from buying U.S. processors and software after it was caught violating U.S. rules for reexport to Iran and North Korea. The company was forced to pay a $1 billion fine and retain a compliance team chosen by the United States as part of the deal to lift U.S. restrictions. Another telling example has been the lobbying by the United States instructing European and Asian allies to shun hardware equipment manufactured by China's premiere tech firm Huawei. Huawei holds about 15 percent of the smartphone market worldwide; it is uniquely positioned to dominate the 5G equipment market and provides much of the hardware used to support the internet in many countries around the world. The company's equipment is cheaper than that of Western rivals Nokia and Ericsson, partly because of its ties to and subsidies from the Chinese state. The Trump administration told allies it is concerned that the Chinese government would be able to pressure Huawei to grant access to its equipment to spy on or disrupt American communications systems. The rise of Huawei's marine division represents an additional threat. At present,

388 submerged cables sit under the ocean and transport data and voice between continents. Western telecommunications firms have built many of the undersea cables in today's system, but increasingly, Chinese firms are moving into the business. Huawei Marine built a subsea cable from Brazil to Cameroon.[17]

You might be asking yourself, "Doesn't software encrypt data that flows over Chinese hardware systems?" The answer to that would be yes, but that is where the "Do you think China will ever have hostile intentions?" question comes in. We have all heard of cases of credit card fraud or bank fraud, or maybe we have experienced the hassle of identity theft. Now imagine if you were driving in an autonomous vehicle and a hostile nation hacked the U.S. 5G system on purpose to cause death and destruction. You would have no way to override your Waymo robo-taxi. It could take you anywhere or stop dead, as in a Steven King novel. To try to imagine the chaos that could be created, one has only to read about the time a Google Maps error took a hundred Colorado drivers down a dirt road by mistake, only to leave them stuck in the mud.[18]

When Chinese president Xi Jinping took power, he immediately set upon establishing himself as the chair of a Communist Party central group on internet security and data. He established a new agency charged with controlling online content and bolstering cybersecurity. Among Xi's aims were to build an "impregnable" cyber defense system, give China a greater voice in internet governance, foster more world-class companies, and lead the globe in advanced technologies."[19] China has been trying to reduce its dependence on U.S. technology and, in doing so, raise its own game. China's military has developed its cyber capability in recent years and beefed up the country's cyber defense, while simultaneously promoting an alternative to the U.S. vision of a global, open internet. Through its Digital Belt and Road initiative, China offers authoritarians the hardware and methodology to champion a nationalized internet, controlled by the national government and able to censor content that enters the country from global sources.

In light of the embarrassing Edward Snowden affair, which exposed America's own eavesdropping, China's government has created regulations to oversee critical digital infrastructure, including the requirement that foreign companies store data relevant to their Chinese operations within China's borders and thereby its jurisdiction. The Digital Silk Road initiative gives China a platform to spread this sovereign model and raises the possibility of a globally divided internet and cloud system, resembling the Berlin Wall and the so-called Iron Curtain that curtailed trade between the West and Soviet satellite countries. One of the largest and most powerful Chinese firms, Alibaba, has not only bought its way into the Pakistani network but launched a "digital free trade zone" to promote trade between China and Malaysia and Thailand.[20] Alibaba also has a footprint in cities in Africa, Laos, Sri Lanka, and Turkey. The more countries that link their telecommunications, cloud, and Internet of Things via Chinese companies and equipment, the higher the risk to U.S. companies or entities trading with those countries that China could exploit a backdoor cyber channel. Certainly, China must feel the same way about U.S. firms.

In the latest round of the U.S.-China trade war, the Trump administration made a statement by showing it was willing to deny China vital access to U.S. microchips in its actions against ZTE. It has also made it difficult for Chinese telecommunications companies to do business in the United States. The Trump administration blocked China from buying U.S. semiconductor companies and banned the sale of Huawei and ZTE smartphones on U.S. military bases. It remains unclear how that geopolitical move, combined with the 2020 coronavirus crisis, will influence the trajectory of the U.S.-Chinese rivalry in cyberspace. China is trying to dominate in e-commerce and voice and face recognition software as well as be premiere in self-driving vehicles, 5G, and managing smart cities. The country's severe restrictions during the height of the coronavirus outbreak gave just a taste of what an overwhelming use of digital tracking of its citizens and their movements within cities could mean for personal liberty and freedom of movement. The United States has a stake in ensuring that there is a different, but defensible, system to harness the technologies to improve the quality of life and sustain civil society and free enterprise, without sacrificing democratic values. China would like to mobilize and export a statist system. China and the United States have yet to agree on a full set of norms of state behavior in the cyber domain, including ground rules that would codify and define proportionality and rights to cyber self-defense.

A NEW STYLE OF GEOPOLITICAL COERCION

All this new cyber gamesmanship has raised the immediate question whether a new kind of geopolitical coercion could form around the increasing cross-border linkages of national electricity grids and via the threat of a cyberattack on national electricity systems. In the age of clean energy, more energy use will shift to electrification, and trade in renewable energy often promotes electricity trading because system stability can benefit from cross-border balancing of supply and demand. Such is the case in Northern Europe's Nord Pool, in which electric power is exchanged on a market basis, allowing a greater concentration of variable renewable energy to be integrated into the interconnected power grid of nine countries. The system has allowed Denmark to sell excess wind power to neighboring countries, including Norway, and to buy more flexible surplus hydropower when the wind is not blowing. The U.S. state of Vermont and Canada have found similar synergies. Europe has also studied connecting its grid to North Africa and the Middle East, which have large potentials to supply utility-scale solar energy, while China is keen to set up linkages in Asia. India is already trading electricity with Bangladesh, while hydro plants in Laos balance the electricity grid in Thailand. But what if an interconnected nation decides to threaten a strategic denial of electricity services? Could curtailment of needed electricity be used to extract geopolitical concessions?

Over the past decades, we have adjusted to the risk of an oil supply disruption. In oil, we have learned how to cope, utilizing inventory, conservation, and lifestyle changes to adjust before the loss of supplies translates with a significant time lag into a corresponding shutdown of oil-fueled homes and cars. We have weeks to prepare before we get to ground zero, given long tanker transit times, large pipeline fill, large storage hubs, and strategic government stockpiles.

By contrast to oil, a cutoff of electricity by a neighboring country or cyber intrusion instantaneously leads to blackouts at the consumer level because of the differing physical properties of electricity (except in cases where battery storage might provide some relief). I have been there, in the world of no electricity, on many occasions—in the aftermath of hurricanes in Houston, in the face of faulty equipment in northern California, after an ice storm in New England. You learn to cope, eating food out of a can and using the water you hopefully stored in your bathtub once you realized a problem was coming. My Houston neighbors maintained one analog phone, which was handy if you wanted to call an airline to see if you could fly somewhere else until electricity was restored—that is, if you had sufficient gasoline to get to the airport, because gasoline pumps need electricity to dispense fuel. There was always the risk that law and order would break down, leading to the debate whether it was smarter to go stay with a friend in a high-rise with better security or whether that would increase the chances that someone would come and trash your house. In a word, an electricity cutoff is a bad thing. We often take electricity for granted because it seems so ubiquitous that we fail to recognize how many vital infrastructure systems require it. Communications systems, fuel systems, and health-care infrastructure all rely on electricity, so any shutdown of the grid can have cascading effects with dire consequences.

During the Cold War, the Soviet Union's link to electricity grids in Eastern and Central Europe reduced those countries' scope for independent action. To lessen the possibility of crippling electric power cutoffs by Russia, today's Estonia, Latvia, Lithuania, and Poland are transitioning to interconnections to the EU grid in the hope of diversifying away from Russia. The move comes in the wake of a 2015 event in which Russian hackers were able to cut off power to three Ukrainian electricity distribution firms.

The practicality of electricity coercion will be a function of control and design. In a system like Europe's, no single actor exercises control over the entire transmission network. Even in a complex system in which a number of North African and Middle Eastern countries could form a consortium to export solar power to Europe, an organized denial of service would be hard to implement. The expected renewable energy systems will come equipped with electricity storage systems and probably substantial capacity reserves, reducing the likelihood that a single electricity supplier could extort Europe with a threat of blackouts.[21]

Further influencing the future geopolitics of clean energy is the fact that electricity is unlikely to remain a unidirectional business, in which one country serves as the supplier and another as the buyer. In the digital age, prosumer electricity culture will be different, in that all countries might be both sellers and buyers simultaneously. Also, countries that import electricity will still have the option to develop their own rooftop solar and other localized renewables and storage technologies to promote more energy security. Additionally, remaining fossil fuel facilities will serve as backup for a long time. As the MIT economist Sergey Paltsev notes, aging traditional fossil fuel energy infrastructure and new installations of renewable energy could coexist for a long time into the future, reducing the leverage that either will have on consumers.[22] Moreover, the speed at which utility-scale solar can be constructed and its relatively lower upfront capital costs are a natural blocker to electricity coercion.

Still, countries are thinking about the strategic positioning of electrical infrastructure management. Serving as a hub can be economically and geopolitically advantageous, as recent vying for natural gas infrastructure routing between

Germany and Ukraine has already demonstrated. Power struggles could develop over who owns and has decision rights over transnational grids and their management.[23] But regional governance treaties and a neutral regional grid operator offer an attractive mechanism of choice to promote cross-border electricity trade. The Association of Southeast Asian Nations (ASEAN) countries, for example, are working together to create this kind of regulatory framework to undergird a cross-border power grid in Southeast Asia. Europe's Nord Pool is owned by Euronext, the pan-European stock exchange, and the continental Nordic and Baltic countries transmission system operators. China's proposed Global Energy Interconnection Development and Cooperation Organization (GEIDCO), which is backed by its State Grid Corporation and promoting a global grid concept, has yet to gain traction.

The bottom line is that the geopolitics of green energy can be a friendlier place if regional bodies oversee transmission and policy and greater interdependence promotes peaceful relations and greater shared interests. The problem is that, to date, existing geopolitical pathologies linked to concerns about cyberattacks appear to dominate considerations about the integrity and security of both national and transnational electricity networks. To obviate the problem will require strong regional and multinational institutions that regulate trade and enforce global rules and norms, requiring stronger diplomatic efforts and global governance.

U.S. LEADERSHIP IN A GREENING GLOBAL ECONOMY

The "America First" trade and diplomatic orientation of the Trump administration has made it more difficult for the United States to play a major role in building multinational coalitions in clean energy and promoting an institutionalized process to defend norms of behavior in cyberspace. The consequence is increased insecurity in the digitalized lifestyle of average Americans. While the containment of malevolent tendencies, from Beijing to Tehran, has to be part of any U.S. policy toward digital energy tech, an isolationist U.S. posture vis-à-vis America's traditional alliance system raises the risk that the more benign and positive characteristics of global clean energy trade cannot emerge as the dominant trend. Without U.S. global leadership, it will be difficult for new technologies' geopolitical potential to be realized to produce a better world than the one in which conflicts over oil have thwarted peaceful relations among nations. If the United States is not successful in reestablishing its leadership in global cleantech trade and does not take an active role in promoting the accompanying global institutions, it will be to the detriment of U.S. companies, products, and America's long-range international stature.

As China stakes out its position in the green energy market, U.S. policy makers face a formidable task. U.S. clean energy and technology companies currently have a global edge, but without a supportive policy atmosphere to foster markets at home and abroad, the United States could inadvertently cede its premiere economic role and add new risks to its national security. The Trump administration set the United States back by withdrawing from active global engagement on climate change and zeroing in on traditional energy at the expense of promoting American green energy technologies. As more countries impose carbon taxes or pricing, U.S. exports of fossil energy could be penalized and the market for U.S. oil and gas could shrink.

The United States needs a major reset. Computer-assisted, automated energy innovation is a compelling national interest. Not only will the digital energy revolution create new markets, industries, and companies, but it will also dictate which nations have the most cost-effective supply chains and manufacturing productivity. It will also decisively dictate military readiness and access to space. The United States needs to lead in this area rather than cede the effort to other governments that are willing to commit public funds and regulatory environments to ensure that their national digital champions remain globally competitive.

Conclusion

Recommendations for the United States

In my lifetime, the structure of the international world order has undergone major changes. The Cold War was characterized by spheres of influence between two superpowers, the United States and the Soviet Union. After the fall of the Soviet Union, American foreign policy experts had difficulty deconstructing this way of thinking, but eventually they settled on extolling the virtues of the liberal democratic order. This liberal order involves multinational institutions designed to promote economic, political, diplomatic, and strategic architectures that encourage trade, economic development, and a well-functioning international monetary system. The United Nations, the World Bank, the World Trade Organization, and the G20 were cornerstones of this structure for the U.S.-led multinational system. These institutions still function today, but U.S. leadership in them is waning.

In the two decades after the Cold War ended, the presumption that societies around the world would increasingly liberalize was a driving premise of U.S. foreign policy. The calamitous U.S. war in Iraq, it was hoped, would bring some form of representative democracy to the Middle East. A decade after the start of the Arab Spring protests, a darker reality of repression and conflict is unfolding. Years of U.S. economic engagement with China has similarly not led to liberal political transformation of the Chinese Communist Party system. Trade has increased, but if anything, China has consolidated back to a centralized authoritarian structure reminiscent of bleaker times.

It is against this geopolitical backdrop that future U.S. foreign policy must now pivot away from old tenets. Rapid technological change means the tools of war are changing, and with those changes come different strategies about how to sustain access to the energy that is needed to drive a complex economy and power a modern military. The United States is just waking up to the reality that digital advancements mean it can produce a lot more oil and gas domestically. But America's leaders must also look to the future of energy transformations to make sure the United States is positioned to respond to other kinds of technological changes that are coming in the energy world. The United States has to consider how climate change might alter the kinds of energy resources and the production and distribution infrastructure that will be most desirable in the coming decades. The United States needs to be positioned for the reality that automation is intensifying the competition for fewer jobs that will be left to share in global manufacturing and services. The United States will need different, more advanced tools to protect its energy infrastructure from extreme weather and cyberattack. This requires not just asking questions, but asking the right questions. Narratives that the cheapest, best-performing technologies will win without government intervention are patently false; in fact, government intervention often prevents moving to the cheapest, best-performing technologies. Incumbent technologies are often protected in numerous ways, including masked government subsidies, the failure of retail consumer prices to account directly for externalized environmental costs, and the benefit of depreciated infrastructure and long-term sales contracts.

NEW GLOBAL REALITIES

The United States needs to adjust to new global realities. First, to maintain its global influence and power, the United States has to embrace the digital revolution in energy technologies, even if it has the potential to lessen demand for American oil and gas. The genie is already out of the bottle on these technologies. There is no benefit to allowing traditional energy incumbents to push the United States to go backward to save jobs. This is a formula to transfer those jobs to other countries that will be glad to fund or overtake U.S. intellectual property and move promising technologies forward, first in their own countries and later in the form of export products. These products will then go back to the United States as imported goods for American use made by workers in other countries.

Second, the U.S. embrace of the digital energy revolution must be done in a manner that preserves and promotes the best possible future for sustainability and the protection of individual rights. The United States needs to lead not only technologically, but also in the best practices for deployment. It is important that the United States be a leader in creating the guardrails to the integration of automation and data analytics into energy and transportation infrastructure.

To get the full benefit of energy innovation, the United States will need to make many policy choices on how best to regulate emerging digital energy technologies such as on-demand travel services, self-driving vehicles, electricity storage, and the Internet of Things. First and foremost, U.S. policy toward artificial intelligence, automated vehicles and drones, e-commerce, and smart, computer-assisted household electric and appliance systems must consider the potential of these technologies to reduce carbon emissions in key sectors such as transportation, manufacturing, and electricity.

A variety of emerging digital energy technologies now offer a unique opportunity to transition and modernize existing energy and transportation infrastructure in a manner that promotes sustainability and locks in cleaner, more efficient energy and transport systems for decades to come. At the dawn of the twentieth century, different policy considerations, focused mainly on national defense and economic growth, led to choices that created infrastructure path dependencies that eventually led to urban congestion, air pollution, and global warming. Digital energy could be used to reverse these trends, or they could exacerbate them. The public policy context in which new technologies become widely deployed will be highly material to the promotion of their environmental sustainability. It should not be assumed that the technologies are inherently carbon-saving; they can be carbon-saving if guideposts to make them so accompany deployment. The United States needs to lead by example in regulating the use of automation, e-commerce, and digital electricity applications to ensure that their widespread adoption promotes a reduction in pollutants, including carbon emissions.

To the extent that the United States and other countries are able to benefit from the advent of energy-saving devices, the Internet of Things, and advanced logistics to reduce oil use, geopolitical fallout will have to be considered. The energy-saving potential of digital energy is already clouding the economic and geopolitical future of many petrostates, with deleterious effects on regional and global peace and stability. It is not enough for the United States to look at this situation as an excuse to disengage. The United States needs to prepare for this possible future and think about ways to create a softer landing for its allies and new responses to oil-rich adversaries.

Finally, the United States needs to reconsider how to approach China as a peer competitor. The old days of the Cold War were simpler in that regard. Russia had oil, and the United States did not. Therefore, the United States wanted oil prices to be lower and Russia to have a smaller share of the supplier universe. The logic of a Cold War with China is more complex. Not only are China's digital products intertwined with the environmental and economic development goals of many countries around the world, but Beijing, with its Belt and Road Initiative, is also well placed to promote trade into strategic infrastructure alliances. China has become the top trading partner for more than two-thirds of the world's nations.[1] It has a broad industrial plan to dominate emerging digital technologies in renewable energy, advanced vehicle and mobility network services, and additive manufacturing, and it has shown a willingness to do so by taking undue advantage of the openness to the U.S. education, investment, and export control systems. To build its globalist image, China's government has declared its intention to reach net zero emissions by 2060.

It is not enough simply to close the door to Chinese intellectual property theft or to impose restrictions on technologies that have dual strategic uses. The U.S. federal government has a positive role to play as well in fostering American technological achievement and incentivizing investment in critical industries. Energy innovation is a vital national interest. What is needed is a major effort to fund both basic science and public-private partnerships for clean energy, automation, digital networks, cybersecurity, and additive manufacturing.

To date, political leadership has been sorely lacking. The U.S. Congress has been tinkering at the edges, but a comprehensive national effort at innovation is needed. In her comprehensive analysis of the policies that can drive cleantech innovation and deployment, the former White House official and academic researcher Kelly Sims Gallagher concluded that access to affordable finance and policies that create demand for the deployment and use of cleantech are most important.[2] My experience in California was consistent with this finding. The state's low-carbon fuel standard, which mandates targets increasingly lowering the carbon intensity of fuel used in the state, incentivized investment in alternative fuels, including related innovative technologies. By sending a price signal that low-carbon innovation would be rewarded, California became a hub for the development and deployment of new low-carbon technologies. One study shows that the standard, which created a market in which sales of fuels that are below regulated levels generate credits, was nearly as efficient as a carbon tax when combined with a price ceiling, which is in effect in California.[3] But instead of just promoting market efficiency, the study found that the low-carbon fuel credits promoted more investment and sales of new, greener fuels and yielded a larger production response than a straight carbon tax.

LEADING BY EXAMPLE

Beyond fostering cleantech, the United States also needs to lead by example in regulating emerging technologies to ensure that they are utilized to promote national security and individual rights, not the opposite. It is the U.S. government's job to defend privacy, freedom of speech, and personal security of its citizens against the encroachment of foreign adversaries. The U.S. government of late has been lacking in fulfilling this role.

In 1957, Russia launched the world's first artificial satellite, *Sputnik*, into space to the shock of the American public, beginning one of the largest science competitions of modern times, the Space Race. Congress passed the 1958 National Defense Education Act, which authorized more than $1 billion in funding to "insure trained manpower of sufficient quality and quantity to meet the national defense of the United States."[4] The program, which spawned a new generation of American scientists and engineers now nearing retirement from public life, led to technological breakthroughs that have allowed the United States to dominate the global competition for economic and military achievement for several decades. For example, not many Americans give much thought to how the Global Positioning System (GPS) that guides their daily movements came to be. I am sure many people assume that a clever person at Apple made it up from scratch and turned it into an app. In fact, the GPS concept was first developed by U.S. scientists who were trying to come up with a way to track *Sputnik*'s orbit around the earth. Scientists noticed subtle changes in the frequency of the satellite's radio signal depending on whether it was closer to or farther away from their tracking equipment and developed a mapping technique to predict where the satellite was going. That same science allows GPS receivers on earth to calculate their own position by timing signals sent from satellites in space. Now we use the technology to avoid traffic jams.

Because every four-year-old with an iPad can offer a parent insights on where to turn to get to the toy store, I find it is hard to impress on my new generation of students the hypothetical of how problematic it would have been if Russia had developed GPS access and the United States had not. That is what would have happened if the United States had failed to rally to the national challenge of the race to the moon versus the Soviet Union because it was expensive and required publicly collected taxes to be paid to scientists. In today's divided America, spending money to beat a foreign country in technology development seems anachronistic. Many Americans believe that technology has commercial drivers, will happen anyway, and can be purchased from another country for a price. Intellectual property is notoriously hard to defend in today's porous global borders. Even instructions for making a nuclear weapon can be downloaded from the internet. Americans take for granted the U.S. superiority in weapons systems and everyday devices and just assume that the jobs, wealth, and security they provide for America's citizens will continue whether Americans pay tax dollars for science or not. Most Americans are not aware that the founders of the autonomous vehicle team at Google only developed autonomous vehicles in response to a U.S. Department of Defense contest or that the solar car competitions that students participate in could one day be important for America's defense via solar- and battery-powered equipment in space.

This time around, maintaining U.S. innovation culture will be just as important to maintaining America's power and influence globally as it has been in past eras of rapid technological change. The United States can decide not to lead on the technologies that will be needed to arrest climate change, but that means other countries will. The consequences of falling behind in energy science and engineering will have a negative ripple effect in other ways as well, if U.S. products and services fall out of step with global standards and specifications. China has already made headway in locking up important positions in global product standards setting organizations such as the International Organization for Standardization (ISO), which facilitates international trade by publishing technical standards for everything from food safety to environmental and technical performance of everyday appliances, and the International Telecommunications Union (ITU), a body comprised of 193 governments, 800 companies, and various academic and nongovernmental organizations, which allocates global radio spectrum and satellite orbits and recommends global technical standards for information and communications technologies. Dropping out of the Paris accord would have ended U.S. leadership in working groups that could determine how carbon border tariffs might work or future global consensus on environmentally oriented standards for vehicles and fuels. The United States' decision to reverse course and remain in the Paris accord is correct. As part of that process, the

United States should reengage its leadership in global technology R & D efforts to achieve cost breakthroughs in energy technologies such as carbon capture and storage and other clean energy solutions that do not have dual-use applications.

LEADERSHIP BEGINS WITH DOMESTIC ENERGY REGULATORY REFORM

But the United States cannot lead in international forums unless it is already leading at home. Domestically, the United States needs to adopt the kind of regulations and policies that promote energy's digital future while also protecting democratic governance and addressing climate change. Adjustments are needed in energy market design and regulatory policies that not only promote energy innovation but also protect against unintended negative consequences to the environment and privacy rights. China has looked to American and European models in constructing its own market economy, and this remains a strength for U.S. positive engagement with China and beyond.

Digital innovation has the potential to improve the resiliency of the electricity sector in the face of cyber intrusion and natural disasters, but it will require a major reform of the incentive structure for electric utilities and the regulations that shape electricity-pricing policies. Under the current system in most U.S. states, utilities use preferential pricing to large electricity users to reduce their usage through demand curtailments or interruptible load programs during sudden surges in demand, such as during heat waves or when supplies are disrupted by accident or severe weather. Such load management techniques can be expensive as well as inconvenient because the customer may be required to change usage at a moment's notice.

New policies are needed that allow utilities to participate in the cost savings and revenue gains from installing storage that can balance supply and demand on the grid and optimize system performance. Mini-grids that can permanently or temporarily delink from the grid can save money for both utilities and consumers by displacing the need for large-scale equipment to relieve location-specific congestion. These smaller, smart systems can avoid higher marginal costs during temporary peaks in electricity demand while at the same time promoting low-carbon energy at lower cost. Restructured rate-setting and revenue models for utilities need to be adjusted to allow electricity providers to earn returns from the locational value of batteries and distributed mini-grids. One model could be to allow utilities to serve as owners or integrators of a range of power suppliers—both distributed, small-scale generation and large, centralized power stations. Another possibility is that utilities could function as managers that offer and control automation and communications capabilities, using smart grids and managing electricity sales and purchases on behalf of producers, consumers, and prosumers (parties that both buy from the grid and sell their own renewable power and storage). Consideration should also be given to creating a more just system of residential electricity pricing as we green the grid, rather than leaving society's disadvantaged with undue burdens of the costs of maintaining the grid.

More programs are also needed to promote the installation of smart telemetry, smart metering, and blockchain for transactional accounting. To facilitate more flexible electricity markets, states should require utilities and other distributed energy provider companies to provide customers with their own detailed usage data, including net metering data, as well as to aggregate and share anonymized data for use by local government to enhance resource planning and community aggregation. State governments should also reform regulatory barriers that currently prevent digital platform companies from taking part in retail electricity markets by offering software and other data services.

Beyond electricity reform, federal and state authorities are just now beginning to consider restrictions on the use of automated vehicles. For the United States to lead on autonomous vehicles, it needs to have more than technical superiority. It also needs to lead in framing the rules of the road for the use of self-driving technology. Federal, state, and local government should cooperate in developing reporting standards for driverless vehicles and ride hailing to allow for access to information on safety, fuel use, level of occupancy, average fleet emissions, and role in traffic flow. Vehicle companies and autonomous fleet providers should be required to disclose to users what data are collected and how the privacy of that data is protected, as well as how the company will use the data. The privacy of travel data for individual customers should be protected by law through legal restrictions that ensure anonymity of data and its aggregation used in reporting standards. Autonomous vehicle regulation should also include emission standards for fleet businesses and other pricing mechanisms that promote conservation, such as road pricing or fuel fees. Bans on the use of traditional internal combustion engines for autonomous fleets should also be phased in over time to lower the greenhouse gas emissions of robo-trucks and taxis.

PROTECTING AND PROMOTING
AMERICAN INNOVATION CULTURE

The United States should expand the U.S. Department of Energy regional centers of innovation program to parts of the United States where jobs are needed and create new incubators that tap a broad range of funding partners, such as institutional investors, pension funds, insurance companies, foundations, private endowments and family offices, and mutual funds. Regions with underused factories and skilled workforces, such as in the Rust Belt, should be targeted for the establishment of new technology business clusters to produce smart inverters, electrolyzers, batteries, and self-driving vehicles. Government agencies such as the Department of Defense can serve as early adopters of technologies coming from the research collaboratives. As part of this effort, public and private industry funding should be tapped to stimulate retraining initiatives at research universities, trade schools, and community colleges to train workers for new fields. A new scholarship program should be established for American-born graduate students who agree to work for a set number of years at national labs upon graduation. Corporations should adopt reverse mentoring programs and cross-training between recruits and experienced workers to share knowledge to promote innovation and inclusion.

The United States government could also actively investigate adding new public-private energy R & D partnerships that are modeled after the original paradigm of Sematech (Semiconductor Manufacturing Technology), a successful consortium of fourteen American advanced semiconductor manufacturers, equipment and materials suppliers, universities, and government partners. Sematech was formed in 1987 in Austin, Texas, as a partnership between the U.S. government and the American semiconductor industry to restore the U.S. lead in semiconductors, reestablish supply chains and materials infrastructure, and reduce reliance on Japan, which had overtaken the U.S. industry.[5] Launched in combination with a trade agreement that reduced Japanese competition, Sematech received public funds from the U.S. military and created a road map to compress miniaturization cycles, lower costs, and reduce product defects. The Department of Defense contribution was made on national security grounds because foreign control of essential computing inputs was considered a threat to the U.S. military's preeminence. At the time that Sematech was formed, U.S.

companies' share of the global semiconductor materials market had sunk to 17 percent. U.S. companies' share of critical lithography equipment that transferred integrated circuit patterns onto semiconductors had fallen from 71 percent of the global market to less than a third by 1988. The Sematech venture helped bring the U.S. semiconductor industry back to a leading position globally and speeded innovation within the electronics and computing sector, enabling many of the technologies discussed in this book. The model continues on, including a new partnership in 2003 to promote commercial advancements in nanotechnology and chip fabrication. The model could apply to several kinds of energy initiatives that would maintain or restore U.S. technical leadership, such as advanced nuclear power, hydrogen-related technology, or battery materials.

In the international sphere, the United States must recognize that it cannot disengage from global problems without putting its own citizens at risk. That message is a hard one in today's political culture when domestic issues are front of mind for most voters. Still, if the shock waves of coronavirus, the U.S.-China trade war, and escalating violence in the Middle East showed anything, it is that the United States cannot easily cut itself off from global events and imagine that the impact will not reach U.S. shores. U.S. foreign policy will need to reflect the changes that the digital energy future is going to bring to the global stage. To do that, the United States needs to get prepared.

A GLOBAL PLAZA ACCORD FOR OIL

The long-run trajectory for oil could result in increased instability in major oil-producing nations. To counter this, the United States needs a multipronged approach. The United States should stay the course on policies designed to lower oil demand, even though it has its own domestic oil supply. Promoting alternative fuels, such as hydrogen, natural gas, renewable natural gas, and electricity in cars and trucks, and regulating new technologies like robo-taxis and ride-hailing services can free up U.S. oil for export to countries that are less able to transition away from oil quickly. This posture can garner geopolitical benefits while at least lowering the U.S. contribution to emissions.

But as demand for oil wanes in the decades to come, the economic and political prospects for many petrostates will worsen, potentially leading to heightened political instability and conflict. Those conditions could easily be accompanied by a global sovereign credit crisis, in which the already high debt levels of oil-exporting states become increasingly problematic. The United States and multilateral agencies such as the World Bank and the International Monetary Fund need to work with countries to prepare them to make reforms and adjustments in the hopes of producing a softer landing.

The United States can start with continued diplomatic efforts to assist regional institutions such as the Organization of American States (OAS) to resolve internal problems in oil-producing states such as Venezuela. In the Middle East, as countries begin to feel the pinch of lower oil revenues, the United States should redouble international efforts to slow the sale of arms to all parties in the region by all actors, including Russia and China, and to press regional allies to shift spending to development efforts. In the Middle East and beyond, Venezuela is a pressing example of why petrostates need to diversify their economies away from oil in line with technology opportunities that can help the region cope with rising temperatures and water and food scarcity.

As the trend line for a decline in oil use takes hold, there could be an opening for the United States to assert leadership in conversations about a Plaza Accord style agreement on oil in the context of ongoing global climate negotiations. The United Nations-backed Green Climate Fund, which is financing climate adaptation, clean energy, and energy efficiency projects in low-income economies to assist them in meeting climate agreement pledges, has amassed close to $10 billion for climate aid to the world's poorest nations. That fund reflects the recognition that industrial countries gained their wealth by producing emissions that have already accumulated in the atmosphere. But to date, there has been little consideration of how to balance climate and development goals for oil-dependent economies, particularly for new oil states like Guyana, Mauritania, and Suriname.

The United States got a taste of the oil problem when global demand suddenly collapsed in early 2020 amid the first months of the COVID-19 pandemic. The U.S. White House had to lend its authority to a process by which oil producers from many countries, but primarily Russia and Saudi Arabia, agreed to lower oil production to prevent a severe meltdown in sovereign credit markets for oil-producing states and other negative consequences from the dramatic collapse in oil prices.

The immediate success of the OPEC plus agreement, coordinated with the G20 countries, to reverse a potentially dire outcome for fragile oil-producing states in the early months of 2020 set a new precedent that could influence deliberations in a future round of climate negotiations. One question for international climate policy makers down the road could be how to modulate the impact of climate risk on the oil-producing nations whose economies are most overly dependent on oil revenues to meet national budgetary requirements. To date, deliberations regarding international compensation for countries leaving stranded oil assets unproduced have been considered unachievable on a practical and financial level. However, the G20 acknowledgment that a wide array of oil-producing states needed to restrict output to avoid a severe oversupply of oil in 2020 raises the possibility that some form of international intervention under the auspices of a climate agreement could be constructed to limit the amount of oil placed into global markets.

In the past, the United States has had a firm policy that oil supply be determined by competitive market conditions, but as the economic consequences of decarbonization begin to affect important oil-dependent economies in the developing world, the United States may need to reverse its historical opposition to multilateral dialogue regarding international oil policies. If the United States takes a stronger stance on mastering its own oil-saving technologies as a core economic interest, it will be in a better position to consider whether wealthier economies with a long-standing history of oil production and use should limit new oil development to make room for continued oil sales from poorer nations that have less economic maneuverability. One reason for a more flexible U.S. diplomatic stance would be the recent acknowledgment that the failure of fragile oil states can not only damage global sovereign credit markets but also add to the burden of required international peacekeeping and humanitarian services. It seems possible that the economic and geopolitical trade-offs represented by a smaller, more efficient U.S. oil industry, in a world where oil demand in the United States and globally is retreating, might be less costly to wider U.S. national interests in the future than the negative geopolitical consequences of a greatly oversupplied global oil situation.

A MORE NUANCED CHINA POLICY

The United States also needs a more nuanced policy toward China. There is no question that the United States needs to do better to safeguard its technological advances against China's intellectual property theft and to push back on aggressive Chinese state regulatory policies that try to force technology transfer by American firms to Chinese entities. But the United States should prioritize and focus those efforts on controlling technologies that are ranked and properly vetted as critical to U.S. national security or specifically contributing to China's abuse of human rights.

At the same time the United States is safeguarding its own strategic technologies, Washington should look for opportunities to collaborate with China on bilateral research initiatives that focus on technologies that do not have strategic applications but are important to common global interests, such as carbon capture and storage, direct air capture, clean water technologies, health, and technologies that make food supplies safer and more resilient. By doing so, the United States can hope to promote favorable terms of peaceful coexistence and prevent a situation in which China's leadership replaces economic priorities with a more nationalistic geopolitical focus to mobilize its population for its own preservation.

In the defense sphere, the United States and China need a stronger dialogue on rules of engagement and deterrence for space and for cyber to establish clear and transparent codes of conduct and signed autonomous weapons arms control agreements. It is pressing that the United States and China agree to this set of obligations for cyber behaviors that are permissible in normal times and what actions should be banned. Once this was established, the two powers could go forward to promote a multinational understanding of such norms. Most important is to identify agreed limits on disruptive acts in cyberspace, both in peacetime and in war, especially consequential attacks that would have an impact on civilians. The same applies to bioterrorism attacks, which are outside the scope of this book. It will be important to establish national obligations to prevent subnational groups from within one's own borders from carrying out cyberattacks on other countries. Such an international framework is advisable before the United States and China expand the digital realm to our city streets and connected, automated vehicles; to a smart, connected electricity grid; and to industrial devices that will manufacture the goods that people need.

All in all, however, the best way to deter a rising China from threatening U.S. interests is by simultaneously forging a more visible, concerted national effort in science and technology, especially where digital energy innovation is concerned, and demonstrating U.S. leadership in important global issues of common interest such as climate change, global health, and stability of the global economic institutions. Promoting a stronger United States is certain to produce a better outcome than trying to weaken China; the latter approach, based on recent history, is likely to fail. At the same time, the United States can exercise global leadership by example by demonstrating progressive standards for digital technology that place strict limits on emissions from automated vehicles and protect personal data involved in other kinds of digital applications to ensure privacy, human rights, and free speech.

Finally, to create and sustain a globally competitive United States, the country needs to engage a new generation of Americans to fill graduate programs in science and engineering and to utilize their education in public service. Expanding existing programs like the U.S. Department of Energy's Office of Science Graduate Student Research, which provides supplemental scholarships for U.S. graduate students to pursue part of their PhD dissertations at a U.S. national lab, is one way to support greater study on energy science and engineering. An expanded GI Bill for digital education would be another.

It will be impossible to achieve the level of cybersecurity needed to utilize the potential of autonomy, big data, and the Internet of Things if Americans are not willing to train and use their skills to protect the cyber domain of these products, not just in corporate ventures but in the rank and file of the U.S. government both at the federal and local level. The dichotomy between the tech world and the U.S. Department of Defense comes from failing to develop a shared understanding of when the United States should use force, of what kind, and to what ends. This will entail a fuller debate not only on the ramifications of preemptive action but also regarding government's role in protecting the privacy and freedoms of its citizens in a globalized digital domain. Only with confidence in the government's ability to keep our networks safe can we expand to the miraculous potential that digital energy might have in changing the world for the better.

When I began the research for this book, I had a wonderful opportunity to sit with the leadership team of a well-known philanthropy, funded by the success of a Silicon Valley billionaire, to talk about my endeavor to highlight the solutions the tech industry might bring to energy and climate change, but also to caution that the result was not a given. We were seven like-minded people of different generations, all of whom were dedicating their professional efforts to the subject of energy and climate change. Our excitement grew as they suggested I think about all the different kinds of projects one could do, beyond my book, to influence people to link their love for tech and their smart devices to the hard task of using less carbon-intensive energy in their daily lives. And then one member of the group hit upon a catchy slogan: What if we could construct an educational campaign titled "The End of Oil"? For sure, the group surmised, that approach could get a lot of attention.

I went home and thought about their idea. And then it hit me. It is hard to achieve something if you cannot picture the end state. What would a world that used no oil actually look like? Honestly, it is pretty hard to imagine, considering today's infrastructure and lifestyle. The innovations discussed in this book begin to show the outlines of what technologies could get us there: cities with public transport coordinated with non-oil robo-vehicles, distributed electricity grids that link to centralized networks to best tap renewables and new storage technologies, and intelligent logistics and 3D printing to shrink supply chain transportation distances. These are among the technologies that could organize a digital energy future around lower carbon emissions. But as the analysis and futuristic musing on the digital energy so well demonstrate, it is not an easy lift. When I try to think about completely eliminating plastics from daily life, the task of eliminating all oil becomes a bit more like science fiction than science and engineering.

A successful U.S. digital energy policy would be one that excites a new generation of Americans to study science not just to get a job but to be part of a national mission. To do that, the U.S. Congress would have to allocate sufficient public funding to early-stage science and development to convince students that it is worth studying to be in energy tech. The level of funding needed, in my modest opinion, would be easiest to achieve by putting a price on carbon and targeting some of the government's intake from issuing carbon credits (or from taxes, if it is a tax) toward fostering investable regional innovation ecosystems that pair government with industry, national labs, universities, and local colleges. A national effort must involve corporate champions, the way Europe's new battery alliance is doing, because ultimately the private sector is in the best position to deliver new technologies to market at scale. Any serious effort needs to have a road map for stakeholders and clear national priorities and targets, like those laid out during the Sematech experiment in the 1980s. It is important not to forget that the self-driving electric cars that might transform mobility services came originally from a Pentagon contest.

A national industrial policy around future tech must also be married with regulatory frameworks that align to explicit and clear societal goals. The lesson of the early 1900s is that national security concerns alone might not take us to the most desirable path. Long-range environmental and social impacts are equally important. Resilience to climatic events is another must-do in my book for what technologies to develop and how to deploy them, as is social inclusion. Ride sharing or distributed energy solutions that leave lower-income citizens with deteriorating services and rising day-to-day costs is an undesirable outcome. Society need not sacrifice its well-being on these other measurements in the name of national defense.

While goals for the regulation of the digital domain can and should be set through a democratic process, I, for one, would like to see personal data privacy and public interests better protected before we move ahead with digitizing even more aspects of daily life. Over the past decade, social media could have been better at promoting democracy if early regulations had bound its use in ways that protected the values that are beneficial to human well-being and human rights.

By creating an atmosphere in which digital innovation can thrive to serve human well-being, instead of using machines to take it away, the United States has a unique opportunity to serve the world as a counterexample to authoritarian nations that might rival U.S. capabilities in manpower, finance, and ambition but offer products and services with unpleasant strings attached. The United States must distinguish itself not only in its continued ingenuity, but in an ingenuity that solves global problems rather than driving them.

Notes

ACKNOWLEDGMENTS

1. Richard E. Smalley, "Future Global Energy Prosperity: The Terawatt Challenge," *Material Matters Bulletin* 30 (2005), https://cohesion.rice.edu/NaturalSciences/Smalley/emplibrary/120204%20MRS%20Boston.pdf.

INTRODUCTION

1. Daniel Yergin, *The Prize* (New York: Free Press, 2008).
2. Burkhard Bilger, "Auto Correct: Has the Self-Driving Car at Last Arrived?," *New Yorker*, November 17, 2013, https://www.newyorker.com/magazine/2013/11/25/auto-correct.
3. Bilger, "Auto Correct."
4. Yohei Matsuo, Daisuke Maruyama, and Tatsuya Goto, "Entire Japan Inc to Be Outspent by 5 US Tech Giants in R&D," *Nikkei Asian Review*, February 2, 2020, https://asia.nikkei.com/Spotlight/Datawatch/Entire-Japan-Inc-to-be-outspent-by-5-US-tech-giants-in-R-D.
5. Timothy Martin, "American Tech Firms Are Winning the R&D Spending Race with China," *Wall Street Journal*, October 30, 2018.

1. LESSONS FROM HISTORY: NOTHING IS INEVITABLE

1. John S. Watson, "The Energy Economy," speech delivered at the University of Chicago, October 13, 2010, https://www.chevron.com/stories/the-energy-economy.
2. Maurice E. Stucke and Ariel Ezrachi, "The Rise, Fall and Birth of the U.S. Antitrust Movement," *Harvard Business Review*, December 15, 2017, https://hbr.org/2017/12/the-rise-fall-and-rebirth-of-the-u-s-antitrust-movement. Nobel Prize–winning economist Kenneth Arrow is among those who argue that competition breeds innovation whereas monopolistic firms do not have financial incentive to innovate. Kenneth J. Arrow, "Economic Welfare and the Allocation of Resources for Invention," in *The Rate and Direction of Inventive Activity: Economic and Social Factors*, ed. Richard R. Nelson (Princeton, N.J.: Princeton University Press, 1962), 609–626. Other research, based on J. A. Schumpeter's classic *Capitalism, Socialism and Democracy* (New York: Harper & Row, 1942), argues that

market power gives big firms the profitability and confidence to engage in long-run R & D spending.

3. Richard Nelson and Nathan Rosenberg, eds., *National Innovation Systems: A Comparative Analysis* (Oxford: Oxford University Press, 1993).

4. "Fly Speculations," *New York Times*, July 10, 1898, https://timesmachine.nytimes.com /timesmachine/1898/07/10/102089270.pdf.

5. August W. Giebelhaus, "History of Oil Industry," in *Concise Encyclopedia of History of Energy*, ed. Cutler J. Cleveland (San Diego, Calif.: Elsevier Science, 2004).

6. Michael Brian Schiffer, *Taking Charge: The Electric Automobile in America* (Washington, D.C.: Smithsonian Institution Press, 1994).

7. Giebelhaus, "History of Oil Industry."

8. Jeff Guinn, *The Vagabonds* (New York: Simon and Schuster, 2019).

9. Michael S. Carolan, "Ethanol Versus Gasoline: The Contestation and Closure of a Socio-Technical System in the USA," *Social Studies in Science* 39, no. 3 (2009): 421–448.

10. Colin Schultz, "London Had All-Electric Taxis in 1897," *Smithsonian Magazine*, July 2, 2012, https://www.smithsonianmag.com/smart-news/london-had-all-electric-taxis-in-1897 -230098/.

11. Richard, "Arrival of Electric Taxis in NYC in July 1897," UPS Battery Center, July 23, 2018, https://www.upsbatterycenter.com/blog/arrival-of-electric-taxis-new-york-1897/.

12. Schiffer, *Taking Charge.*

13. Schiffer, *Taking Charge.*

14. Schiffer, *Taking Charge.*

15. Zachary Shahan, "Henry Ford's Wife Wouldn't Drive Ford Model T, Kept Her Electric Car," Clean Technica, April 11, 2014, https://cleantechnica.com/2014/04/11/henry-fords-wife -wouldnt-drive-model-t-kept-electric-car/.

16. Richard Rhodes, *Energy* (New York: Simon & Schuster, 2018), 210–211.

17. Simon Romero, "Wielding Rocks and Knives, Arizonans Attack Self-Driving Cars," *New York Times*, December 31, 2018.

18. Douglas Brinkley, *Wheels for the World* (New York: Penguin Books, 2003).

19. Brinkley, *Wheels for the World.*

20. Ashlee Vance, "Tesla Loses a Founder, and a Piece of Its Soul," *Bloomberg*, July 26, 2019.

21. Edwin Black, *Internal Combustion: How Corporations and Governments Addicted the World to Oil and Derailed the Alternatives* (New York: St. Martin's Griffin, 2007).

22. Black, *Internal Combustion.*

23. Brinkley, *Wheels for the World.*

24. Paul Israel, "Was Jobs an Edison for Our Time?," *CNN Digital*, October 7, 2011.

25. Black, *Internal Combustion.*

26. Black, *Internal Combustion.*

27. "Storage Battery Test," *New York Times*, March 8, 1913.

28. Schiffer, *Taking Charge.*

29. Carolan, "Ethanol Versus Gasoline."

30. Daniel Yergin, *The Prize* (New York: Free Press, 2008).

31. Yergin, *The Prize.*

32. Brinkley, *Wheels for the World.*

33.   "Ford, Henry," The National Aviation Hall of Fame, https://www.nationalaviation.org /our-enshrinees/ford-henry/.

34.   "Ford Model 1918 3-ton (M1918)," Military Factory, March 8, 2017, https://www.military factory.com/armor/detail.asp?armor_id=679.

35.   Garrett Fisk, "Henry Ford and the World Wars," Michigan Tech University, October 12, 2015, https://ss.sites.mtu.edu/mhugl/2015/10/12/henry-ford/.

36.   Brinkley, *Wheels for the World*, 212.

37.   Thomas E. Jeffrey, " 'Commodore' Edison Joins the Navy: Thomas Alva Edison and the Naval Consulting Board," *Journal of Military History* 80 (2016): 411–445.

38.   Jeffrey, " 'Commodore' Edison Joins the Navy."

39.   Jeffrey, " 'Commodore' Edison Joins the Navy"; "Hydrogen Leak Suspected," *New York Times*, January 16, 1916, http://edison.rutgers.edu/E-2%20Explosion.pdf.

40.   Jeffrey, " 'Commodore' Edison Joins the Navy."

41.   Jeffrey, " 'Commodore' Edison Joins the Navy."

42.   Brinkley, *Wheels for the World*.

43.   Hal Bernton, "The Godfather of Gasohol Is . . . Henry Ford!" *Washington Post*, August 5, 1979, https://www.washingtonpost.com/archive/opinions/1979/08/05/the-godfather-of -gasohol-ishenry-ford/ca98c17b-3112-4f80-b98a-7b06ed6a735b/?noredirect=on&utm_term =.16828d6994a9.

44.   Carolan, "Ethanol Versus Gasoline."

45.   Carolan, "Ethanol Versus Gasoline."

46.   Bernton, "The Godfather of Gasohol."

47.   Jonathan Kwitny, "The Great Transportation Conspiracy," *Harper's*, February 1981, http://www.brooklynrail.net/images/NationalCityLinesConspiracy/Harpers_Magazine _Feb_1981.pdf.

48.   United States v. National City Lines Inc. E. Al, 269 U.S. 337 (1948).

49.   Jonathan Rose, *The Well-Tempered City* (New York: Harper Wave Books, 2016), 105.

50.   Hiroko Tabuchi, "How the Koch Brothers Are Killing Public Transit Projects Around the Country," *New York Times*, June 19, 2018, https://www.nytimes.com/2018/06/19/climate /koch-brothers-public-transit.html.

2. REVOLUTIONIZING THE LINK: ENERGY AND ADVANCED ECONOMIC DEVELOPMENT

1.   Carol Graham and Soumya Chattopadhyay, "(Un?)Happiness and Gasoline Prices in the United States," Global Economy and Development, Brookings, September 2010.

2.   Vaclav Smil, *Energy and Civilization: A History* (Cambridge, Mass.: MIT Press, 2017).

3.   Simon Kuznets, *Economic Growth of Nations: Total Output and Production Structure* (Cambridge, Mass.: Belknap Press of Harvard University Press, 1971); Hollis B. Chenery and Moises Syrquin, *Patterns of Development, 1950–1970* (Oxford: Oxford University Press, 1975).

4.   Douglas F. Barnes and Willem M. Floor, "Rural Energy in Developing Countries: A Challenge for Economic Development," *Annual Review of Energy and the Environment* 21, no. 1 (1996): 497–530.

5.   Alex Epstein, *The Moral Case for Fossil Fuels* (New York: Portfolio, 2014).

6. Kenneth B. Medlock III and Ronald Soligo, "Economic Development and End-Use Energy Demand," *Energy Journal* 22, no. 2 (2001): 77–105.

7. Daniel Sperling and Deborah Gordon, *Two Billion Cars* (Oxford: Oxford University Press, 2009).

8. Kelly Sims Gallagher, *The Globalization of Clean Energy Technology: Lessons from China* (Cambridge, Mass.: MIT Press, 2017).

9. Lutz Kilian, "The Economic Effects of Energy Price Shocks," *Journal of Economic Literature* 46, no. 4 (2008): 871–909.

10. Erik Brynjolfsson and Andrew McAfee, *The Second Machine Age: Work, Progress, and Prosperity in a Time of Brilliant Technologies* (New York: Norton, 2014).

11. Andrew Hargadon, *Sustainable Innovation* (Stanford, Calif.: Stanford University Press, 2015).

12. Richard Lester, "America's Energy Innovation Problem (and How to Fix It)," Working Paper 09-007, Massachusetts Institute of Technology, November 2009, http://web.mit .edu/nse/lester/files/EIP_09-007.pdf.

13. Gregory C. Unruh, "Understanding Carbon Lock-In," *Energy Policy* 28 (2000): 817–830.

14. Alec Ross, *The Industries of the Future* (New York: Simon & Schuster Paperbacks, 2016).

15. Klaus Schwab, *The Fourth Industrial Revolution* (New York: Crown Business, 2016).

16. Richard Nelson and Nathan Rosenberg, eds., *National Innovation Systems: A Comparative Analysis* (Oxford: Oxford University Press, 1993).

17. Nelson and Rosenberg, *National Innovation Systems*.

18. Richard Rhodes, *Energy* (New York: Simon & Schuster, 2018).

19. Ashlee Vance, "Tesla Loses a Founder, and a Piece of Its Soul," *Bloomberg*, July 26, 2019.

20. Jean-Jacques Servan-Schreiber, *The American Challenge* (New York: Atheneum Press, 1968).

21. Constantine Samaras, William J. Nuttall, and Morgan Bazilian, "Energy and the Military: Convergence of Security, Economic, and Environmental Decision-Making," *Energy Strategy Reviews* 26 (2019).

22. David C. Mowery, "Military R & D and Innovation," in *Handbook of the Economics of Innovation*, ed. Bronwyn H. Hall and Nathan Rosenberg (Amsterdam: North-Holland, 2010), 1219–1256.

23. Robert D. Atkinson and Caleb Foote, "Is China Catching Up to the United States in Innovation," Information Technology and Innovation Foundation, April 8, 2019.

24. Dan Prud'homme and Max von Zedtwitz, "The Changing Face of Innovation in China," *MIT Sloan Management Review*, June 12, 2018.

25. Prud'homme and von Zedtwitz, "The Changing Face of Innovation in China."

26. Dan Murtaugh, "China Tries to Revive Economy with $205 Billion of Projects in 2020: Report," *Bloomberg News*, May 15, 2020.

27. Gabriel B. Collins and Andrew S. Erickson, "Economic Statecraft: Options for Reducing U.S. Overdependence on Chinese-Supplied Materials and Medications," Baker Institute Report, April 23, 2020, https://www.bakerinstitute.org/research/economic-statecraft -options-reducing-us-overdependence-chinese-supplied-materials-and-medications/.

28. Sarah Ladislaw, "The United States Needs an Energy Industrial Strategy, and Everyone Knows It," Center for Strategic and International Studies, May 5, 2020, https://www.csis .org/analysis/united-states-needs-energy-industrial-strategy-and-everybody-knows-its.

3. CHINA'S ENERGY STRATEGY

1. Laura Silver, Kat Devlin, and Christine Huang, "U.S. Views of China Turn Sharply Negative Amid Trade Tensions," Pew Research Center, August 2019, https://www.pewresearch.org/global/2019/08/13/u-s-views-of-china-turn-sharply-negative-amid-trade-tensions/.

2. Amy Myers Jaffe, "Green Giant," *Foreign Affairs* 97, no. 11 (2018): 83–93.

3. Michael Klare, *Resource Wars: The New Landscape of Global Conflict 2001* (New York: Henry Holt, 2001).

4. Jaffe, "Green Giant."

5. General Office of the State Council, "Twelfth Five-Year Plan" for Energy Development, The Central People's Government of the People's Republic of China, January 23, 2013, http://www.gov.cn/zwgk/2013-01/23/content_2318554.htm.

6. Richard Pérez-Peña, David D. Kirkpatrick, and Michael Crowley, "Trump Says Iran Appears Responsible for Saudi Attack but That He Wants to Avoid War," *New York Times*, September 16, 2019.

7. Declan Walsh and Ben Hubbard, "With U.S. Help No Longer Assured, Saudis Try a New Strategy: Talks," *New York Times*, December 26, 2019.

8. Global Commission on the Geopolitics of Energy Transformation, "A New World: Geopolitics of Energy Transformation," IRENA, January 2019, https://www.irena.org/publications/2019/Jan/A-New-World-The-Geopolitics-of-the-Energy-Transformation.

9. Darrell M. West and Qi Ye, "Integrating Digital Technologies and Energy Management in China," Brookings Institution Working Paper, April 5, 2017; Andrew Stocking and Terry Dinan, "China's Growth in Energy Demand," Congressional Budget Office, June 2015.

10. Elizabeth C. Economy, *The Third Revolution: Xi Jinping and the New Chinese State* (Oxford: Oxford University Press, 2018).

11. Will Mathis, "Clean Energy Investment Is Set to Hit $2.6 Trillion This Decade," *Bloomberg*, September 5, 2019.

12. "New SIPRI Data Reveals Scale of Chinese Arms Industry," SIPRI, January 27, 2020, https://www.sipri.org/media/press-release/2020/new-sipri-data-reveals-scale-chinese-arms-industry.

13. Kelly Sims Gallagher, "Foreign Technology in China's Automobile Industry: Implications for Energy, Economic Development, and Environment," China Environment Series, Woodrow Wilson International Center for Scholars, 2003.

14. Michael J. Dunne, "The Dark Horse: Will China Win the Electric, Automated, Shared Mobility Race?," in *Three Revolutions*, ed. Daniel Sperling (Washington, D.C.: Island Press, 2018).

15. Michael J. Dunne, "China's Electric Vehicle Leaders: Who Are They?" *Forbes*, March 30, 2018.

16. Rose Yu, "China Fines Five Auto Makers for Electric-Vehicle Subsidy Fraud," *Wall Street Journal*, September 8, 2016.

17. China Association of Automobile Manufacturers, "Economic Operation of the Automotive Industry in 2019," Industry Information Department of China Automobile Association, January 13, 2020, http://www.caam.org.cn/chn/1/cate_3/con_5228367.html.

18. Bradley Berman, "Beijing Shifts from EV Subsidies to Setting Quotas for Automakers," *electrek*, December 6, 2019, https://electrek.co/2019/12/06/beijing-shifts-from-ev-subsidies -to-setting-quotas-for-automakers/.

19. Liu Yuanyuan, "China Installed More Than 1000 EV Charging Stations per Day in 2019," Renewable Energy World, January 13, 2020, https://www.renewableenergyworld.com/2020/01/13 /china-installed-more-than-1000-ev-charging-stations-per-day-in-2019/#gref.

20. Kartikeya Singh, "Pathways for Developing a Natural Gas Vehicle Market," *CSIS*, March 2019.

21. Singh, "Pathways for Developing a Natural Gas Vehicle Market."

22. Brian Eckhouse, "The U.S. Has a Fleet of 300 Electric Buses. China Has 421,000," *Bloomberg News*, May 15, 2019.

23. Eckhouse, "The U.S. Has a Fleet of 300 Electric Buses. China Has 421,000."

24. Mark Clifford, "Chinese Government Subsidies Play a Major Part in Electric Car Maker BYD's Rise," *Forbes*, July 26, 2016.

25. Henry Sanderson, "Electric Cars: China Powers the Battery Supply Chain," *Financial Times*, May 22, 2019.

26. "Who Is Winning the Global Lithium Ion Battery Arms Race?," Benchmark Mineral Intelligence, January 26, 2019.

27. Bianji Hongyu, ed., "China Building Traction Battery Recycling System as NEV Develops Fast," *People's Daily Online*, February 28, 2019, http://en.people.cn/n3/2019/0228 /c90000-9550975.html.

28. Mario Pagliaro and Francesco Meneguzzo, "Lithium Battery Reuse and Recycling: A Circular Economy Insight," *Heliyon* 5 (2019).

29. Akihide Anzai, "China Scrambles to Tap EV Battery Recycling Opportunity," *Nikkei Asian Review*, April 4, 2019.

30. Winnie Zhu et al., "How China Overpowered the U.S. to Win the Battle for Rare Earths," *Bloomberg News*, June 10, 2019.

31. Simon Webb, Lisa Shumaker, and Jonathan Oatis, eds., "U.S. Dependence on China's Rare Earth: Trade War Vulnerability," *Reuters*, June 27, 2019.

32. Ernest Scheyder, "Texas Rare Earths Mine Developers to Build U.S. Refinery," *Reuters*, December 16, 2019.

33. Gregory Allen, "Understanding China's AI Strategy," Center for a New American Security, February 6, 2019.

34. Christopher Wray, "FBI Director Christopher Wray's Opening Remarks: China Initiative Conference," transcript by CSIS, February 6, 2020.

35. Lingna Yan, "China Issues Mid- and Long-Term Plan for the Automobile Industry," King and Spalding, May 1, 2017.

36. Bo Zhao, "Connected Cars in China: Technology, Data Protection and Regulatory Responses," in *Grundrechtsschutz im Smart Car*, ed. Alexander Roßnagel and Gerrit Hornung (Wiesbaden: Springer Vieweg, 2019).

37. Kyle Wiggers, "Baidu Secures Licenses to Test Self-Driving Cars in Beijing," Venture Beat, December 31, 2019.

38. Zhao, "Connected Cars in China."

39. James Kynge, Louise Lucas, and Sue-Lin Wong, "Huawei Looks to Self-Driving Cars in Bid to Broaden AI Focus," *Financial Times*, June 12, 2019.

40. Sarah Dai, "One of the World's Top Coders, Known as Godfather, Is Backing a Chinese Self-Driving Car Start-Up," *South China Morning Post*, February 7, 2018.

41. John VerWey, "Chinese Semiconductor Industrial Policy: Prospects for Future Success," United States International Trade Commission, *Journal of International Commerce and Economics*, August 2019.

42. Kensaku Ihara, "Taiwan Loses 3,000 Chip Engineers to 'Made in China 2025,'" *Nikkei Asian Review*, December 3, 2019.

43. Sheryl Tian and Tong Lee, "China Races Ahead of the U.S. in Battle for 5G Supremacy," *Bloomberg*, August 1, 2019.

44. Tian and Lee, "China Races Ahead of the U.S. in Battle for 5G Supremacy."

45. U.S.-China Economic and Security Review Commission, *2018 Report to Congress*, November 2018, 221.

46. U.S.-China Economic and Security Review Commission, *2018 Report to Congress*, 222.

47. Economy, *The Third Revolution*.

48. Gregory C. Allen, "Understanding China's AI Strategy," CNAS, February 6, 2019.

49. Rebecca Chao, "Why Do Chinese Billionaires Keep Ending Up in Prison?" *Atlantic*, January 29, 2013.

50. Daisuke Wakabayashi and Scott Shane, "Google Will Not Renew Pentagon Contract That Upset Employees," *New York Times*, June 1, 2018.

51. Dan Lamothe, "Pentagon Chief Overhauls Silicon Valley Office, Will Open Similar Unit in Boston," *Washington Post*, May 11, 2016.

52. Thomas L. Friedman, "Our One-Party Democracy," *New York Times*, September 8, 2009.

53. Economy, *The Third Revolution*

54. David Stanway, "China Cuts Smog but Health Damage Already Done: Study," *Reuters*, April 2018, https://www.reuters.com/article/us-china-pollution-health/china-cuts-smog-but-health-damage-already-done-study-idUSKBN1HO0C4.

55. Charlie Campbell, "China's Aging Population Is a Major Threat to Its Future," *Time*, February 7, 2019, https://time.com/5523805/china-aging-population-working-age/.

56. Nicole Hao, "China's Private Sector Pessimistic About 2020 Economic Outlook," *Epoch Times*, January 15, 2020.

57. Richard McGregor, "How the State Runs Business in China," *Guardian*, July 25, 2019.

58. McGregor, "How the State Runs Business in China."

59. Cindy Li and Sean Creehan, "The State Strikes Back: The Diminishing Role of China's Private Sector," Federal Reserve Bank of San Francisco, July 12, 2019.

60. "Xi's Wider Fight with U.S. Is Only Just Beginning After Trade Deal," *Bloomberg News*, January 17, 2020.

61. Kurt M. Campbell and Jake Sullivan, "Competition Without Catastrophe," *Foreign Affairs* 98, no. 5 (2019).

62. Campbell and Sullivan, "Competition Without Catastrophe."

63. Office of Director of National Intelligence, "National Intelligence Strategies of the United States of America," 2019.

64. John Hemmings, "Restructuring Order: The Geopolitical Risks in China's Digital Silk Road," *Asia Policy* 15, no. 1 (2020).

65. James Kynge et al., "How China Rules the Waves," *Financial Times*, January 12, 2017.

66. Center on Global Energy Policy and David Sandalow, *Belt and Road Initiative Green Development Conference Report*, Columbia University and Renmin University, November 2017.

67. Deborah Brautigam, "Misdiagnosing the Chinese Infrastructure Push," *American Interest*, April 4, 2019, https://www.the-american-interest.com/2019/04/04/misdiagnosing-the-chinese-infrastructure-push/.

68. Nicholas Casey and Clifford Krauss, "It Doesn't Matter If Ecuador Can Afford This Dam. China Still Gets Paid," *New York Times*, December 24, 2018.

69. Dylan Gerstel, "It's a (Debt) Trap! Managing China-IMF Cooperation Across the Belt and Road," *New Perspectives in Foreign Policy*, issue 16 (2018).

70. Michael Beckley, "The United States Should Fear a Faltering China," *Foreign Affairs*, October 28, 2019.

4. MEET THE JETSONS: REVOLUTIONARY
TRANSPORT VIA AUTOMATION AND DATA

1. Burkhard Bilger, "Autocorrect," *New Yorker*, November 18, 2013.

2. Bilger, "Autocorrect."

3. Bilger, "Autocorrect."

4. State of California Department of Motor Vehicles, *Autonomous Vehicle Disengagement Reports 2018*, 2018.

5. "Waymo Gets $8 Mln Grant to Help Expand Operations in Michigan," *Reuters*, January 22, 2019.

6. State of California Department of Motor Vehicles, *Autonomous Vehicle Disengagement Reports 2018*.

7. Mike Snider, "Waymo Will Give Shoppers Rides to Walmart with Its Self-Driving Cars," *USA Today*, July 25, 2018.

8. Peter Valdes-Dapena, "GM's New Electric Car Battery Tops Tesla's," CNN Business, March 5, 2020.

9. Susan Shaheen and Nelson D. Chan, "Ridesharing in North America: Past, Present, and Future," *Transport Reviews* 32 (2012): 93–112.

10. "Ford Invests in ARGO AI, a New Artificial Intelligence Company, in Drive for Autonomous Vehicle Leadership," Ford, February 10, 2017.

11. Lindsay Funicello-Paul, "Navigant Research Leaderboard: Smart City Suppliers," Navigant Research, November 6, 2017.

12. Samuel Schwartz and Karen Kelly, *No One at the Wheel: Driverless Cars and the Road of the Future* (New York: Public Affairs, 2018), 4.

13. Daniel Fagnant and Kara Kockelman, "The Travel and Environmental Implication of Shared Autonomous Vehicles Using Agent-Based Model Scenarios," *Transportation Research Part C* 40 (2014): 1–13.

14. David Schrank et al., "2015 Urban Mobility Scorecard," Texas A&M Transportation Institute, August 2015, https://static.tti.tamu.edu/tti.tamu.edu/documents/mobility-scorecard-2015.pdf.

15. International Energy Agency, "Digitization & Energy," November 2017, https://www.iea.org/reports/digitalisation-and-energy.

16. Ziru Li, Yili Hong, and Zhongju Zhang, "Do On-Demand Ride-Sharing Services Affect Traffic Congestion? Evidence from Uber Entry," SSRN, September 14, 2016, https://papers.ssrn.com/sol3/papers.cfm?abstract_id=2838043.

17. Steven B. Gehrke, Alison Felix, and Timothy Reardon, "Fare Choices: A Survey of Ride-Hailing Passengers in Metro Boston," Metropolitan Area Planning Council, February 2018.

18. Alan Jenn, "Emissions Benefits of Electric Vehicles in Uber and Lyft Services," National Center for Sustainable Transportation, August 1, 2019.

19. Frances Sprei, "Disrupting Mobility," *Energy Research & Social Science* 37 (2018): 238–242.

20. Peter Fox-Penner et al., "Long-Term U.S. Transportation Electricity Use Considering the Effects of Autonomous Vehicles: Estimates and Policy Observations," *Energy Policy* 122 (2018): 203–213.

21. Molly D'Agnostino, Paige Pellaton, and Rebecca Ruff, "California Readying Rules for Automated Vehicle Ride-Hailing," *Streetsblog California*, May 4, 2020, https://cal.streetsblog.org/2020/05/04/california-readying-rules-for-automated-vehicle-ride-hailing/.

22. California Air Resources Board, "SB 1014 Clean Miles Standard: 2018 Base-Year Emissions Inventory Report," December 2019.

23. California Air Resources Board, "SB 1014 Clean Miles Standard: 2018 Base-Year Emissions Inventory Report."

24. Ferry Grijpink et al., "The Road to 5G: The Inevitable Growth of Infrastructure Cost," McKinsey & Company, February 2018, https://www.mckinsey.com/industries/telecommunications/our-insights/the-road-to-5g-the-inevitable-growth-of-infrastructure-cost.

25. Bernard Marr, "The Brilliant Ways UPS Uses Artificial Intelligence, Machine Learning and Big Data," *Forbes*, June 15, 2018.

26. Zia Wadud, Don MacKenzie, and Paul Leiby, "Help or Hindrance? The Travel, Energy and Carbon Impacts of Highly Automated Vehicles," *Transportation Research Part A: Policy and Practice* 86 (2016): 1–18.

27. Dimitri Weideli, "Environmental Analysis of US Online Shopping," MIT Center for Transportation and Logistics, 2013.

28. Rosamond Hutt, "The World's Largest Bus System Is Starting to Go Electric," World Economic Forum, June 17, 2019.

29. Lisa Rayle et al., "App-Based, On-Demand Ride Services: Comparing Taxi and Ridesourcing Trips and User Characteristics in San Francisco," Working Paper, University of California Transportation Center, November 2014.

30. Gehrke, Felix, and Reardon, "Fare Choices."

31. Thomas Black, "Where's My Flying Car? The Lowdown on Personal Flight: Quick Take," *Bloomberg*, August 8, 2019.

32. "Amazon Unveils Futuristic Plan: Delivery by Drone," *60 Minutes Overtime*, CBS News, uploaded December 1, 2013, https://www.cbsnews.com/news/amazon-unveils-futuristic-plan-delivery-by-drone/.

33. Joshuah K. Stolarroff et al., "Energy Use and Life Cycle Greenhouse Gas Emissions of Drones for Commercial Package Delivery," *Nature Communications* 9, no. 409 (2018).

5. ALEXA: BEAM ME UP CLEAN ENERGY

1. Tomas Kellner, "Fired Up: GE Successfully Tested Its Advanced Turboprop Engine with 3D-Printed Parts," *GE Reports*, January 2, 2018, https://www.ge.com/reports/ge-fired-its-3d-printed-advanced-turboprop-engine/.

2. Avetik Chalabyan et al., "How 3-D Printing Will Transform the Metals Industry," McKinsey & Company, August 2017.

3. Leendert A. Verhoef et al., "The Effects of Additive Manufacturing on Global Energy Demand: An Assessment Using a Bottom-Up Approach," *Energy Policy* 112 (2018): 349–360.

4. Erin McCullough and Nedal T. Nassar, "Assessment of Critical Minerals: Updated Applications of an Early-Warning Screening Methodology," *Mineral Economics* 30, no. 3 (2017): 257–272.

5. California ISO, "Impacts of Renewable Energy on Grid Operations," https://www.caiso.com/Documents/CurtailmentFastFacts.pdf.

6. Nalin Kulatilaka Leonardo Santiago Pirooz Vakili, "Reallocating Risks and Returns to Scale Up Adoption of Distributed Energy Resources," *Energy Policy* 69 (2014): 566–574.

7. IRENA International Renewable Energy Agency, "Innovation Outlook: Smart Charging for Electric Vehicles," May 2019, https://www.irena.org/publications/2019/May/Innovation-Outlook-Smart-Charging.

8. Chris Bronk, "What 5G Means for Energy," *Energy Realpolitik* (blog), Council on Foreign Relations, May 31, 2019, https://www.cfr.org/blog/what-5g-means-energy.

9. Amy Myers Jaffe, "Feasibility of Renewable Natural Gas as a Large-Scale, Low Carbon Substitute," California Air Resource Board, no. 13-307 (2016).

10. Anthony Pettinari et al., "Rethinking Single-Use Plastics," Citi GPS: Global Perspectives & Solutions, August 2018.

11. Anna Hirtenstein, "Oil's Dream to Grow in Plastics Dims as Coke Turns to Plants," *Bloomberg*, January 3, 2018, https://www.bloomberg.com/news/articles/2018-01-02/oil-s-dream-to-expand-in-plastics-dims-as-coke-turns-to-plants.

6. THE ENERGY FUTURE AND THE POSSIBILITY OF PEAK OIL DEMAND

1. Lutz Kilian, "Not All Oil Price Shocks Are Alike: Disentangling Demand and Supply Shocks in the Crude Oil Market," *American Economic Review* 99, no. 3 (2009): 1053–1069.

2. Colin J. Campbell and Jean H. Laherrere, "The End of Cheap Oil," *Scientific American* 278 (1998): 78.

3. Kenneth Deffeyes, *Hubbert's Peak: The Impending World Oil Shortage* (Princeton, N.J.: Princeton University Press, 2001).

4. Matthew Simmons, *Twilight in the Desert* (Hoboken, N.J.: John Wiley and Sons, 2006). Simmons argued that even oil giant Saudi Arabia was reaching the limits of its oil production capability.

5. Matthew Martin and Javier Blas, "Aramco IPO Prospectus Flags Peak Oil Demand Risk in 20 Years," *Bloomberg*, November 10, 2019.

6. U.S. Energy Information Administration, "What Drives Crude Oil Prices: Demand OECD," https://www.eia.gov/finance/markets/crudeoil/demand-oecd.php.

7. Energy Intelligence Group, "Oil Market Intelligence," September 2018, http://www.energyintel.com/pages/about_omi.aspx.

8. "Daily Chart: Developing Economies Are Catching Up Ever More Slowly," *Economist*, June 4, 2016.

9. Jim Krane, *Energy Kingdoms: Oil and Political Survival in the Persian Gulf* (New York: Columbia University Press, 2019).

10. Global Agenda Council on the Future of Oil and Gas, "Future Oil Demand Scenarios," World Economic Forum, April 2016.

11. Equinor, "Energy Perspectives 2019: Delaying Climate Action Increases the Challenge," 2019, https://www.equinor.com/en/how-and-why/energy-perspectives.html.

12. Adam R. Brandt et al., "Peak Oil Demand: The Role of Fuel Efficiency and Alternative Fuels in a Global Oil Production Decline," *Environmental Science & Technology* 47 (2013): 8031–8041.

13. Brandt et al., "Peak Oil Demand."

14. Daniel Scheitrum, Amy Myers Jaffe, and Lew Fulton, "Changing Oil Market Fundamentals and Implications for OPEC Production Strategy," *IAEE Energy Forum: Bergen Special Issue* (2016).

15. Lewis Fulton, Pierpaolo Cazzola, and Francois Cuenot, "IEA Mobility Model (MoMo) and Its Use in the ETP 2008," *Energy Policy* 37, no. 10 (2009): 3758–3768.

16. Lee Schipper and Marie-Lilliu Celine, "Transportation and CO2 Emissions: Flexing the Link—A Path for the World Bank," Environmental Department Papers—Paper No. 69 (Paris: International Energy Agency, 1999).

17. Yilei Sun and Brenda Goh, "China Auto Sales Fall 14.6 Percent on Year in April, 10th Month of Decline," *Reuters*, May 12, 2019, https://www.reuters.com/article/us-china-autos-caam/china-auto-sales-fall-14-6-on-year-in-april-10th-month-of-decline-idUSKCN1SJ0FO.

18. Anurag Kotoky, "India Just Posted the Worst Car Sales Data in Eight Years," *Bloomberg Quint*, May 13, 2019.

19. Austin Brown, Jeffrey Gonder, and Brittany Repac, *An Analysis of Possible Energy Impacts of Automated Vehicles* (Basel: Springer International Publishing, 2014).

20. Susan Shaheen, "Shared Mobility: The Potential of Ride Hailing and Pooling," UC Berkeley Transportation Sustainability Research Center, March 1, 2018.

21. Scheitrum et al., "Changing Oil Market Fundamentals."

22. Daniel Spitzer, "ICE-Free Cities: Global Strategies for Creating Sustainable Urban Transport," *Natural Resources & Environment* 33 (2018): 8–11.

23. Christian Brand, "Beyond 'Dieselgate': Implications of Unaccounted and Future Air Pollutant Emissions and Energy Use for Cars in the United Kingdom," *Energy Policy* 97 (2016): 1–12.

24. Paul Hockenos, "End of the Road: Are Diesel Cars on the Way Out in Europe?," *Yale Environment 360*, April 12, 2018.

25. Athlyn Cathcart-Keays, "Will We Ever Get a Truly Car-Free City?," *Guardian*, December 9, 2015.

26. Anders Tønnesen et al., *Europeiske Byer Med Bilfrie Sentrum* (Oslo: Transportøkonomisk Institutt, 2016).

27.   Clifford Atiyeh, "Americans Are Keeping Their Cars Longer and Longer," *Car and Driver*, August 24, 2018.

28.   Calculations and projections are based on the ASIF methodology, which relates vehicle stock, activity, efficiency, and energy content to emissions rate and energy consumption. A generic form of the ASIF-based equations for passenger light duty vehicle (PLDV) projections is:

$$G = \Sigma_{m,f}\, P_{m,f}\, A_{m,f}\, C_{m,f}\, E_{m,f}$$

Where G is the total energy consumption, P is the vehicle stock, A is the level of activity per vehicle, C is the energy consumption rate per unit of service provided, and E is the energy density per unit of fuel, assessed across all modes (m) and fuels (f). Costs of substitution in modalities of travel and for electrification of vehicles were used in the analysis.

29.   International Energy Agency, *Energy Technology Perspectives 2017*, June 2017, https://doi .org/10.1787/energy_tech-2017-en.

30.   Atif Mian and Amir Sufi, "The Effects of Fiscal Stimulus: Evidence from the 2009 Cash for Clunkers Program," *Quarterly Journal of Economics* 127 (August 2012): 1107–1142.

31.   David Shepardson, "Senate Democrat Schumer Proposes Plan to Swap Gas Cars for Electric Vehicles," *Reuters*, October 24, 2019.

32.   Fred Dews, "Cash for Clunkers: More Costly, Less Effective," *Brookings*, November 7, 2013.

33.   OPEC Secretariat, "World Oil Outlook," 16th International Energy Forum Ministerial, April 2018.

34.   OPEC Secretariat, "World Oil Outlook."

35.   Harumi Ito and Darin Lee, "Comparing the Impact of the September 11th Terrorist Attacks on International Airline Demand," *International Journal of the Economics of Business* 12 (2005): 225–249.

36.   Occo Roelofsen et al., "Is Peak Oil Demand in Sight?," McKinsey & Company, June 24, 2016, https://www.mckinsey.com/industries/oil-and-gas/our-insights/is-peak-oil-demand-in -sight.

37.   Jan Stewart and Edward Westlake, "Houston Roundtable: The Cost of Oil's Changing Cycles Cornerstone," Council on Foreign Relations, May 7, 2019.

38.   Meghan L. O'Sullivan, *Windfall* (New York: Simon & Schuster, 2017).

39.   Daniel Yergin and Martin Hillenbrand, *Global Insecurity* (Boston: Houghton Mifflin, 1982).

40.   Kaz Miyagiwa and Yuka Ohno, "Oil and Strategic Development of Substitute Technology," James A. Baker III Institute for Public Policy, Rice University, May 2000.

41.   Martin Hoffert et al., "Advanced Technology Pathways to Global Climate Stability: Energy for a Greenhouse Planet," *Science* 298 (2002): 981–987.

42.   Malte Meinshausen et al., "Greenhouse-Gas Emission Targets for Limiting Global Warming to 2 Degrees C," *Nature* 458 (2009): 1158–1163.

43.   Paul A. Griffin and Amy Myers Jaffe, "Are Fossil Fuel Firms Informing Investors Well Enough About the Risks of Climate Change?," *Journal of Energy & Natural Resources Law* 36 (2018).

44.   Kevin Crowley, "Exxon Aims for $15-a-Barrel Costs in Giant Permian Operation," *Bloomberg*, March 14, 2019, https://www.bloomberg.com/news/articles/2019-03-14/exxon -aims-for-15-a-barrel-costs-in-giant-permian-operation.

45. Robert Barsky and Lutz Kilian, "Oil and the Macroeconomy Since the 1970s," *Journal of Economic Perspectives* 18, no. 4 (2004): 115–134.

46. Mahmoud El-Gamal and Amy Myers Jaffe, "The Coupled Cycles of Geopolitics and Oil Prices," *Economics of Energy and Environmental Policy* 7, no. 2 (2018).

47. Christophe McGlade and Paul Ekins, "The Geographical Distribution of Fossil Fuels Unused When Limiting Global Warming to 2 Degrees C," *Nature* 517 (2015): 187–190.

48. Scheitrum et al., "Changing Oil Market Fundamentals."

49. Amy Myers Jaffe, "Emerging-Market Petrostates Are About to Melt Down," *Foreign Affairs*, April 2, 2020. https://www.foreignaffairs.com/articles/2020-04-02/emerging-market-petrostates -are-about-melt-down.

7. ENERGY INVESTOR DYSTOPIA

1. Greta Thunberg, "'You Did Not Act in Time': Greta Thunberg's Full Speech to MPs," *Guardian*, April 2019, https://www.theguardian.com/environment/2019/apr/23/greta-thunberg -full-speech-to-mps-you-did-not-act-in-time.

2. Coral Davenport, "Climate Change Poses Major Risks to Financial Markets, Regulator Warns," *New York Times*, June 11, 2019.

3. Amy Myers Jaffe, "Emerging-Market Petrostates Are About to Melt Down," *Foreign Affairs*, April 2, 2020.

4. Amy Myers Jaffe, "Financial Herding Must Be Checked to Avert Climate Crashes," *Nature Energy* 5 (2020): 101–103.

5. Paul A. Griffin and Amy Myers Jaffe, "Are Fossil Fuel Firms Informing Investors Well Enough About the Risks of Climate Change?," *Journal of Energy & Natural Resources Law* 36 (2018).

6. Judge Alsup in *City of Oakland v. BP et al.* 3:17-cv-06011 ND Ca, Document 283, Filed 25 June 2018.

7. "How to Deal with Worries About Stranded Assets," *Economist*, November 24, 2016, https://www.economist.com/special-report/2016/11/24/how-to-deal-with-worries-about -stranded-assets.

8. Giles Parkinson, "Citigroup Predicts $100 Trillion in Stranded Assets If Paris Summit Succeeds," *CleanTechnica*, August 26, 2015.

9. Malte Meinshausen et al., "Greenhouse Gas Emission Targets for Limiting Global Warming to 2 Degrees C," *Nature* 458 (2009): 1158–1163.

10. Christophe McGlade and Paul Ekins, "The Geographical Distribution of Fossil Fuels Unused When Limiting Global Warming to 2 Degrees C," *Nature* 517 (2015): 187–190.

11. Nicholas Silver, "Blindness to Risk: Why Institutional Investors Ignore the Risk of Stranded Assets," *Journal of Sustainable Finance & Investment* 7 (2017): 99–113.

12. Atif Ansar, Ben Caldecott, and James Tilbury, "Stranded Assets and the Fossil Fuel Divestment Campaign: What Does Divestment Mean for the Valuation of Fossil Fuels?," Smith School of Enterprise and the Environment, October 2013.

13. Brad M. Barber, *Monitoring the Monitor: Evaluating CalPERS' activism*, University of California, Davis, November 2006, https://investedinterests.com/wp-content/uploads/2018/03 /Monitoring_the_Monitor_-_Evaluating_CalPERS_Activism_-_Barber1.pdf.

14. Nancy Meyer et al., "Deflating the 'Carbon Bubble,'" HIS Markit, May 26, 2015.

15.   Harry Dempsey, "Why U.S. Energy Investors Are Experiencing a Crisis of Faith," *Financial Times*, August 28, 2019.

16.   Leslie Hook, "Clean Power Stocks Outperform Fossil Fuel Peers During Pandemic," *Financial Times*, May 28, 2020.

17.   Silver, "Blindness to Risk"; Jan Bebbington et al., "Fossil Fuel Reserves and Resources Reporting and Unburnable Carbon: Investigating Conflicting Accounts," *Critical Perspectives on Accounting* 66 (2019).

18.   Richard R. Nelson, *National Innovation Systems* (New York and London: Oxford University Press, 1993).

19.   World Bank Group, "State and Trends of Carbon Pricing 2019," June 6, 2019.

20.   Paul A. Griffin, David H. Lont, and Yuan Sun, "The Relevance to Investors of Greenhouse Gas Emissions Disclosures," *Contemporary Accounting Research* 34 (2017): 1265–1297.

21.   CDP, "More Than Eight-Fold Leap Over Four Years in Global Companies Pricing Carbon Into Business Plans," October 12, 2017, https://www.cdp.net/en/articles/media/more-than-eight-fold-leap-over-four-years-in-global-companies-pricing-carbon-into-business-plans.

22.   Katie Fehrenbacher, "A Biofuel Dream Gone Bad," *Fortune*, December 4, 2015.

23.   Liqian Ma, "Risks and Opportunities from the Changing Climate," Cambridge Associates, December 2015, http://www.cambridgeassociates.com/our-insights/research/risks-and-opportunities-from-the-changing-climate-playbook-for-the-truly-long-term-investor/.

24.   William Nordhaus and James Tobin, "Is Growth Obsolete?," *National Bureau of Economic Research* 5 (1972), https://www.nber.org/chapters/c7620.pdf.

25.   William Nordhaus, "Revisiting the Social Cost of Carbon," *Proceedings of the National Academy of the Sciences of the United States of America* 114 (2017): 1518–1523.

26.   Nicholas Stern, "The Economics of Climate Change," *American Economic Review* 98 (2008): 1–37; Simon Dietz et al., "Reflections on the Stern Review (1): A Robust Case for Strong Action to Reduce the Risks of Climate Change," *World Economics* 8 (2007): 121–68; William Nordhaus, "Critical Assumptions in the Stern Review on Climate Change," *Science* 317 (2007): 201–202; Richard S. J. Tol, "Estimates of the Damage Costs of Climate Change: Part 1. Benchmark Estimates," *Environmental and Resource Economics* 21 (2002): 47–73.

27.   Kenneth Gillingham, Richard G. Newell, and William A. Pizer, "Modeling Endogenous Technological Change for Climate Policy Analysis," *Energy Economics* 30 (2008): 2734–2753.

28.   Richard Newell, Adam Jaffe, and Robert Stavins, "The Induced Innovation Hypothesis and Energy-Saving Technological Change," *Quarterly Journal of Economics* 114 (1999): 941–975. This article provides empirical evidence that higher energy prices are associated with faster improvements in energy efficiency.

29.   Johannes Bollen, Ton Manders, and Paul Veenendaal, "How Much Does a 30 Percent Emissions Reduction Cost?," CPB Netherlands Bureau for Economic Policy Analysis, September 2004, https://www.cpb.nl/sites/default/files/publicaties/download/how-much-does-30-emission-reduction-cost-macroeconomic-effects-post-kyoto-climate-policy.pdf.

30.   Ian Sue Wing, "Induced Technological Change in Computable General Equilibrium Models for Climate Change Policy Analysis" (PhD diss., Massachusetts Institute of Technology, 2004).

31. Interagency Working Group on Social Cost of Carbon, United States Government, "Technical Support Document: Social Cost of Carbon for Regulatory Impact Analysis—Under Executive Order 12866," February 2010, https://obamawhitehouse.archives.gov/sites/default/files/omb/inforeg/for-agencies/Social-Cost-of-Carbon-for-RIA.pdf.

32. *Zero Zone, Inc., et al. v. United States Department of Energy et al.*, United States Court of Appeals for the Seventh Circuit, http://media.ca7.uscourts.gov/cgi-bin/rssExec.pl?Submit=Display&Path=Y2016/D08-08/C:14-2159:J:Ripple:aut:T:fnOp:N:1807496:S:0.

33. Richard Price, Simeon Thornton, and Stephen Nelson, "The Social Cost of Carbon and the Shadow Price of Carbon: What They Are, and How to Use Them in Economic Appraisal in the UK," Munich Personal RePEc Archive, December 2007, https://mpra.ub.uni-muenchen.de/74976/1/MPRA_paper_74976.pdf.

34. Sharon Kelly, "How America's Clean Coal Dream Unravelled," *Guardian*, March 2, 2018.

35. James Conca, "Net Zero Natural Gas Plant—The Game Changer," *Forbes*, July 31, 2019.

36. Intergovernmental Panel on Climate Change, *Carbon Dioxide Capture and Storage* (New York: Cambridge University Press, 2005), https://www.ipcc.ch/site/assets/uploads/2018/03/srccs_wholereport-1.pdf.

37. Intergovernmental Panel on Climate Change, *Carbon Dioxide Capture and Storage*.

38. 26 U.S.C. §45Q (2019).

39. Dominic Woolf et al., "Sustainable Biochar to Mitigate Global Climate Change," *Nature Communications* 1 (2010).

40. Sabine Fuss et al., "Betting on Negative Emissions," *Nature Climate Change* 4 (2014): 850–853.

41. Nils Johnson, Nathan Parker, and Joan Ogden, "How Negative Can Biofuels with CCS Take Us and at What Cost? Refining the Economic Potential of Biofuel Production with CCS Using Spatially-Explicit Modeling," *Energy Procedia* 63 (2014): 6770–6791.

42. Mathias Fridahl and Mariliis Lehtveer, "Bioenergy with Carbon Capture and Storage (BECCS): Global Potential, Investment Preferences, and Deployment Barriers," *Energy Research and Social Science* 42 (2018): 155–165.

43. Geoffrey Morgan, "Billionaire-Backed Carbon Engineering to Build First 'Negative Emissions' Facility," *Calgary Herald*, March 21, 2019.

44. Jeff Tollefson, "Sucking Carbon Dioxide from Air Is Cheaper Than Scientists Thought," *Nature*, June 7, 2018, https://www.nature.com/articles/d41586-018-05357-w.

45. Tollefson, "Sucking Carbon Dioxide from Air."

46. Harvard School of Engineering, "Calculating Solar Geoengineering's Technical Costs," November 2018, https://www.seas.harvard.edu/news/2018/11/calculating-solar-geoengineering-s-technical-costs.

47. Muyu Xu and Michael Martina, "China Expects First Trade in National Emissions Scheme in 2020," *Reuters*, March 30, 2019.

48. Jack Barkenbus, "The Electric Vehicle Revolution Will Come from China, Not the US," *The Conversation*, May 14, 2019.

49. Pippa Stevens, "Here's How the World's Largest Money Manager Is Overhauling Its Strategy Because of Climate Change," *CNBC*, January 14, 2020.

50. Paul Stevens, "The International Oil Companies: The Death of the Old Business Model," Chatham House, May 2016.

51.   Ensieh Shojaeddini et al., "Oil and Gas Company Strategies Regarding the Energy Transition," *Progress in Energy* 1, no. 1 (2019).

52.   Mohammad S. Masnadi et al., "Global Carbon Intensity of Crude Oil Production," *Science* 361 (2018): 851–853.

53.   Glenn-Marie Lange et al., *The Changing Wealth of Nations: Measuring Sustainable Development in the New Millennium* (Washington, D.C.: World Bank, 2011).

8. THE LOSERS: THE CHANGING GEOPOLITICS OF OIL

1.   Axel Pierru, James Smith, and Hossa Almutairi, "OPEC's Pursuit of Market Stability," *Economics of Energy and the Environment*, June 2020.

2.   Robert Mabro, "OPEC and the Price of Oil," *Energy Journal* 13, no. 2 (1990): 1–17.

3.   Dermot Gately, "OPEC's Incentives for Faster Growth," *Energy Journal* 25, no. 2 (2004): 75–96.

4.   Ronald Soligo, Amy Myers Jaffe, and Peter Mieszkowski, "Energy Security," Working Paper, James A. Baker III Institute for Public Policy, Rice University, April 1997.

5.   Amy Myers Jaffe and Ronald Soligo, "Market Structure in the New Gas Economy: Is Cartelization Possible?," in *Natural Gas and Geopolitics from 1970 to 2040*, ed. David G. Victor, Amy M. Jaffe, and Mark H. Hayes (New York: Cambridge University Press, 2006).

6.   Anjili Raval and David Sheppard, "OPEC Is Stuck in a Production-Cutting Cycle It Cannot Get Out Of," *Financial Times*, July 2, 2019, https://www.ft.com/content/68e3c3bc-9cce-11e9 -9c06-a4640c9feebb.

7.   Annie Lowrey, "Obama Finds Oil in Markets Is Sufficient to Sideline Iran," *New York Times*, March 20, 2012.

8.   Kenneth Medlock, Amy Myers Jaffe, and Meghan O'Sullivan, "The Global Gas Market, LNG Exports, and the Shifting U.S. Geopolitical Presence," *Energy Strategy Review* 5 (2014): 14–25.

9.   Jennifer Jacobs, "Trump Says 'No Time Pressure' on Iran as EU Calls for Restraint," *Bloomberg*, June 27, 2019.

10.   Grant Smith, Olga Tanas, and Dina Khrennikova, "In a Sated Oil Market, Saudi Arabia Attack Sinks Without Trace," *Bloomberg*, October 3, 2019.

11.   Steven A. Cook, "This Is the Moment That Decides the Future of the Middle East," *Foreign Policy*, September 17, 2019.

12.   Tatiana Mitrova and Tim Boersma, "The Impact of US LNG on Russian Natural Gas Export Policy," Center on Global Energy Policy, Columbia University, December 2018.

13.   Ali Al-Shihabi, "The Case for a New Saudi Oil Policy in a Reborn Global Energy Market," Al Arabiya English, April 21, 2020.

14.   John Micklethwait et al., "Saudi Arabia Plans $2 Trillion Megafund for Post-Oil Era: Deputy Crown Prince," *Bloomberg*, April 1, 2016.

15.   Justin Scheck, Rory Jones, and Summer Said, "A Prince's $500 Billion Desert Dream: Flying Cars, Robot Dinosaurs and a Giant Artificial Moon," *Wall Street Journal*, July 25, 2019.

16.   Jim Krane, *Energy Kingdoms: Oil and Political Survival in the Persian Gulf* (New York: Columbia University Press, 2019).

17. Simon Shen, "The 'China Complex' That Is Haunting the Russian Far East," *EJI Insight*, September 20, 2017.

18. Kent Calder, *Asia's Deadly Triangle: How Arms, Energy and Growth Threaten to Destabilize Asia-Pacific* (London: Nicholas Brealey, 1999); Michael Klare, *Resource Wars: The New Landscape of Global Conflict* (New York: Henry Holt, 2001).

19. Steven A. Cook, "Mohammed bin Salman Is Worse Than a Criminal. He's a Symbol," *Foreign Policy*, December 4, 2018.

20. Andrew L. Gulley, Nedal T. Nassar, and Sean Xun, "China, the United States and the Competition for Resources That Enable Emerging Technologies," *PNAS* 16 (2018): 4111–4115.

21. Cook, "Mohammed bin Salman."

22. Mahmoud A. El-Gamal and Amy Myers Jaffe, "The Coupled Cycles of Geopolitics and Oil Prices," *Economics of Energy and Environmental Policy* 7, no. 2 (2018): 1–15.

23. The Lofoten Declaration, August 2017, http://www.lofotendeclaration.org/#read.

24. Alex Lenferna, "Can We Equitably Manage the End of the Fossil Fuel Era?," *Energy Research and Social Science* 35 (2018): 217–223.

25. Richard Milne, "Norway Resists Growing Environmental Pressure Over Oil," *Financial Times*, December 19, 2019.

9. GEOPOLITICS OF A GREENING ECONOMY

1. Emmanuel Hache, "Do Renewable Energies Improve Energy Security in the Long Run?," *International Economics* 156 (2018): 127–135.

2. Julian Kettle, "Mining Sector Faces Energy Transition Conundrum," *Financial Times*, February 18, 2020.

3. Michael Klare, *The Race for What's Left* (New York: Picador, 2012).

4. Meghan O'Sullivan, Indra Overland, and David Sandalow, "The Geopolitics of Renewable Energy," HKS Faculty Research Working Paper Series RWP17-027, June 2017.

5. Indra Overland, "The Geopolitics of Renewable Energy: Debunking Four Emerging Myths," *Energy Research & Social Science* 49 (2019): 36–40.

6. Andre Manberger and Bengt Johansson, "The Geopolitics of Metals and Metalloids Used for the Renewable Energy Transition," *Energy Strategy Reviews* 26 (2019).

7. Manberger and Johansson, "The Geopolitics of Metals and Metalloids."

8. Zhang Yan, Yilei Sun, and Brenda Goh, "Exclusive: Tesla in Talks to Use CATL's Cobalt-Free Batteries in China-Made Cars—Sources," *Reuters*, February 18, 2020.

9. Colin Beresford, "GM Unveils Battery with Capacity Twice as Big as Tesla's," *Car and Driver*, March 4, 2020, https://www.caranddriver.com/news/a31226611/gm-ultium-electric -vehicle-battery-revealed/.

10. Keith Bradsher, "Amid Tension, China Blocks Vital Exports to Japan," *New York Times*, September 22, 2010.

11. Felix Chang, "The New Long March: Trade War Between China and the United States," Foreign Policy Research Institute, Asia Program, June 7, 2019.

12. Overland, "The Geopolitics of Renewable Energy."

13. Manberger and Johansson, "The Geopolitics of Metals and Metalloids."

14.   Dave Keating, "Europe Launches Multibillion-Euro Initiative for Electric Car Batteries," *Forbes*, May 2, 2019.

15.   Carole Mathieu, "The European Battery Alliance Is Moving Up a Gear," Edito Energie, French Institute of International Relations, May 2, 2019.

16.   Laura Millan Lombrana, Chris Reiter, and Richard Weiss, "Europe Floors It in the Race to Dominate Car Batteries," *Bloomberg*, February 2, 2020.

17.   James Stavridis, "China's Next Naval Target Is the Internet's Underwater Cables," *Bloomberg*, April 16, 2019.

18.   Meghan Lopez, "From Detour to Disaster: Google Maps Got Dozens of Colorado Drivers in a Mud Mess on Sunday," *Denver Channel*, June 24, 2019. https://www.thedenverchannel .com/news/local-news/from-detour-to-disaster-google-maps-got-dozens-of-colorado -drivers-in-a-mud-mess-on-sunday.

19.   Adam Segal, "When China Rules the Web," *Foreign Affairs* 97, no. 5 (2018).

20.   Segal, "When China Rules the Web."

21.   Johan Lilliestam and Saskia Ellenbeck, "Energy Security and Renewable Electricity Trade—Will Desertec Make Europe Vulnerable to the 'Energy Weapon'?" *Energy Policy* 39, no. 6 (2011): 3380–3391.

22.   Sergey Paltsev, "The Complicated Geopolitics of Renewable Energy," *Bulletin of the Atomic Scientists* 72, Issue 6 (2016): 390–395.

23.   Daniel Scholten and Rick Bosman, "The Geopolitics of Renewables: Exploring the Political Implications of Renewable Energy Systems," *Technological Forecasting and Social Change* 103 (2016): 273–283.

CONCLUSION: RECOMMENDATIONS FOR THE UNITED STATES

1.   Kurt M. Campbell and Jake Sullivan, "Competition Without Catastrophe: How America Can Both Challenge and Coexist with China," *Foreign Affairs*, September/October 2019.

2.   Kelly Sims Gallagher, *The Globalization of Clean Energy Technology: Lessons from China* (Cambridge, Mass.: MIT Press, 2014).

3.   Daniel Scheitrum, "Impact of Intensity on Alternative Fuel Adoption: Renewable Natural Gas and California's Low Carbon Fuel Standard," *Energy Journal* 41 (2020).

4.   National Defense Education Act, H.R. 13247, 85th Congress (1958).

5.   Robert D. Hof, "Lessons from Sematech," *MIT Technology Review*, July 25, 2011.

Bibliography

Ansar, Atif, Ben Caldecott, and James Tilbury. "Stranded Assets and the Fossil Fuel Divestment Campaign: What Does Divestment Mean for the Valuation of Fossil Fuels?" Oxford University, Smith School of Enterprise and the Environment, October 2013.

Arrow, Kenneth J. "Economic Welfare and the Allocation of Resources for Invention." In *The Rate and Direction of Inventive Activity: Economic and Social Factors*, ed. Richard R. Nelson, 609–626. Princeton, N.J.: Princeton University Press, 1962.

Barber, Brad M. "Monitoring the Monitor: Evaluating CalPERS' Activism." University of California, Davis, November 2006.

Barnes, Douglas F., and Willem M. Floor. "Rural Energy in Developing Countries: A Challenge for Economic Development." *Annual Review of Energy and the Environment* 21, no. 1 (1996): 497–530.

Barsky, Robert, and Lutz Kilian. "Oil and the Macroeconomy Since the 1970s." *Journal of Economic Perspectives* 18, no. 4 (2004): 115–134.

Bebbington, Jan, Thomas Schneider, Lorna Stevenson, and Alison Fox. "Fossil Fuel Reserves and Resources Reporting and Unburnable Carbon: Investigating Conflicting Accounts." *Critical Perspectives on Accounting* 66 (January 2020).

Black, Edwin. *Internal Combustion: How Corporations and Governments Addicted the World to Oil and Derailed the Alternatives*. New York: St. Martin's Griffin, 2007.

Bollen, Johannes, Ton Manders, and Paul Veenendaal. "How Much Does a 30 Percent Emissions Reduction Cost?" CPD Netherlands Bureau for Economic Policy Analysis, 2004.

Brand, Christian. "Beyond 'Dieselgate': Implications of Unaccounted and Future Air Pollutant Emissions and Energy Use for Cars in the United Kingdom." *Energy Policy* 97 (2016): 1–12.

Brandt, Adam R., Adam Millard-Ball, Matthew Ganser, and Steven M. Gorelick. "Peak Oil Demand: The Role of Fuel Efficiency and Alternative Fuels in a Global Oil Production Decline." *Environmental Science and Technology* 47 (2013): 8031–8041.

Brinkley, Douglas. *Wheels for the World*. New York: Penguin Books, 2003.

Bronk, Chris. "What 5G Means for Energy." *Energy Realpolitik* (blog), Council on Foreign Relations, May 31, 2019. https://www.cfr.org/blog/what-5g-means-energy.

Brown, Austin, Jeffrey Gonder, and Brittany Repac. "An Analysis of Possible Energy Impacts of Automated Vehicles." In *Road Vehicle Automation*, ed. Gereon Meyer and Sven Beiker, 137–153. Basel: Springer International, 2014.

Brynjolfsson, Erik, and Andrew McAfee. *The Second Machine Age: Work, Progress, and Prosperity in a Time of Brilliant Technologies.* New York: Norton, 2014.

Calder, Kent. *Asia's Deadly Triangle: How Arms, Energy and Growth Threaten to Destabilize Asia-Pacific.* London: Nicholas Brealey, 1999.

Campbell, Colin J., and Jean H. Laherrere. "The End of Cheap Oil." *Scientific American* 278 (1998): 78.

Carolan, Michael S. "Ethanol Versus Gasoline: The Contestation and Closure of a Socio-Technical System in the USA." *Social Studies of Science* 39 (2009): 421-448.

Chenery, Hollis B., and Moises Syrquin. *Patterns of Development.* Oxford: Oxford University Press, 1975.

Chernow, Ron. *Titan: The Life of John D. Rockefeller, Sr.* New York: Random House, 1998.

Cook, Steven A. "Mohammed bin Salman Is Worse Than a Criminal. He's a Symbol." *Foreign Policy*, December 4, 2018.

——. "This Is the Moment That Decides the Future of the Middle East." *Foreign Policy*, September 17, 2019.

Deffeyes, Kenneth. *Hubbert's Peak: The Impending World Oil Shortage.* Princeton, N.J.: Princeton University Press, 2001.

Dietz, Simon, Chris Hope, Nicholas Stern, and Dimitri Zenghelis. "Reflections on the Stern Review (1): A Robust Case for Strong Action to Reduce the Risks of Climate Change." *World Economics* 8 (2007): 121-168.

Economy, Elizabeth C. *The Third Revolution: Xi Jinping and the Chinese State.* Oxford: Oxford University Press, 2018.

El-Gamal, Mahmoud A., and Amy Myers Jaffe. "The Coupled Cycles of Geopolitics and Oil Price." *Economics of Energy and Environmental Policy* 7, no. 2 (2018): 1-15.

——. *Oil, Dollars, Debt, and Crises: The Global Curse of Black Gold.* Cambridge: Cambridge University Press, 2010.

Epstein, Alex. *The Moral Case for Fossil Fuels.* New York: Portfolio Hardcover, 2014.

Esty, Daniel C., ed. *A Better Planet: Forty Big Ideas for a Sustainable Future.* New Haven, Conn.: Yale University Press, 2019.

Fagnant, Daniel, and Kara Kockelman. "The Travel and Environmental Implications of Shared Autonomous Vehicles Using Agent-Based Model Scenarios." *Transportation Research Part C* 40 (2014): 1-13.

Fox-Penner, Peter, Will Gorman, and Jennifer Hatch. "Long-Term U.S. Transportation Electricity Use Considering the Effects of Autonomous Vehicles: Estimates & Policy Observations." *Energy Policy* 122 (2018): 203-213.

Fridahl, Mathias, and Mariliis Lehtveer. "Bioenergy with Carbon Capture and Storage (BECCS): Global Potential, Investment Preferences, and Deployment Barriers." *Energy Research and Social Science* 42 (2018): 155-165.

Fulton, Lewis, Pierpaolo Cazzola, and Francois Cuenot. "IEA Mobility Model (MoMo) and Its Use in the ETP 2008." *Energy Policy* 37, no. 10 (2009): 3758-3768.

Fuss, Sabine, Josep G. Canadell, Glen P. Peters, Massimo Tavoni, Robbie M. Andrew, Philippe Ciais, Robert B. Jackson, et al. "Betting on Negative Emissions." *Nature Climate Change* 4 (2014): 850–853.

Gallagher, Kelly Sims. *The Globalization of Clean Energy Technology.* Cambridge, Mass.: MIT Press, 2017.

Gately, Dermot. "OPEC's Incentives for Faster Growth." *Energy Journal* 25, no. 2 (2004): 75–96.

Giebelhaus, August W. "History of Oil Industry." In *Concise Encyclopedia of History of Energy*, ed. Cutler J. Cleveland. San Diego: Elsevier Science, 2004.

Gillingham, Kenneth, Richard G. Newell, and William A. Pizer. "Modeling Endogenous Technological Change for Climate Policy Analysis." *Energy Economics* 30 (2008): 2734–2753.

Gold, Russell. *The Boom.* New York: Simon & Schuster, 2014.

Griffin, Paul A., and Amy Myers Jaffe. "Are Fossil Fuel Firms Informing Investors Well Enough About the Risks of Climate Change?" *Journal of Energy and Natural Resources Law* 36 (2018).

Griffin, Paul A., David H. Lont, and Yuan Sun. "The Relevance to Investors of Greenhouse Gas Emissions Disclosures." *Contemporary Accounting Research* 34 (2017): 1265–1297.

Guinn, Jeff. *The Vagabonds.* New York: Simon & Schuster, 2019.

Gulley, Andrew L., Nedal T. Nassar, and Sean Xun. "China, the United States and the Competition for Resources That Enable Emerging Technologies." *PNAS* 16 (2018): 4111–4115.

Harford, Tim. *Fifty Inventions that shaped the Modern Economy.* New York: Riverhead Books, 2017.

Hargadon, Andrew. *Sustainable Innovation.* Stanford, Calif.: Stanford University Press, 2015.

Harvey, Hal. *Designing Climate Solutions.* Washington, D.C.: Island Press, 2018.

Heck, Stefan, and Matt Rogers. *Resource Revolution.* New York: Melcher Media, 2014.

Hoffert, Martin, Ken Caldeira, Gregory Benford, David R. Criswell, Christopher Green, Howard Herzog, Atul K. Jain, et al. "Advanced Technology Pathways to Global Climate Stability: Energy for a Greenhouse Planet." *Science* 298 (2002): 981–987.

Intergovernmental Panel on Climate Change. *Carbon Dioxide Capture and Storage.* New York: Cambridge University Press, 2005.

International Energy Agency. "Energy Technology Perspectives 2017." June 2017.

Ito, Harumi, and Darin Lee. "Comparing the Impact of the September 11th Terrorist Attacks on International Airline Demand." *International Journal of the Economics of Business* 12 (2005): 225–249.

Jaffe, Amy Myers. "Feasibility of Renewable Natural Gas as a Large-Scale, Low Carbon Substitute." California Air Resources Board, no. 13–307 (2016).

—. "Financial Herding Must Be Checked to Avert Climate Crashes." *Nature Energy* 5 (2020): 101–103.

—. "The Tech-Enabled Energy Future." Council on Foreign Relations, March 8, 2019.

Jaffe, Amy Myers, and Ronald Soligo. "Market Structure in the New Gas Economy: Is Cartelization Possible?" In *Natural Gas and Geopolitics from 1970 to 2040*, ed. David G. Victor, Amy M. Jaffe, and Mark H. Hayes, 439–464. New York: Cambridge University Press, 2006.

Jeffrey, Thomas E. " 'Commodore' Edison Joins the Navy: Thomas Alva Edison and the Naval Consulting Board." *Journal of Military History* 80 (2016): 411–445.

Johnson, Nils, Nathan Parker, and Joan Ogden. "How Negative Can Biofuels with CCS Take Us and at What Cost? Refining the Economic Potential of Biofuel Production with CCS Using Spatially-Explicit Modeling." *Energy Procedia* 63 (2014): 6770–6791.

Kilian, Lutz. "The Economic Effects of Energy Price Shocks." *Journal of Economic Literature* 46, no. 4 (2008): 871–909.

—. "Not All Oil Price Shocks Are Alike: Disentangling Demand and Supply Shocks in the Crude Oil Market." *American Economic Review* 99, no. 3 (2009): 1053–1069.

Klare, Michael. *Resource Wars: The New Landscape of Global Conflict.* New York: Henry Holt, 2001.

Krane, Jim. *Energy Kingdoms: Oil and Political Survival in the Persian Gulf.* New York: Columbia University Press, 2019.

Kuznets, Simon. *Economic Growth of Nations: Total Output and Production Structure.* Cambridge, Mass.: Belknap Press of Harvard University Press, 1971.

Lange, Glenn-Marie, Kirk Hamilton, Giovanni Ruta, Lopa Chakraborti, Deval Desai, Bram Edens, Susana Ferreira, et al. *The Changing Wealth of Nations: Measuring Sustainable Development in the New Millennium.* Washington, D.C.: World Bank, 2011.

Lenferna, Alex. "Can We Equitably Manage the End of the Fossil Fuel Era." *Energy Research and Social Science* 35 (2018): 217-223.

Lester, Richard. "America's Energy Innovation Problem (and How to Fix It)." Working Paper 09-007, Massachusetts Institute of Technology, 2009.

Mabro, Robert. "OPEC and the Price of Oil." *Energy Journal* 13, no. 2 (1990): 1-17.

Masnadi, Mohammad S., Hassan M. El-Houjeiri, Dominik Schunack, Yunpo Li, Jacob G. Englander, Alhassan Badahdah, Jean-Christophe Monfort, et al. "Global Carbon Intensity of Crude Oil Production." *Science* 361 (2018): 851-853.

McCullough, Erin, and Nedal T. Nassar. "Assessment of Critical Minerals: Updated Applications of an Early-Warning Screening Methodology." *Mineral Economics* 30, no. 3 (2017): 257-272.

McGlade, Christophe, and Paul Ekins. "The Geographical Distribution of Fossil Fuels Unused When Limiting Global Warming to 2 Degrees C." *Nature* 517 (2015): 187-190.

Medlock, Kenneth B., III, Amy Myers Jaffe, and Meghan O'Sullivan. "The Global Gas Market, LNG Exports, and the Shifting U.S. Geopolitical Presence." *Energy Strategy Review* 5 (2014): 14-25.

Medlock, Kenneth B., III, and Ronald Soligo. "Economic Development and End-Use Energy Demand." *Energy Journal* 22, no. 2 (2001): 77-105.

Meinshausen, Malte, Nicolai Meinshausen, William Hare, Sarah C. B. Raper, Katja Frieler, Reto Knutti, David J. Frame, and Myles R. Allen. "Greenhouse-Gas Emission Targets for Limiting Global Warming to 2 Degrees C." *Nature* 458 (2009): 1158-1163.

Mian, Atif, and Amir Sufi. "The Effects of Fiscal Stimulus: Evidence from the 2009 Cash for Clunkers Program." *Quarterly Journal of Economics* 127 (2012): 1107-1142.

Mitrova, Tatiana, and Tim Boersma. "The Impact of US LNG on Russian Natural Gas Export Policy." Center on Global Energy Policy, Columbia University, December 2018.

Miyagiwa, Kaz, and Yuka Ohno. "Oil and Strategic Development of Substitute Technology." James A. Baker III Institute for Public Policy, Rice University, May 2000.

Mom, Gijs. *The Electric Vehicle: Technology and Expectations in the Automobile Age.* Baltimore: Johns Hopkins University Press, 2004.

Mowery, David C. "Military R & D and Innovation." In *Handbook of the Economics of Innovation,* ed. Bronwyn H. Hall and Nathan Rosenberg, 1219-1256. Amsterdam: North-Holland, 2010.

Nelson, Richard R. *National Innovation Systems.* New York: Oxford University Press, 1993.

Nelson, Richard R., and Nathan Rosenberg, eds. *National Innovation Systems: A Comparative Analysis.* Oxford: Oxford University Press, 1993.

Newell, Richard, Adam Jaffe, and Robert Stavins. "The Induced Innovation Hypothesis and Energy-Saving Technological Change." *Quarterly Journal of Economics* 114 (1999): 941-975.

Nordhaus, William. "Critical Assumptions in the Stern Review on Climate Change." *Science* 317 (2007): 201-202.

—. "Revisiting the Social Cost of Carbon." *Proceedings of the National Academy of the Sciences of the United States of America* 114 (2017): 1518–1523.

Nordhaus, William, and James Tobin. "Is Growth Obsolete?" *National Bureau of Economic Research* 5 (1972): 1–80.

O'Sullivan, Meghan L. *Windfall.* New York: Simon & Schuster, 2017.

Pickl, Matthias J. "The Renewable Energy Strategies of Oil Majors—From Oil to Energy?" *Energy Strategy Reviews* 26 (2019).

Price, Richard, Simeon Thornton, and Stephen Nelson. "The Social Cost of Carbon and the Shadow Price of Carbon: What They Are, and How to Use Them in Economic Appraisal in the UK." Munich Personal RePEc Archive, December 2007.

Prud'homme, Dan, and Max von Zedtwitz. "The Changing Face of Innovation in China." *MIT Sloan Management Review*, June 12, 2018.

Rayle, Lisa, Susan Shaheen, Nelson Chan, Danielle Dai, and Robert Cervero. "App-Based, On-Demand Ride Services: Comparing Taxi and Ridesourcing Trips and User Characteristics in San Francisco." Working Paper, University of California Transportation Center, November 2014.

Rhodes, Richard. *Energy.* New York: Simon & Schuster, 2018.

Rose, Jonathan. *The Well-Tempered City.* New York: Harper Wave Books, 2016.

Ross, Alec. *The Industries of the Future.* New York: Simon & Schuster Paperbacks, 2016.

Samaras, Constantine, William J. Nuttall, and Morgan Bazilian. "Energy and the Military: Convergence of Security, Economic, and Environmental Decision-Making." *Energy Strategy Reviews* 26 (2019).

Scheitrum, Daniel, Amy Myers Jaffe, and Lew Fulton. "Changing Oil Market Fundamentals and Implications for OPEC Production Strategy." *IAEE Energy Forum: Bergen Special Issue* (2016).

Schiffer, Michael Brian. *Taking Charge: The Electric Automobile in America.* Washington, D.C.: Smithsonian Institution Press, 1994.

Schipper, Lee, and Marie-Lilliu Celine. "Transportation and CO_2 Emissions: Flexing the Link—A Path for the World Bank." Environmental Department Papers, no. 69. Washington, D.C.: World Bank Group, 1999.

Schrank, David, Bill Eisele, Tim Lomax, and Jim Bak. "2015 Urban Mobility Scorecard." Texas A&M Transportation Institute, August 2015.

Schwab, Klaus. *The Fourth Industrial Revolution.* New York: Crown Business, 2016.

Schwartz, Samuel I., and Karen Kelly. *No One at the Wheel: Driverless Cars and the Road of the Future.* New York: Hachette, 2018.

Servan-Schreiber, Jean-Jacques. *The American Challenge.* New York: Atheneum, 1968.

Shaheen, Susan, and Nelson D. Chan. "Ridesharing in North America: Past, Present, and Future." *Transport Reviews* 32 (2012): 93–112.

Shojaeddini, Ensieh, Stephen Naimoli, Sarah Ladislaw, and Morgan Bazilian. "Oil and Gas Company Strategies Regarding the Energy Transition." *Progress in Energy* 1, no. 1 (July 2019).

Silver, Nicholas. "Blindness to Risk: Why Institutional Investors Ignore the Risk of Stranded Assets." *Journal of Sustainable Finance and Investment* 7 (2017): 99–113.

Sivaram, Varun, ed. *Digital Decarbonization: Promoting Digital Innovations to Advance Clean Energy Systems.* New York: Council on Foreign Relations, 2018.

Smalley, Richard E. "Future Global Energy Prosperity: The Terawatt Challenge." *Material Matters Bulletin* 30 (2005): 412–417.

Smil, Vaclav. *Energy and Civilization: A History.* Cambridge, Mass.: MIT Press, 2017.

Soligo, Ronald, Amy Myers Jaffe, and Peter Mieszkowski. "Energy Security." Working Paper, James A. Baker III Institute for Public Policy, Rice University, April 1997.

Sperling, Daniel. *Three Revolutions.* Washington, D.C.: Island Press, 2018.

Sperling, Daniel, and Deborah Gordon. *Two Billion Cars.* Oxford: Oxford University Press, 2009.

Spitzer, Daniel. "ICE-Free Cities: Global Strategies for Creating Sustainable Urban Transport." *Natural Resources and Environment* 33 (2018): 8–11.

Sprei, Frances. "Disrupting Mobility." *Energy Research and Social Science* 37 (2018): 238–242.

Stern, Nicholas. "The Economics of Climate Change." *American Economic Review* 98 (2008): 1–37.

Stevens, Paul. *International Oil Companies: The Death of the Old Business Model.* London: Chatham House, 2016.

Stolarroff, Joshuah K., Constantine Samaraset, Emma R. O'Neill, Alia Lubers, Alexandra S. Mitchell, and Daniel Ceperley. "Energy Use and Life Cycle Greenhouse Gas Emissions of Drones for Commercial Package Delivery." *Nature Communications* 9, no. 409 (2018).

Stucke, Maurice E., and Ariel Ezrachi. "The Rise, Fall and Birth of the U.S. Antitrust Movement." *Harvard Business Review,* December 15, 2017.

Sue Wing, Ian. "Induced Technological Change in Computable General Equilibrium Models for Climate Change Policy Analysis." PhD diss., Massachusetts Institute of Technology, 2001.

Summons, Matthew. *Twilight in the Desert.* Hoboken: Wiley, 2006.

Tol, Richard S. J. "Estimates of the Damage Costs of Climate Change. Part 1: Benchmark Estimates." *Environmental and Resource Economics* 21 (2002): 47–73.

Tollefson, Jeff. "Sucking Carbon Dioxide from Air Is Cheaper Than Scientists Thought." *Nature,* June 7, 2018.

Tønnesen, Anders, Sunniva Frislid Meyer, Eva-Gurine Skartland, and Hanne Beate Sundfør. *Europeiske Byer Med Bilfrie Sentrum.* Oslo: Transportøkonomisk Institutt, 2016.

Tooze, Adam. "Why Central Banks Need to Step Up on Global Warming." *Foreign Policy,* July 20, 2019.

Unruh, Gregory C. "Understanding Carbon Lock-in." *Energy Policy* 28 (2000): 817–830.

Van de Graaf, Thijs, and Michael Bradshaw. "Stranded Wealth: Rethinking the Politics of Oil in an Age of Abundance." *International Affairs* 94 (2018): 1309–1328.

Verhoef, Leendert A., Bart W. Buddeb, Cindhuja Chockalingam, Brais García Nodar, and Ad J. M. van Wijk. "The Effects of Additive Manufacturing on Global Energy Demand: An Assessment Using a Bottom-Up Approach." *Energy Policy* 112 (2018): 349–360.

Wadud, Zia, Don MacKenzie, and Paul Leiby. "Help or Hindrance? The Travel, Energy and Carbon Impacts of Highly Automated Vehicles." *Transportation Research Part A: Policy and Practice* 86 (2016): 1–18.

Wagner, Gernot, and Martin L. Weitzman. *Climate Shock: The Economic Consequences of a Hotter Planet.* Princeton, N.J.: Princeton University Press, 2015.

West, Darrell M., and Qi Ye. "Integrating Digital Technologies and Energy Management in China." Brookings Institution, April 5, 2017.

Woolf, Dominic, James E. Amonette, F. Alayne Street-Perrott, Johannes Lehmann, and Stephen Joseph. "Sustainable Biochar to Mitigate Global Climate Change." *Nature Communications* 1 (2010).

Yergin, Daniel. *The Prize.* New York: Simon & Schuster, 1991.

Yergin, Daniel, and Martin Hillenbrand. *Global Insecurity.* Boston: Houghton Mifflin, 1982.

Index

Printed and bound by CPI Group (UK) Ltd, Croydon, CR0 4YY

03/06/2024

14509865-0001